MIS Cases in Action

MIS Cases in Action

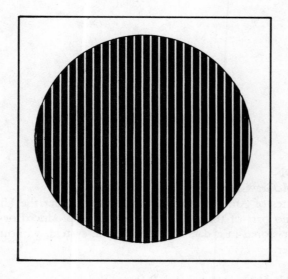

Jamal Munshi
University of Arkansas

McGraw-Hill Publishing Company

New York St. Louis San Francisco Auckland Bogotá
Caracas Hamburg Lisbon London Madrid Mexico Milan
Montreal New Delhi Oklahoma City Paris San Juan
São Paulo Singapore Sydney Tokyo Toronto

Dedicated to Tamara and Erick

MIS: CASES IN ACTION

Copyright © 1990 by McGraw-Hill, Inc. All rights reserved.

Printed in the United States of America. Except as permitted under the United States Copyright Act of 1976, no part of this publication may be reproduced or distributed in any form or by any means, or stored in a data base or retrieval system, without the prior written permission of the publisher.

2 3 4 5 6 7 8 9 0 MAL MAL 8 9 4 3 2 1 0 9

ISBN 0-07-044026-3

This book was set in Galliard by Kathleen Baldonado.
The editor was Karen M. Jackson. The production supervisor was Phil Galea.
The cover was designed by Simmon Factor. The interior was designed by Lorna Cunkle.
The artist was Graphics Plus.
Development and project supervision were done by Cole and Associates.
Malloy was printer and binder.

Library of Congress Cataloging-in-Publication Data

Munshi, Jamal.
  MIS:cases in action / Jamal Munshi
    p. cm.
  ISBN 0-07-044026-3
  1. Management information systems-Case studies. I. Title.
T58.6.M865 1990
658.4'038-dc20   89-7946

Contents

Preface

MIS students, whether undergraduate or graduate, are often at a disadvantage when it comes to relating what they learn in the classroom to practical, real-world conditions. This situation seems to go hand in hand with the lack of satisfactory teaching materials for MIS, particularly casebooks.

MIS: Cases in Action is a by-product of the frustration I experienced as an instructor in not being able to find the "right" materials for my students. For years I searched for appropriate case studies that would adequately amplify the concepts developed in the textbooks and in lectures and that would truly bring MIS to life for students. Sadly, almost all the case material available comes across as contrived and is woefully out-of-date. Students today can quickly differentiate what is real from what is not and what is dated from what is current.

In developing this book, therefore, it became apparent that to be successful, I would have to find a way to bring the "real world" into the classroom. What better way to put students in touch with the world outside the classroom than through the use of actual cases involving real people and organizations making decisions and solving problems? Through this simple medium students are presented with real-life situations and decisions in MIS.

In the case studies I have selected, I have sought to demonstrate all the different forms of what we call "MIS" so that students can learn what MIS looks like, what goes on in an MIS department, why, as MIS managers, we do what we do, and what sorts of decisions we have to make.

Presenting a diversity of examples is important, since MIS encompasses concepts from management, accounting, marketing, finance, psychology, systems analysis, database design, computer programming, project management, and information technology. I have also presented a variety of organizations and situations to emphasize the diversity found in MIS.

During the selection process, I paid as much attention to the decision maker as to the system details. One of the key benefits of case studies is the insight they provide into the decision maker's role. For this reason, I wanted to work with decision makers who would emphasize answers to this question: "What do MIS managers or analysts have to take into account in making routine decisions?" In cases that highlight projects conceived and designed by end users, a similar line of reasoning was followed: What are the decision-making criteria? What kinds of decisions have to be made and what is taken into account in making them?

Part 1 of *MIS: Cases in Action* begins with an overview of the case method and its use in solving MIS problems. Part 1 includes a definition of MIS, an explanation of what a case study is and some methods for solution, a discussion of MIS issues, instruction on how to read cases, and a look at the components of decision making.

Part 2 contains a complete sample case, Advanced Pressure Vessels, Inc., which includes all the elements found in the subsequent cases.

Part 3, *Cases for Solution,* covers a diverse series of six medium-length studies (Fireman's Fund, Bechtel Power, Parker Compumoter, Apple Computer, Autodesk, Taylor-Dunn) and two longer cases (Wal-Mart Stores, Tyson Foods). Each case is developed with sufficient background depth to bring students into contact with the reality of the actual situations faced by managers, analysts, and end users.

Whether a specific case emphasizes competitive advantage, strategic planning, or critical success factors, all the cases underscore the "nowness" of today. The cases selected include such topics as expert systems, electronic data interchange (EDI), executive information systems, applications engineering, office automation and workstations, and the new world of end-user computing.

Case questions for solution have been shaped to challenge the student's imagination, to test learning, and to encourage the development of problem-solving skills.

Part 4, *Topics in Information Technology,* provides technical information useful in developing solutions to the case questions. Drawn from a variety of sources, the information in this section expands upon the background material found in each case.

In Part 5, buzzwords and acronyms are explained briefly in glossary format.

MIS: Cases in Action comes with an Instructor's Manual that contains ideas for lectures, sample case solutions, and test items. A template disk in IBM PC-compatible, OS-2, and Apple Macintosh formats is also available.

In the twelve months or so that I have been working on this book I have met some remarkable people. I have seen the gleam in their eyes as they described their new ideas and the frustration on their brows as we investigated the contents of their in-baskets. The experience has been, without doubt, one of the most interesting of my life.

Through *MIS: Cases in Action,* I have sought to shrink the distance between the classroom and the fascinating world of MIS. In this effort, I have had the assistance of many fine people. The following persons and organizations have been particularly helpful:

Tom Porter, Director of Telecommunications
Apple Computer, Inc.

Peter O'Dell, MIS Manager
Patricia Peper, Publications Coordinator
Autodesk, Inc.

Steve McIntyre, Information Services
George Belonogoff, Information Services

Larry P. Miller, Public Relations
Bechtel Power Corporation

Chris McDermot, Director, R & D, Artificial Intelligence
Sandy Johnson, Project Manager, *Underwriter Adviser*
John M. Kozero, Director of Financial Communication
Fireman's Fund Insurance Company

Leonard Luna, Applications Engineer
Scott Johnson, President
Parker Compumotor Division

Robert Cammack, Vice-President, Engineering
Taylor-Dunn Corporation

Stan McClure, Programming Manager
Dan Snyder, Vice-President, MIS
Tyson Foods, Inc.

Sheldon Breiner, Chairman and CEO
Syntelligence, Inc.

Mark A. Schmidt, Director of Information Technology and Planning
Wal-Mart Stores, Inc.

Professor David Douglas, Chairman, CIS/QA Department
College of Business, University of Arkansas

Jim Walker
MIS Designer

Special thanks are due to Karen Jackson and Terry McGillen at McGraw-Hill and to
Brete Harrison, Barbara Pickard, and Lorna Cunkle at Cole and Associates, whose
encouragement and support were essential in finishing the manuscript.

— *Jamal Munshi*
Fayetteville, Arkansas

P.S. As you use *MIS: Cases in Action,* I would appreciate receiving your comments
and suggestions for future editions. I can be reached through my BITNET address:
JM24747@UAFSYSB.

PART 1

The Case Method As Used in MIS

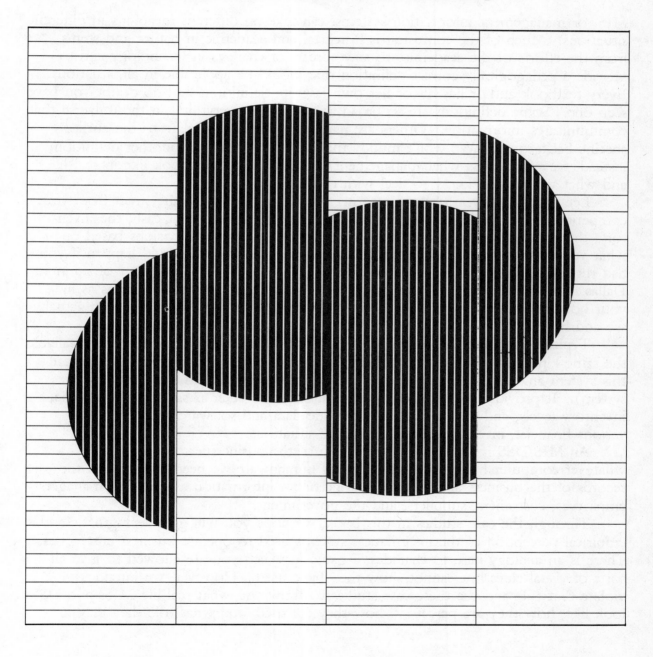

What Is MIS?

MIS in Practice: A Pragmatic Approach

MIS, or management information systems, can take on different meanings in different situations. Much of the confusion is historical and academic in nature and stems from the efforts of the academics to stay abreast of changes in technology and to provide a pedagogically correct definition that would be applicable in all situations. Every textbook author has his or her own favorite definitions and no doubt you have seen one. Some definitions are so broad as to include everything in the universe that communicates information. Others are narrow in scope and relate to the author's specific background. We won't muddy the water here with yet another definition; instead, we will discuss what management information systems look like in real life and what we need to know to deal with them.

Let us say that you operate a corner hot dog stand across the street from your competition. Everything is in front of you, your customers, your cash, the inventory, the competitive situation. You can make quick business decisions based on what you see and hear while you run this business. But what would happen if you had thousands of hot dog emporia all over the country? Sitting in your office in Dallas in a high rise you need to make the same sorts of business decisions as in your hot dog stand days, but you can't make them based on real things you actually see and hear.

Typically, in America today you would use a computer system to make available the same kinds of information available on your large business empire. Let us call this system an MIS/DSS, (management information system and decision support system). It provides to managers routine information such as sales, costs, income, inventory levels, and may additionally provide data and software tools to model various financial, inventory, and competitive situations.

An MIS/DSS is an electronic extension of the businessperson. It includes whatever computer hardware, software, and humanware we need to maintain the records of the business and to make the pertinent information available to managers, employees, customers, suppliers, and the government.

Through the case studies in this book, we hope you will gain a pragmatic and empirical perception of the information systems used to operate business enterprises. There is an analogy here to charades, a game in which you are allowed to give all sorts of visual clues but cannot show the object itself. However, we intend to violate that rule and use these case studies to show you what real-life MISs and DSSs look like, how they are perceived, how they are used, and what role they play in overall business management. And, through the case solution questions, we will help you comprehend the technology and the decision-making situations that business managers must deal with in designing, implementing, and using these systems.

What you need to know to be able to make these decisions is in your MIS textbook. Three important aspects of the study of MIS that will be useful are information technology, systems analysis, and database management systems. These are discussed briefly below.

Information Technology

Information technology and its associated terminology are in a state of evolutionary change. Rapid advances have augmented the bridge between what technology can provide and what business managers will use. As a consequence, effective business managers need to remain current both in terms of the technology available and in terms of the lexicon of the computer industry. Otherwise, they will find themselves at a serious disadvantage when there is the need to evaluate alternative technologies.

Managers in this situation usually proceed through the "three stages of ignorance" as described by a colleague of mine, Dr. Dub Ashton, professor of marketing at the University of Arkansas. These stages are fear, blind faith, and disillusionment.

In the fear stage the ignorant manager is suspicious of information technology and tries to avoid computers. The firm suffers from the lack of appropriate information technology and may forfeit competitive advantage. Alternatively, the manager may entrust technically oriented subordinates and consultants to manage the system and the information it provides, thereby compromising his or her managerial effectiveness.

When managers progress beyond the fear stage, they usually enter the stage of "blind faith." Information technology becomes akin to witchcraft, which they do not understand but which they believe will do wonderful things for the firm. This situation leads to such exaggerated expectations that it invariably results in the third stage: disillusionment, frustration, and anger.

The case studies we have selected for you illustrate relevant technology in the field of business information management. The case solution questions present the sort of technology issues and decisions that you would have to resolve as a business manager today.

What we see from these cases is the evolution of a radical and exciting view of computer systems. The focus has shifted from the computer to the human interface from the programmer to the user. This reformation has resulted principally from the microcomputer. The combination of low cost, small size, rugged design, and ease of use has made it the workstation of choice and has encouraged the use of local area networks. According to the new thinking, the network is the system, the micro is the workstation, and everything else, including mainframes with high computing power, is simply network devices, which must be accessed transparently within the micro metaphor the user understands.

Systems Analysis

Computer systems are tools, perhaps uninteresting in themselves but, in the hands of the right person, very useful in a wide variety of applications. In computer systems, as in all tools, a technology gap can exist between the tool and the application.

Say that you are a hammer sales representative. You wish to sell a hammer to a house builder but know nothing of construction and are unsure of exactly how your product might be used in such an activity. The builder, on the other hand, knows how to build houses and could benefit greatly from your product but either does not know that it exists or is not sure how to use it or how it could be a benefit. This is what we mean by a gap between technology (hammer) and application (housebuilding).

Systems analysts are professionals who are trained to span this gap. Systems analysis consists of understanding the application, knowing the information technology, and bringing the appropriate technology to bear upon the application. By "systems analysis" we are here referring to the entire systems development life cycle of analysis, design, procurement, and implementation or the alternative method of prototyping.

This is a central theme in the study of MIS. As a business manager, there are many situations in which you will need to be a systems analyst or deal with one. In any case, since you already know your business — "the application" — you are ideally suited to be your own systems analyst. All you need to know are the availability of information technology and the methods used by systems analysts.

Two methods discussed in your textbook are the systems development life cycle (SDLC) and the prototyping method. The SDLC consists of the following recognizable activities:

1. *Systems analysis.* Identify information needs and design the logical system. This includes the user interface and a hypothetical system that would relate the user interface to the actual data set.

2. *Systems design.* Design the physical system. Specify what hardware and software will be used to realize the logical system you designed in step 1.

3. *Procurement.* Purchase all hardware and software that will be needed, write software that will be developed in-house, and write specs and obtain consultants for software that will be developed out-of-house.

4. *Implementation.* Bring the system up onsite and convert the business activities to the new system to realize the benefits promised in step 1.

It is prudent here to caution against excessive reliance on technology to solve business problems. You must try to avoid the Stuart Greene jinx that says, "When the only tool you've got is a hammer, everything looks like nails" (Stuart Greene, "Network Services: Where the Action Is" in *Apple Viewpoint* September 9, 1988). The corollary to data is this: "When the only tool you've got is data processing, everything looks like data." Frequently, you will run into analysts who try to solve all business problems by throwing technology at them, the philosophy being, "You have a problem because you are deficient in technology," and "If you throw enough technology at your problem it is bound to go away." This is not a good approach to MIS systems analysis.

Database Management

If a MIS does have a heart, it is certainly the database, and so it is not surprising that the study of database management is an important part of your MIS course. In some of these case studies you will see that setting up the right database structure is the key to a successful MIS implementation.

Relational database systems, popularized by such programs as dBASE IV, Revelation, Foxbase, Oracle, SLQ/DS, Informix, and DB2, have become the work-horses in many organizations. So it is not only important, but may be sufficient, to understand databases only in terms of the relational database structure.

A relational database can best be described as a collection of relations. Each of these relations can be thought of as a two-dimensional table consisting of rows and columns, with each column containing a column heading unique to that table. Some people find it useful to think of these tables as "files" since many of the programs (most notably dBASE IV) use an OS file to store each relation. We will use the file metaphor here. An MIS database will typically have several files such as the customer file, the payroll file, the inventory file, and so on.

Each column in the tables is called a *field* and stores the same kind of data. The column heading is the field name and, together with the file name, uniquely identifies this kind of data. Typical field names found in business databases are "customer name," "part number," "unit price," "purchase order number," etc. Each column contains the same kind of data, but the numbers in different rows refer to different instances of data: different customers, suppliers, parts, etc. Each instance is represented by a row in our tabular representation and is referred to as a *record*. A specific instance of a given field, i.e., one piece of data, is normally referred to as a *data item*.

Now you can think of a database as consisting of many files (typically 5 to 25; for example, "customer file"), with each file having several fields (typically 4 to 20;

for example, "zip code") and many, many records (typically 1000 to 10,000). (See Figure CS.1.)

Each file contains at least one key by which a unique record can be identified and perhaps one or more foreign key fields by which its relationship to the other files in the database is established. For example, in the customer file, we can assign customer numbers to each customer as a key field. A secondary key can be a field called *credit rating* which contains numbers from 1 to 10. This points to a small credit-rating file with "credit rating" as the key field. For each credit rating the file may contain data describing whether credit can be extended, for how much, for how long, and whether payment terms will include early payment discounts or late payment penalties. It is these keys that tie a collection of files or relations into a cohesive and functioning database.

The design of a database properly starts with establishing what reports it will be asked to generate, identifying all the fields that will be needed, and assigning these to an orderly organization of files. It is important to separate the user views from the physical view. The users are presented with the data in an organization that is most convenient to their interpretation and use, while the distribution of data among files is determined by considerations of data redundancy, data integrity, and speed of access.

What Is a Case Study?

The Structure of a Case

A case is a decision-making situation with a large number of facts that you must sort through and separate into components for analysis. You must then synthesize these components into a solution. A large amount of information is supplied in each case study, although not all the information may be relevant to the case solution. As part of the case study exercise, you are required to separate the germane from the extraneous, the relevant from the irrelevant, the material from the circumstantial. Case studies are designed to mimic real-life situations. In real life, not only is there no guarantee that all the information you have is relevant, but there is no guarantee that you have all the information you need. Sometimes you will have to make a reasonable assumption to come up with a case solution.

Figure CS.1
Sample of a Relational Database

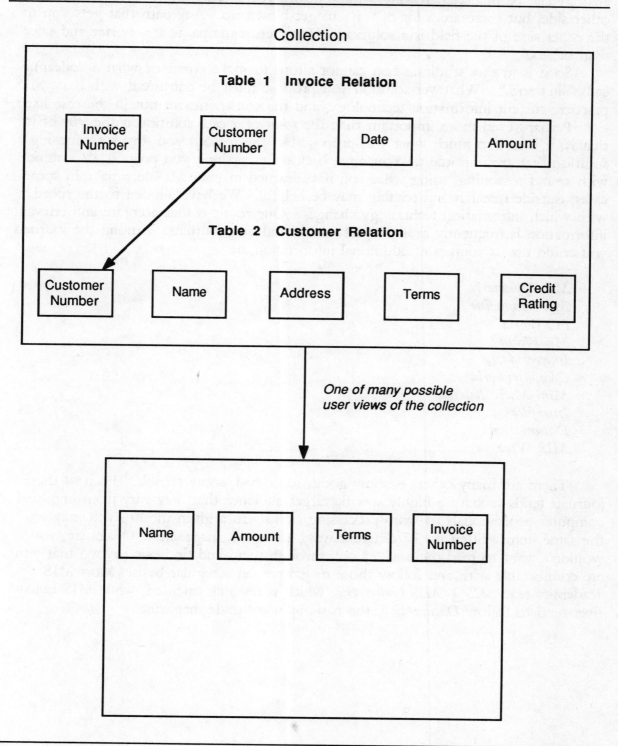

Collection

Table 1 Invoice Relation

| Invoice Number | Customer Number | Date | Amount |

Table 2 Customer Relation

| Customer Number | Name | Address | Terms | Credit Rating |

*One of many possible
user views of the collection*

| Name | Amount | Terms | Invoice Number |

In some ways, a case study presents an unstructured problem for which there is usually no single right answer but for which there are many wrong answers. An analogy can be made to crossing a mine field. There is no single right path to the other side, but there are a lot of ways to get blown up. Any path that gets you to the other side of the field is a solution. However, some paths are shorter and safer than others.

So it is in case studies. You cannot afford to make errors or what a colleague calls "ain't so's." Whatever solution you propose must be consistent with basic MIS practice, current information technology, and the constraints set out in the case itself.

Perhaps even more important than the *what* of a case solution is the *why* of it; that is, it is not so much what you propose but the reasons you give for choosing a solution that are important. You must back up everything you propose or assume with sound reasoning, using what you have learned in your MIS lectures. In some cases, outside research and reading may be helpful. We have alluded to the speed with which information technology changes. One result is that accurate and relevant information is frequently available only in the industry journals. Among the journals you could use as sources of additional information are

MIS Quarterly
Byte Magazine
PC World
MacWorld
Infoworld
Computerworld
Mini-Micro Journal
Interface
Datamation
MIS Week

There are many others — some good, some bad, some terrible. Each of these journals tends to have a highly specific target audience that may vary from high-end computer professionals to word-processing clerks. In a given month, you may see the same item written up 17 different ways in various magazines. Of course, you wouldn't want to read them all. Look through them and find one or two that you are comfortable with and follow those magazines on a regular basis. Most MIS academics read *MISQ (MIS Quarterly)*, which is research-oriented, while MIS executives tend to follow *Datamation*, the basic industry trade magazine.

What's in a Case Study?

A case study is a narrative that describes a particular business situation. It is a story and, like a story, may tend to ramble at times, but it always has a theme and a moral. To help you find these easily, each case has been organized rather loosely according to the following topics:

Company Information/Background Data
Situational Data/Assumptions About the System
The Problem (or the Objective)
The Options (and Their Distinguishing Features)

Company Data and Background Information

You may already be familiar with some of these companies and completely unaware of others. In any case, we assume no such familiarity. This background section provides as much information as we felt you would need to view the specific MIS problem in its proper perspective.

Usually, you will find a description of the size and regional base of the company and financial information from the most recent annual reports. You will also find some information about the company's products and its relative position in its market and industry. Based on this information, you can assess the size, strength, and technical sophistication of the company. The MIS solutions proposed should not violate these basic precepts.

For instance, it is not appropriate to propose that a corner grocer purchase a $100,000 VAX system. The grocer hasn't the space, the finances, the technical sophistication, or the MIS information needs to justify obtaining such a system. This is a rather extreme example, and you may feel that no one would ever make such a silly error. However, students as well as MIS consultants do make such errors, albeit on a finer scale.

Situational Data and Assumptions About the System

In this section of the narrative, we begin to focus on the information system of the company. If the case study involves a specific division or department, then the discussion will be limited to the department being studied. Topics that may be discussed here are organizational structure and issues; past, present, and future information needs; an overview of the information system, including hardware, software, and organization; and information about personalities who may or may not have an impact on the solution.

After reading this section, you should get a feel for what it would be like to work in the department being studied. Doing this will affect not only the type of MIS solution you will propose, but also the reasons you will give to support your decisions. However, in contrast with other MIS case books, the focus of these cases is NOT on organizational issues but on technical ones.

Technical information on the MIS is furnished in this section and augmented as necessary with appendices you can use for quick reference.

Many students have an aversion to prefaces and appendices, assuming that, if the author had intended for them to read the material, it would have been included in the body of the text. As a consequence, a lot of very helpful information in appendices is being overlooked even as you read this sentence. To avoid this situation, we have dropped the word appendix from our vocabulary. You will find the technical reference material in Part 4 of this book, "Topics in Information Technology."

The Problem

We will use the MIS textbook definition of the word *problem*. A problem is the gap between the existing state of the world and the desired state of the world. By *world* we mean the particular system or situation under study. Several aspects of this definition need scrutiny.

First, a gap can be created by two means: either the existing state can deteriorate or the desired state can be changed by the person who perceives the problem. In the former state we would have a *problem* as we understand the word in the vernacular. Something has gone bad and needs to be fixed, i.e., restored to its original and desired state. In the latter, we do not have a problem in the traditional sense but we have set for ourselves a new objective. However, in our context, this too is a problem.

Second, what the problem is and whether one even exists depend largely on the attitude of the speaker, since the nature of the problem depends mostly on his perception of the current state and his expectations of the desired state.

Third, if you take a systemic view of things, it is easy to see, in terms of this definition, why problems are dynamic in nature. The gap may never be closed if the speaker's view of the current state or of the desired state changes directly as a result of our attempt to solve the problem.

For example, say the problem is that the Golden Gate Bridge, which spans the San Francisco Bay, is too congested. Current state: it takes half an hour to cross during commute hours. Desired state: it takes 5 minutes to cross. Let us look at the possible solution of adding a second deck to the bridge. Assuming no other constraints to population growth in adjacent Marin and Sonoma counties, adding a deck may cause so many people to move to these areas that new traffic bottlenecks appear.

In an almost Heisenbergian sort of way, the solution changes the problem, and the best that we can hope for is that things will incrementally get better as we attempt to solve this progression of problems. The moral of the story is that, in solving MIS cases, we must at least attempt to identify the systemic impact of our proposal.

Problem or Symptom?

It is easy to see that if the problem is not properly identified, the proposed solution will be inappropriate and therefore worthless. In particular, it is important not to accept apparent symptoms as the problem. Thus, an important activity in problem identification is the separation of the symptoms from their cause. What is causing the symptoms is the problem. Remove the cause and the symptoms will also disappear.

However, doing this is easier said than done. For instance, by deciding on causalities beforehand we bring our preconceptions and biases into the solution. Further, it is not clear where the chain of causalities should end. Consequently, don't look for hard-and-fast rules in problem/symptom separation. You will find it a fuzzy exercise, but it is an important one nevertheless.

The separation of symptoms from problems can be viewed as the initial or the exploratory phase of problem resolution. Start with a symptom. Imagine that you are a doctor performing a diagnosis. Ask yourself, "What could cause this symptom? What other symptoms would we find if this were the cause? Are these other symptoms present? If I removed this cause, would these symptoms go away?" At least try to go beyond the first level of symptoms. But by no means should you try to find the ultimate cause. We'll leave that to the theologians.

More Than One Problem?

Problem identification will vary depending on the course material being used as a context in the case assignment. Since there is no predetermined problem built into these cases, problem identification will vary from one class to another and even from one individual to another. However, do not allow this to become a source of anxiety. Your answer does not have to match anyone else's. It just has to be consistent with your MIS course work and must be supported by sound reasoning and judgment.

It should also be expected that a single case solution will identify more than one (unrelated) problem. If these problems are unrelated, they can't be symptoms of a common problem and must be treated as different problems needing resolution. In such a case, these problems should be treated in parallel and interactions between the parallel proposals should be assessed. (If the "problems" are related, then they are symptomatic and may constitute a syndrome. The cause of the syndrome is the problem.)

Case Study Solutions

There are three rules for writing well. Unfortunately, no one knows what they are.
— Somerset Maugham

Methods of Solution

In some undergraduate courses you may be required only to answer the case questions. However, in more advanced and MBA-level courses, you may be asked to write a report or make a presentation on the case. This section is included to help provide a structure or checklist for analyzing case-study scenarios.

A case solution requires you to do more than write just a critical review of the MIS scenario. You must balance your comments about what is wrong and what is right. Moreover, you must develop a framework for your response that will cover all aspects of the MIS paradigm. You will do this in your own unique way. There is no right or wrong way to organize your case analysis.

However, if you haven't done case studies before and don't know how to get started, then read this section for some helpful suggestions. However, by no means should you construe this as the only approach to case solutions.

First, you must be able to cut through the talk and understand exactly what is going on. You can demonstrate your grasp of the case story by summarizing the MIS events as well as the relevant background information that you decide should be taken into account. In writing this summary, you will want to use the corresponding chapters in the text and your lecture notes as the context.

The context or the framework, or the *paradigm,* is a very important consideration. For example, a dog, in the context of animal physiology, is an arrangement of tissue, organs, circulatory and nervous systems, skeleton, cartilage, hair, nails, fangs, and teeth. In the context of security or crime prevention, a dog is ferocious, strong, protective, loud, obedient, controllable, and trained. You can imagine other contexts such as pet, wildlife, evolution, etc. In working with case studies, you must use the correct context in which to interpret the case scenarios. The appropriate context will be in terms of the definition of MIS and the topics and issues in MIS you are currently discussing in your class. These would normally be in the area of information technology, SDLC, database design considerations, DSS and management issues.

Second, you must develop a particular focus you wish to pursue. A case may involve so many different aspects of MIS that it would be overwhelming to discuss the case without narrowing the focus to specific facets. These may be specified by the instructor (especially in undergraduate courses), since it would be impractical to do a thorough and exhaustive analysis of each case.

Third, you must identify key issues addressed by the case in the particular focus and context in which you have chosen to analyze it. These key issues will relate directly to MIS issues being stressed in the lecture. Some issues in MIS are presented in the next section.

It is now possible to analyze the case in terms of the context, your focus, and the key issues you have raised. The analysis can proceed along these lines: what is the situation, what's right, what's wrong, what would you have done differently, and what do you recommend for the future, given the situation that exists.

Some Issues in MIS

The "Sins" and "Myths" of Ackoff and Dearden

In the time scale of information technology, 5 years ago is ancient and you wouldn't expect articles from decades past to address relevant issues. Yet, some questions raised by Russel Ackoff in 1967 ("Management Information Systems," *Management Science,* 14, December 1967) and John Dearden in 1972 ("MIS Is a Mirage," *Harvard Business Review,* Jan/Feb 1972, pp. 90-99) are so fundamental in scope that they continue to haunt MIS designers.

John Dearden, who is famous for having said that MIS technology is "a mishmash of fuzzy thinking and incomprehensible jargon," strikes a familiar chord in all of us with his Harry Truman style of plain speaking. He raised the issue of whether it was possible or necessary to have a corporation-wide homogenous MIS that was all things to all people. The "MIS experts" would have to be familiar with financial accounting, marketing, legal services, R & D, engineering, and production management to be able to design and operate this overall system. This, he claimed, was impractical. He is credited with expounding the notion, on this basis, that an MIS must be developed by a group (instead of by an individual) composed of experts from each representative discipline.

Russel Ackoff also addresses "people" problems that are not going to go away through technology alone. He complains that MIS designers tend to interpret all business problems as "lack of information" and are inclined to prescribe "more information" for just about any ailment. He points out that there is such a thing as "too much information" and that it is more important to separate relevant information from irrelevant than to obtain more data. He also raises the possibility that managers may not need the information they want, an issue so perverse that it has yet to be addressed in a meaningful way by MIS designers.

Ackoff argues that managers need to understand how information systems work, not just how to use them. This, he claims, will help managers avoid the trap of being controlled by the information system rather than being in control of it. If a manager does not understand how the MIS works, he or she will be intimidated by the technology and jargon, and therefore work with it on the basis of blind faith or fight with it on the basis of suspicion. In either case the manager will lose managerial competence.

Reliance on Technology to Solve Management Problems

Information technology is not a substitute for good management. Poor management decision-making styles and operating procedures should be identified as such and not as an information problem requiring an MIS solution.

The Twin Issues of Management Support and Project Initiation

It is an axiom of MIS that system implementations without management support are doomed. Ideally, MIS or DSS projects should be initiated by management. The worst-case scenario is that of MIS trying to "sell" management on projects conceived, incubated, and hatched entirely by MIS without direct management involvement. The best-case scenario is that of management identifying the need and implementing the solution with MIS assistance. Projects that do not have enthusiastic management support may die on the vine from lack of usage or interest.

End-User Computing

One wonders what John Dearden would say of this phrase. The genesis of this term perhaps goes back to the first awareness of personal computers in the organization by some MIS people. They thought they controlled all of the data in the organization until one day they saw ticking on a manager's desk a CPU that they could not control. Even more alarming was the sight of a disk drive spinning a diskette with data that they neither supplied nor knew anything about. Out popped the *end-user computing* phrase and the gurus of MIS have been trying to define it ever since. The only problem is that they can't agree.

A working definition of the term that is useful in identifying MIS problems and also consistent with its origin is this: if the users are also the developers and the activity is entirely without the involvement and control of the MIS department, the activity is end-user computing.

The reason end-user computing is an issue in MIS is that it violates classical notions of system homogeneity, data integrity, and data security. It is possible that a manager with only a passing knowledge of good programming practice could make consequential business decisions based on a spreadsheet model and on data that have not been tested, validated, or documented in a manner prescribed by the firm. It is also possible that data accumulated at great expense to the firm may become lost when end-users do not follow backup procedures or when they leave the company. When dealing with sensitive data, the issue of theft must also be addressed.

To a large degree these are legitimate concerns. But there are undoubtedly organizational issues that go beyond data integrity. Initially, MIS people saw personal computers as an encroachment on their domain and fought back to retain control of the firm's data. But whether the firm benefits if MIS does or does not control data is not well established. Most authorities agree that the bottom line on personal computers is that they have been phenomenal in increasing managerial productivity and effectiveness. MIS professionals have largely changed their stance on the issue from one of *control* to one of *support*; from confrontation to cooperation. The thrust of the cooperative effort has been to help the PC users with support, training, networking, PC/mainframe link, and software acquisition to alleviate some of the original concerns about end-user computing.

Ad Hoc Reports

We have seen that, as technology and MIS concepts change, we have to come up with new words to describe these changes. What is known as *ad hoc* may seem perfectly natural to you but, compared to traditional MIS designs, was a new idea when it was first used. The best way to understand what ad hoc means in this context and why we even have a word for it is to first look at traditional MIS.

In traditional MIS, the system (hardware, software, and data) was completely separated from the users of the information. The only information managers received from the management information system were periodic reports or printouts from the system. This is why you will find that some managers still refer to all computer-generated information as "printouts"; this form of information used to be their only contact with the computer.

The content of these printouts was fixed and they were printed only at certain times such as month's end or year's end. Managers did not have access to data that were not in the reports and could not access current data until the end of the report period. To correct this predicament, special software was developed so that custom reports could be generated at any time with simple query commands such as "List all engineers with salary greater than $50,000 and location not Houston."

Reports generated in this manner, whether by end users or by data processing (DP) personnel, became known as ad hoc reports. In most cases, these query methods were further refined so that computer novices such as managers might use them directly. In these cases, managers were actually given direct access to the MIS. Because this change was so remarkable when it happened (although we take it for granted nowadays), it was given a name.

When managers first used terminals to look through the MIS data by themselves, it was a novelty. For the first time, a non-DP person was using the computer directly (except for data entry). Some definitions of end-user computing, therefore, go back to this time and encompass direct usage of any computing facility by users of information.

MIS: Just a Fancy Name for DP?

Although MIS textbooks take a very broad view of the definition of MIS, the perception in the industry varies widely. Most still consider MIS to be the DP department, or the "keepers of the data"; essentially a transaction processing system that periodically generates reports. These are the so-called data-oriented systems and as such are not *management* information systems by current textbook standards, since we now require that a management information system be designed for the primary purpose of providing information to managers.

DP systems are designed primarily for recording and storing transaction data. The reports generated are not set up to be easily comprehensible to managers but rather to be convenient and comprehensive to the satisfaction of the DP department. Managers could glean from these reports what they could understand. In one extreme case, the DP department offered a short course on reading and understanding a project cost-analysis report. If managers have to take a course just to be able to read the report, the report must not have been designed for them. Renaming the DP department MIS does not make it so. MIS must be geared toward informing managers.

Piecemeal Changes and Backlog

Particularly during the implementation and maintenance phases of the systems development life cycle, the MIS user interface and report formats undergo evolutionary change, much of which is initiated by users through program change requests originating in different departments and functional areas. Some of them may be redundant, while others may actually be contradictory.

MIS programming managers must meet these user needs. They may process requests on a piecemeal basis or may collect them until they identify some patterns and spec out an overall programming change that will satisfy a number of related requests. In any case, MIS programming managers then assign a programmer to the task of making these changes, set a timetable, and allocate man-hours, machine time, and other resources to the programming project. The program changes are then coded, usually in a common procedural business language such as COBOL. The program must then be thoroughly tested, validated, and documented, processes not normally appreciated by the users making the requests.

During periods when the number of change requests is high (during maintenance and implementation), a larger programming staff may be needed. If the programming staff is not large enough or if the changes are not managed in an organized manner, the change requests begin to pile up in the in-box and the programmers begin to fall behind, sometimes by months and even years. The backlog has encouraged and may be alleviated by end-user computing, either by managers utilizing the mainframes directly via user-friendly interfaces or by utilizing personal computers.

Most MIS programming managers avoid piecemeal changes for two reasons. First, consider marginally different requests A and B that could both be satisfied with a compromise format C. But if the programming manager goes ahead and programs A first, he or she would then have to write another program for B. Had the manager waited for B and seen the commonalities, he or she might have been able to save valuable programming time.

Second, and more important, as the chief architect of the software the MIS programming manager cannot afford to cede control of the software design to the users. To do so will cause the program to lose all structure and definition and become a cacophony of patchwork.

The Cutting Edge of Technology

Four different circumstances have colluded to keep the American businessperson on the edge of his or her seat always ready to buy the newest and most powerful hardware and software available: rapidly changing technology, falling prices, perceived competitive advantage, and the tax advantages of accelerated depreciation. However, megahertz mania, the rush to buy the media darlings of technology, is more often driven by sex appeal or a desire to stay abreast of new technology than by rational decisions about competitive advantage. Conventional wisdom in MIS is to stay well behind the cutting edge while paying due attention to future growth paths and technological obsolescence. The more important considerations are those of software ware availability and support, hardware compatibility, industry acceptance, and flexibility.

Prototype or Sloppy Design?

Prototyping (PTTP) is an alternative to the traditional SDLC that is considered by many to be cheaper, faster, and better suited to the user. The difference between SDLC and PTTP is simply this: In SDLC, you try to get it right the first time but you don't, so you iterate until you do. In PTTP, you don't try to get it right the first time but instead rely on iterations. There are more iterations but, it is argued, the time you save in the front end more than makes up for that. And because there are more iterations (resulting from the user's actually trying to use the system), the effect is one of enhanced conformity.

The method works well in many applications, especially if the prototype is a development system and there is an identifiable implementation phase when the development system is removed and the working system is brought online. However, when the prototype is itself the working system (in various stages of completion) there is no clear implementation stage and the iterations may continue even when the system is apparently in use.

A risk of PTTP is that initial hardware and software decisions may be made without sufficient analysis. Much of the information normally obtained at the front end of an SDLC crops up in the middle of a PTTP, and by that time commitments to certain hardware and software configurations have already been made. Reluctance to "change horses in midstream" forces the developer to slosh through to a suboptimal design. A related criticism of PTTP is that, by giving it a name, we sanction sloppy designs thrown together with little or no planning or forethought.

What Do Managers Do and How Do They Do It?

MIS designs that focus only on information needs and ignore the manager's cognitive and decision-making styles will not be used. Or, if they are used, it will be only on a perfunctory basis — an obligatory run made for the record. It is, therefore, imperative that any interface to the MIS built for managers be designed only after the systems analyst has acquired information on what managers do and how they do it. The system must adapt to the managers. Too often, analysts design systems to suit themselves with the idea that as long as they provide what they consider to be a friendly user interface, enough documentation, and lots of training, then they can force anyone to adapt to the system as they have built it. This problem is a serious flaw in MIS design and is even more acute in DSS and Executive Information System (EIS) design.

System Diagrams

Your textbook discusses systems theory and systems diagrams, effective diagnostic tools that can be used to gain a basic understanding of how an organization works and what it does. These representations, called IPO (Input-Process-Output) diagrams, serve two functions: they are helpful in grasping the essentials of the business or data environment being described, and they are useful in formulating the dataflow diagrams that are used in developing the database designs and the overall MIS strategy.

Briefly, a *systemic* view of a business or an information system is one that looks at the business as a *system* performing a *process* that transforms *inputs* to *outputs* using *resources*. Further, the system consists of *subsystems* (each a smaller process with its own inputs and outputs) that are interconnected via these input and output paths. Ultimately, all inputs come from and all outputs go to the *environment* of the firm, which consists of customers, suppliers, government agencies, competitors, data sources, the marketplace for goods and labor, etc.

The real value of the so-called systems approach is the diagrams. These offer a way of collecting and organizing information about a business in a visual format that is easy to decipher so that the MIS analysts can understand how the business of the firm is carried out. Once the systems diagrams are drawn correctly and to the satisfaction of the managers, the analyst can then easily extract the dataflow diagrams from them.

Dataflow Diagrams

A simplified systems diagram and the corresponding dataflow diagram are shown in Figure CS.2. Refer to your textbook for additional examples. A dataflow diagram is

Figure CS.2
Dataflow Diagram

System Diagram

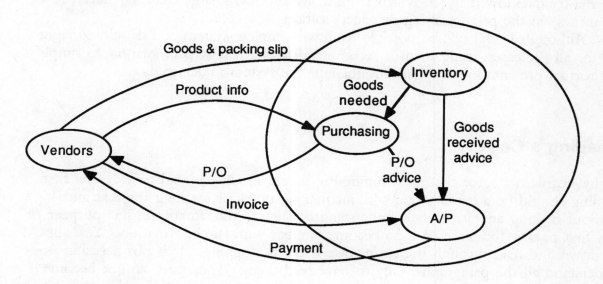

The Corresponding Data Flows

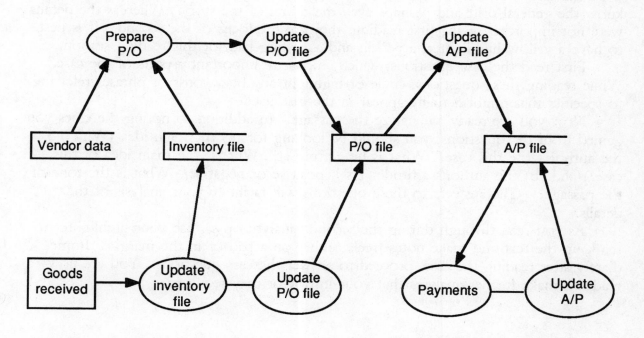

essentially a systems diagram that shows only data flows, a skeletal picture of the entire firm showing all sources and uses of data and their interconnections.

A good dataflow diagram is indispensable in MIS design and an effective aid in case study analysis. It offers a pictorial view of the database structure and is useful as documentation. When changes are made to the system, they are easily recorded on the master dataflow diagram which is normally kept on a large drafting sheet (24 x 36 inches) in the programming manager's office.

Although it will not be possible to draw complete system and dataflow diagrams for all the cases, using them is recommended as a first step in analysis to simplify the textual presentation and gain insight into the system under study.

Reading a Case

Many instructors agree that, as a minimum, a case should be read twice. The first reading should be a cursory one without making notes or marking the text and without making any attempt to understand or analyze the situation. The purpose of this first pass at the material is to become familiar with the information. You should sit down and read through the entire case without stopping. It is not necessary to understand all the paragraphs, only to have read them. Therefore, do not become bogged down rereading paragraphs that you don't understand. Following this initial reading, put away your case book for several hours or for a day if time allows.

The second reading should be an analytical one. You now have some idea of what the case is about, having read it through as if it were a story. Therefore, you know the general drift and perhaps even the moral of the story. Whereas the details were not important in the first reading, they are the focus of the second. It is best to have a yellow highlighter, a pencil, and a writing pad for this reading session.

First read the case questions, which emphasize important aspects of the case. While reading these questions, circle or highlight any buzzwords or phrases referring to specifics that might actually appear in the case itself.

Now you are ready to analyze the passage. In addition to noting the clues you gained from the questions, you should be looking for (a) the main idea (Why did the author write this case? What is he getting at? What is the main idea of this case?) and (b) the author's attitude (Is it positive or negative? What is the tone of the passage?) The answers to these questions will facilitate your analysis of the details.

As you read through during the second (analytic) pass, use your highlighter to mark up the text and make notes freely, either on a pad or in the margins. Immediately after reading the case, proceed to answer the case questions. You are now ready to make further analyses that your instructor may require.

Components of a Decision

Because a case is essentially a decision-making situation, we can examine it according to the components of a decision. These are

The decision maker	Who is the decision maker?
The problem	What is the problem?
Boundaries and constraints	What is the problem space?
	What is the solution space?
The alternatives	What are the options?
The attributes	On what basis are these alternatives to be compared?
The decision process	How are these alternatives to be compared?

Who is the decision maker?

The problem definition and the feasible solutions depend a great deal on who the decision maker (DM) is. The solution methods proposed must address the role and position of the DM within the organization, his or her technical expertise, and his or her cognitive and decision-making style. It must weigh whether the decision maker is risk-averse, conservative or progressive, and what his or her overall objectives are likely to be. Only then can we view the current situation in the correct perspective so that our perception of the problem and our proposed solution will be relevant.

Most of the cases in this book do not delineate the decision maker exactly but leave a wide area of flexibility for the instructor. Your instructor may want you to assume the role of a consultant to the DM or to play that role of the decision maker yourself. In either case, you must work within the possible capacities of the DM in the organizational and the philosophical context that has been set in the case description. When you take these criteria into account, the problem definition and solution alternatives you develop are more likely to be realistic in terms of the personalities and organizational settings outlined.

What is the problem?

In addition to verifying that the problem definition is relevant to the decision maker, the problem-definition phase must undertake the separation of symptoms from problems. Since a problem in general is defined to be the difference between the current state and the goal state, a proper beginning to problem definition is identification of these two states. To separate symptoms from their underlying causes (the actual problems), you should pursue the possible reasons for the differences between these states.

Avoid overly ambitious problem definitions and grandiose solutions. Problem definitions that are focused within reasonable bounds can be addressed concretely and realistically, so you can set your boundaries.

What are the boundaries and constraints?

Most decisions can be improved if the decision maker first defines the *problem space* and the *solution space*. Defining the problem space means distinguishing the problem being addressed from those problems, objectives, and potential problems that are to be excluded from this decision-making process. Clear definition of problem boundaries helps you avoid problem definitions that are so large and all encompassing as to be beyond the scope of the subject matter or the point of the case.

The solution space is delimited by a set of constraints, which normally indicate the maximum amount of resources that can be allocated to this problem solution or to minimum performance specifications; that is, they are the limits within which each alternative or option must be proposed.

What are the options?

A decision — any decision — consists of choosing among two or more alternatives. Thus, there must be at least two possible courses of action or there is no decision to be made. Of course, one alternative is to do nothing.

In generating the possible courses of action you must ensure that each alternative is technically, financially, and politically feasible. Some obvious criteria are often overlooked: Does each alternative assume the same current condition? Does every alternative achieve the (same) goal state? What assumptions had to be made to generate these alternatives from the given data? Are these assumptions the same?

On what basis are these alternatives to be compared?

These are the so-called *factors* or *attributes* of the decision. *Factors* are qualities or determinants that relate directly to what we actually need to solve our problem. We then examine each alternative to determine the extent to which the alternative will satisfy that need. In simple structured cases, the comparison of alternatives can be accomplished in a tabular format.

Table CS.1 shows an example decision. A PC network is to be built. The decision boils down to a choice among three network vendors.

In this case, the data speed, customer support, Mac support, etc., are the factors on which these options are being compared. These may or may not be valid factors, based on whether they are relevant to this decision. For example, the factor *Mainframe Links* is not relevant because it is the same in each case, and thus should be removed. Similarly, if the file-server capability is absolutely required, Vendor B should not be considered, and thus is not an option. Since the remaining two vendors both offer file-server capability, this feature is not a factor in the decision.

How are these alternatives to be compared?

If all factors are strictly quantitative in nature, such as cost in dollars, then the alternatives can be compared simply by summing the costs (or present values). The option with the lowest cost or the highest benefit would then be the best alternative.

Table CS.1
Comparison of Network Alternatives

	Options		
Factors	Vendor A	Vendor B	Vendor C
Data Speed	10	3	6
Customer Support	good	excellent	fair
Macintosh Support	future	now	no
Mainframe Links	yes	yes	yes
Cost	$14000	$7000	$6500
File Server	yes	no	yes
Database Server	yes	no	no
Print Spooling	no	poor	good

However, when some of the factors are qualitative, requiring subjective evaluation by the decision maker, the comparison of options requires the use of other techniques. Many of these are intuitive. You may want to use your own methods, but here are some techniques that business managers frequently use:

1. *Weighting*. Assign a number (weight), say, from 1 to 10, to each sub- jective factor to indicate how important the factor is to the decision maker in relation to the other factors. Then rate each option according to each factor, again with an arbitrary rating scale, to indicate how well this option satisfies the requirements of this factor. Compute the weighted sum of subjective factors as the qualitative score of each op- tion. There still remains the problem of comparing the total subjective score to the total cost or quantitative figure. This requires yet another subjective evaluation and is best performed graphically. Plot each option in a two-dimensional qualitative/quantitative space and use a visual inspection to select the best option. An example is provided in Figure CS.3.

2. *Ranking*. Rank the factors according to importance. Compare the options according to the most important factor and discard the worst options. If more than one option remains, use the next important factor, and so on until only one option is left.

3. *Worst aspects*. Compare the worst attribute of each option to a standard or minimum acceptable value and discard the options that do not compare favorably. It is not always easy to determine which is the worst attribute and what the standard ought to be. For example, say we are comparing two wordprocessing programs, A and B, in terms of speed, cost, numbers of features, and ease of use. For each of these factors, we have set a standard value. Program A exceeds our cost standard but meets other criteria well, so cost becomes its worst attribute.

Figure CS.3
Qualitative/Quantitative Space

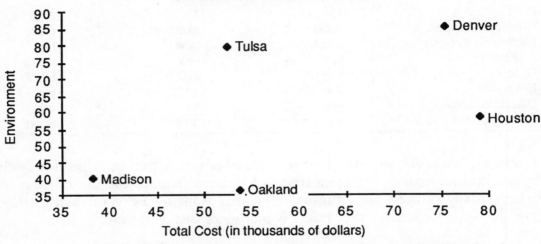

SITE SELECTION DSS: MANUFACTURING PLANT LOCATION
Employee Environment Score plotted against Total Cost
(sites nearer the origin are better)

"Environment" is a subjective rank based on cost of living, traffic, climate,
cultural events, sporting events, etc. "Total Cost" is a quantitative variable.

4. *Multi-dimensional scaling.* Select the two most important attributes, A and B.
    On an xy-plot (the x-axis representing attribute A and the y-axis representing
    attribute B) locate each option. Through visual inspection, discard options that
    plot unfavorably. Repeat with AC, AD, and so on. This technique is useful
    when there are two major factors. In other cases, it can be used to reduce the
    number of factors that must be juggled in making the final choice.

Learning Experiences

These cases are presented to serve as cross-sectional examples of the organizational
role, technology, and infrastructure of MIS in businesses today rather than to necessarily identify and expose problem areas for you to solve. The case study/case
solution approach and the analytical structure it utilizes clearly reveals the lessons you
can learn from MIS professionals. It also presents a simulated decision-making
situation in a managerial role. For the most part, you should view these MIS cases
as success stories, descriptions of some exemplary real-world information systems
from which you can learn a great deal about MIS.

PART 2

Sample Case

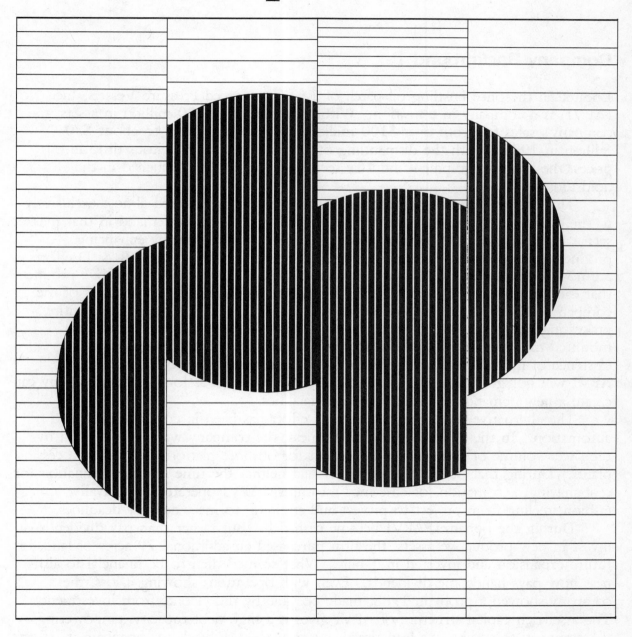

ADVANCED PRESSURE VESSELS, INC.

A User-Oriented Order-Entry System

Company Background

Located in the once bustling oil patch of Texas, Advanced Pressure Vessels, Inc. (APVI) is a company in transition. With approximately $130 million in assets, the company's sales fell from over $100 million in the early eighties to about $70 million in 1988. With the dismantling of OPEC and the precipitous drop in oil prices, the process equipment industry seemed to be firmly entrenched in the doldrums.

This custom pressure vessel manufacturer, which had catered almost exclusively to the domestic oil and gas industry, responded to a slump in demand in that market sector by beefing up the research and development budget and by enhancing productivity and efficiency, primarily through computerization. The R & D efforts are now aimed at entering new and unconventional markets with innovative products that can be produced efficiently, using the enormous fixed productive assets of the company. These include a large fabrication shop and assembly yard where entire processing plants can be pre-assembled and then taken down and shipped as skid-mounted modules. Such facilities are rare and management is convinced of the existence of markets for these services that the firm has hitherto ignored; that is, APVI will not go down with the decline in the oil patch as long as the company can create a new demand for its expertise and facilities.

The alternative (and more important) effort has been in cost reduction and automation. In the heyday of the oil business, the company was overwhelmed by the sheer volume of demand for equipment for offshore platforms and gas processing plants. During that period, the company had neither the time nor the inclination for cost-shaving, automation, or efficiency measures. APVI operated in a cavalier fashion, reeling from project to project and straining to meet delivery deadlines.

During the bonanza, APVI became cash-rich. But rather than pay dividends or invest in new productive assets, the firm purchased an additional 70 acres of land for future expansion and invested in T-bills. What seemed then to be financial foolishness now pays handsome dividends. Even with operations showing a loss, the company showed a profit in 1988, made possible by the income from investments. The asset-rich capital structure of APVI gives it a high debt capacity, empowering the company to survive the lean times and even to raise funds for financing its efforts to enter new markets. The only danger is that its cash-rich and depressed position will invite a leveraged buyout by the financial opportunists of Wall Street. A summary of APVI's financial condition is shown in Table AP.1.

Note in Table AP.1 that assets are supported principally with equity (mostly retained earnings), with very little use of long-term debt. Apparently, much of the earnings have been ploughed into T-bills instead of into the business itself, which, from a purely financial perspective, is highly unusual, to say the least. The income statement shows another anomaly. The pressure vessel business is unable to support the high level of R & D and the operation actually shows a loss. However, this loss is more than compensated for by the income from investments.

The Process Equipment Business

Oil and gas processing frequently requires that fluids be treated at very high pressures – up to 150 times the atmospheric pressure or over 2000 psig (pounds per square inch gauge). Depending on the treatment, the temperature of the fluids can vary from the bitter cold of cryogenic processes (down to -100 degrees F) to the intense heat of chemical reactors (more than 1000 degrees F). In certain cases, the fluids may contain hydrogen sulfide, carbon dioxide, sulfur dioxide, hydrogen, and other gases that are both corrosive and dangerous if leaked. These fluids are processed in large drums called *pressure vessels* that are designed to process gases at very high pressure without leaking or bursting. Most process pressure vessels are built according to standards set by the American Society of Mechanical Engineers (ASME) in the ASME Section 8 Pressure Vessel Code.

The vessel size can vary from 2 feet to 12 feet in diameter and 6 feet to 80 feet in length. The thickness of the steel plates range from three-eighths of an inch to over an inch, depending on the design pressure. The plates are rolled and welded at the APVI fabrication shop. Nozzles and dished heads are purchased and affixed to the vessel by welding. The vessels are then pressure-tested according to ASME specs. APVI engineers, in cooperation with the customers' engineers, ascertain that the vessel will withstand the severity of the service and that its size will be adequate for the desired capacity.

Over the last 40 years, APVI has matured technically beyond mere pressure vessel fabrication, extending its business to include the design and fabrication of small skid-mounted process plants. A skid is a platform, usually 12 feet by 40 feet, made of steel I-beams on which an assembly of pressure vessels and associated equipment, piping, and instrumentation can be built at the APVI shop or yard and then shipped fully assembled. The skid-mounted design minimizes field construction and is particularly attractive for remote or hostile construction sites and off-shore platforms. APVI has been especially successful in this market, and management now seeks to apply the idea of skid-mounting to other applications to enter or create new markets for its services.

Table AP.1
Summary of APVI Financial Statement: Year Ending 12/31/1988

Balance Sheet

Assets

Current Assets

Cash and T-Bills	$ 39,684,000
Accounts Receivable	11,905,000
Inventory	14,821,000
Total Current Assets	**66,410,000**

Fixed Assets

Machinery and Equipment	66,900,000
Buildings	20,757,000
Land	19,369,000
Less accumulated depreciation	(44,031,000)
Net Fixed Assets	**63,085,000**
Total Assets	**$ 129,495,000**

Liability and Equity

Current Liability

Accounts Payable	$ 3,920,000
Other Current Liability	9,793,000
Total Current Liability	**13,713,000**

Long Term Debt

Bonds	7,410,000
Bank Loans	2,000,000
Total Long Term Debt	**9,410,000**

Stockholders' Equity

Common Stock	50,757,000
Retained Earnings	55,615,000
Total Stockholders' Equity	**106,372,000**
Total Support for Assets	**129,495,000**

Income Statement

Sales	$ 71,176,000
Cost of Sales	46,184,000
Selling and Administrative	8,242,000
Research and Development	17,068,000
Income from Continuing Operations	(**318,000**)
Net Interest Income from T-Bills	2,771,000
Net Earnings	2,453,000
Income Tax	682,000
NIAT (Net income after taxes)	**1,771,000**

The APVI Product Divisions

The company is divided into three operating divisions (see Figure AP.1) along product lines. With over 50 employees, the engineered products division (EPD) has the largest staff and is the most technically sophisticated of the three. The personnel consists mainly of design engineers, project engineers, and draftsmen. The group actually operates as an engineering design and construction company and utilizes the pressure vessel group as an internal source for pressure vessels, designing and supplying complete skid-mounted natural gas treating plants.

The division has a sales department (see Figure AP.2) that seeks out construction projects to bid. The proposals department prepares the bid, using engineering design specs prepared for the job by the engineering department. The group may submit 50 to 100 proposals per year, about 10% of which may be successful. These five to ten projects per year generate revenues of $1 million to $2 million each. APVI's future plans are built around the EPD, the newest and most promising operating division of the company.

The old pressure vessel business has been broken off into the pressure vessels division (PVD). The PVD sales department produces a catalog of standard pressure vessels so that regular customers can order by part number. The division also makes custom vessels that are designed by its engineering staff to meet customer specifications. Many of the custom orders are in fact repeat orders from the same customer, while others require only minor modifications to previously made drawings. Historical data play an important role in the operation of the pressure vessels group.

The standard products division (SPD) operates exclusively from the rather large order catalog that its sales staff maintains. Although there is no engineering staff per se, the sales engineers, as they are referred to, are mostly former engineers from the pressure vessels group. The division sells small standardized skid-mounted process units that have been pre-engineered; that is, the customer, assisted by the sales engineer, can pick out a model number for a unit, starting with the process requirements. The standard products include liquids separators, gas dehydrators, and oil field heaters. The catalog contains tables and selection charts to aid the customer in selecting the appropriate process unit. The SPD does not become involved in any custom-engineered job. If an inquiry comes in that cannot be met by a standard product, it is referred to Engineered Products.

As shown in Figure AP.2, each operating division is a semi-autonomous unit with its own sales and engineering staff. The shop acts as a common manufacturing resource that is available to all the divisions. This scheme is complicated by the EPD, which has purchased a competitor's shop to which it has been increasingly shifting its assembly and test operations. Although the shop foreman has openly criticized this high-handed move by EPD, management has been more sympathetic to EPD's scheduling problems created by delays in the shop.

All quotations and proposals prepared by the operating divisions are funneled through the legal and contracts department (usually referred to as just *Contracts*) for

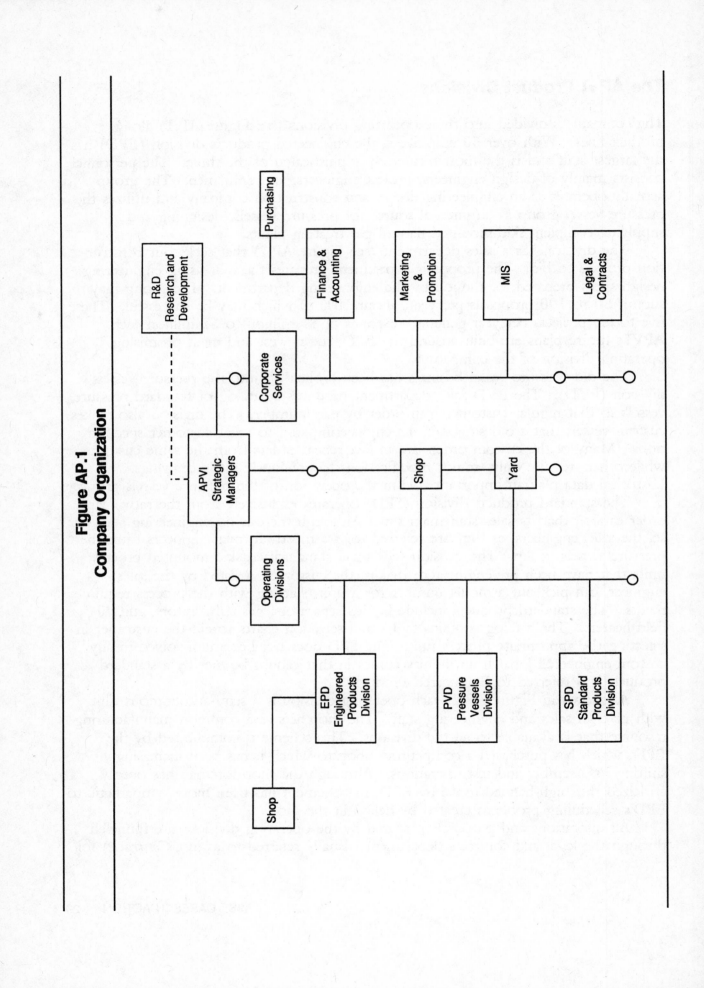

**Figure AP.1
Company Organization**

Figure AP.2
APVI Operating Division

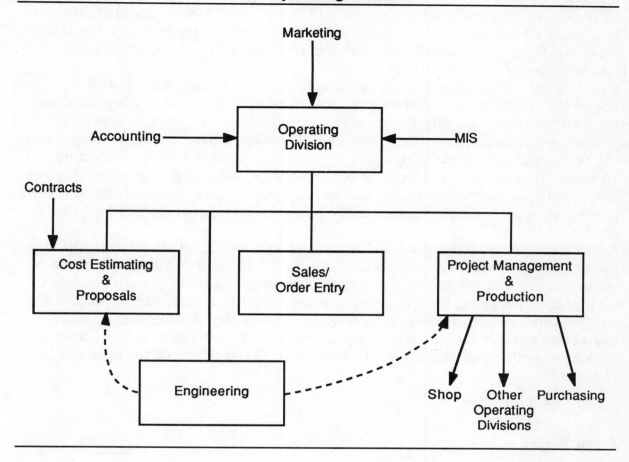

scrutiny before being delivered to customers. In most cases the department's contribution consists of little more than inclusion of boilerplate disclaimer clauses. However, in custom jobs and in dealing with new customers and the U.S. government, the contracts department may become so involved in the proposal process that they take over primary responsibility for the proposal. In such cases, the operating division's role becomes relegated to supplying relevant technical information. Between these extremes are many gray-area cases in which the primary responsibility for the proposal is not clearly established and questions are raised as to who is providing a service to whom. Some division managers have advocated eliminating the contracts department as part of the cost-cutting program.

The research and development group (R & D) is a recent addition to the organization. After feasting for 40 years on the original dehydrator and separator design standards established by the founders, the company has recognized the need for creating new technology to be more competitive in the oil field business, as well as to become more independent of oil and gas production activity. An important milestone in recent R & D efforts has been an improved (and patented) process for extraction of elemental sulfur from hydrogen sulfide, a process now offered by the EPD as a "sulfur plant" option to its desulfurizer plants. A more dramatic outcome of R & D efforts has been the deep-sea submersible vehicle produced for the U.S. Navy and for marine research. The vehicles are designed by the R & D engineers and fabricated at the APVI shop.

It is this vehicle that sparked the imagination of top management with the notion that APVI could and should become more diversified and less dependent on the fortunes of oil. Among the promising new products that R & D may soon produce are safer nuclear waste containers, skid-mounted mobile toxic waste processing plants, and an ultra-fine, high-pressure filtration system for the food industry. However, because these products are unconventional, none of the operating divisions possesses the technology to design and produce them. Thus, the products have been labelled as "experimental" and are actually being produced, marketed, and sold by R & D.

Except for the sulfur plant and some improved metallurgy, the research group has not directly benefitted the operating divisions. Instead, it is quickly becoming its own operating division with its own sales, marketing, engineering, and production departments. However, because it does use the shop and because of its spectacular success with the submersible vehicle, R & D exercises considerable leverage with management and is able to extract very generous R & D budgets. These activities are viewed with a certain amount of suspicion by the managers of the operating divisions.

Data Processing

About 7 years ago, APVI renamed the data processing (DP) department the MIS department and removed it from Accounting (which was renamed Finance). MIS is now a VP-level operation, reporting directly to the president of the company. (see Figure AP.1.) The department consists of approximately 15 MIS professionals organized according to the chart shown in Figure AP.3. The systems engineering group maintains the hardware and the system-level software. The development group is responsible for providing and maintaining the battery of databases and application software that make up the information system from the user's perspective. These programmers are grouped by functional orientation. Because of the technical nature of the business, there is naturally an emphasis on manufacturing and engineering applications. Design and research engineers are heavy users of the system, and providing support for their applications is a major activity of the MIS group.

The MIS hardware environment consists of a mainframe, a mini, and a collection of personal computers. Each system operates in isolation, with no communi-

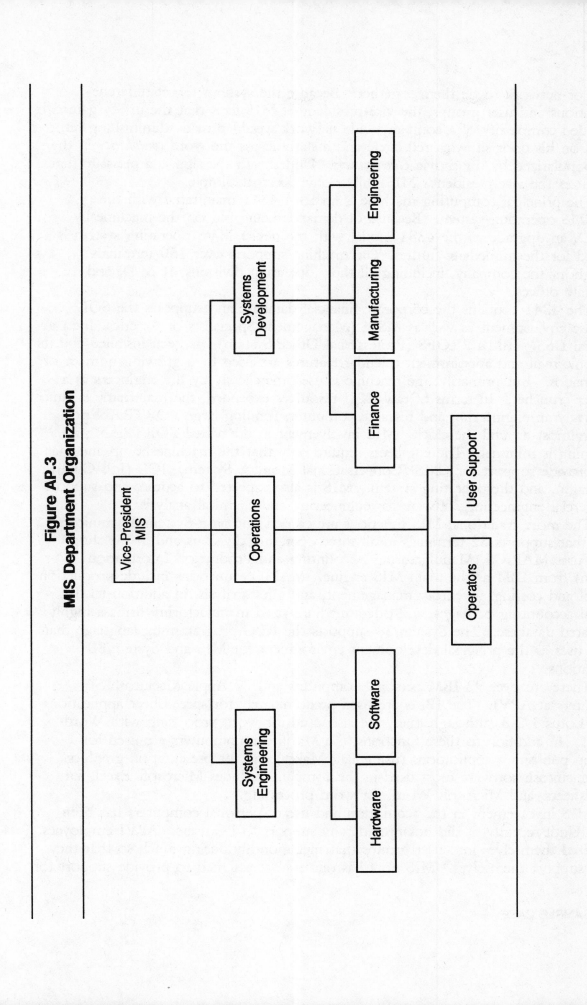

Figure AP.3
MIS Department Organization

cation or network to tie them together. Because the systems target different applications and user groups, the vice-president of MIS feels that the utility gained by the added complexity of a company-wide network would provide diminishing returns. A sign on his door shows a red circle and a slash across the word *complexity* in the style popularized by the movie *Ghostbusters*. Underneath the sign is a message that epitomizes the vice-president's MIS philosophy: Keep It Simple.

The principal computing machine is an IBM 4341 mainframe with the VM/CMS operating system. Because of demands being put on the machine by R & D, an upgrade to the 4381 model with the newer MVS operating system is planned for the immediate future. The machine supports over 150 terminals throughout the company, including all three operating divisions, R & D, and corporate offices.

The 4341 contains the corporate financial database and supports the SQL database environment as well as MSA, (Management Specialists of America, Inc.) a financial DSS. IBM's PROFS (Professional Office System) has been installed and its electronic mail and appointment calendar features are used by a growing number of afficionados. But primarily, the machine is used mercilessly by the engineers as a number cruncher. In terms of raw CPU resources expended, the mainframe is almost exclusively an engineering and research computer, running large FORTRAN programs almost around the clock. MIS involvement in the actual FORTRAN programming is minimal. The engineers require only that the machine be up and that MIS provide support for CMS (Conversational Monitor System), JCL (Job Control Language), and the operating system. MIS is also expected to acquire and support commercial engineering software for engineering and chemical analysis.

The more traditional MIS functions are carried out on a System/38 minicomputer that supports 82 terminals in all three operating divisions and in the shop. APVI uses MAPICS (Manufacturing Accounting and Production Information System) from IBM as the main MIS engine. MAPICS functions include production control and costing, inventory management, and sales analysis, in addition to the normal accounting packages, and offers medium-sized manufacturing firms a highly integrated database. The System/38 supports the RPG programming language that APVI uses as the principal development environment for MIS and System/38 applications.

There are over 92 IBM personal computers and 77 Apple Macintosh SE computers at APVI. The IBMs are used predominately for spreadsheet applications using Lotus 1-2-3, although many are also used for word processing with Word-Perfect. In addition to these functions, the Macintosh computers are used for desktop publishing applications (using PageMaker) and for presentation graphics. The Macintosh software most used in the company includes Microsoft Excel, for spreadsheets, and Microsoft Word, for word processing.

MIS involvement in the acquisition and use of personal computers has been zero. Until recently, it did not provide any support to PC users. APVI employees organized themselves into user groups that met monthly during lunch so that they could support themselves. MIS now has one analyst assigned to provide support for personal computer users and has even linked some of the PCs to the System/38 and the 4341.

Order Entry

Although there are three operating divisions, there are in fact four semi-independent sales entities in the company, if one includes R & D. Each of these operates in a different marketplace and has unique products and order processing information needs. Further, each entity operates an independent sales department. Some divisions deal with one-of-a-kind orders while others deal with standard products. The evolution of the divisions has been sequential so that as each division was spawned, it defined its own order processing needs instead of adopting a system from another division. For all of these reasons, each division has its own order-entry system, and perhaps rightly so. These systems have very little in common, since each was custom-designed and developed to fit the division's order-processing needs.

The three operating divisions use order-entry systems on the System/38, all programmed in RPG. The programs for the pressure vessels and standard products divisions are "canned" commercial order-entry packages purchased from different vendors and are maintained and supported by APVI's MIS programmers. Both programs had to be heavily maintained (changed) to fit the order processing needs of the two divisions and both are geared to different types of businesses and users. As a result, the programs are disparate and have very little in common, either in data structure or in user interface.

The order-entry system for EPD had to meet unique needs. There are only a few orders per year and each order is unique, with a long list of qualifying engineering specifications. Also, EPD managers decided that the order-entry system should be integrated with their proposal-tracking and sales-forecast program. Since these programs were obtained from an outside vendor, the order entry system was purchased from the same vendor to ensure compatibility. An unusual feature of EPD's order-entry system is that each order is broken up into a series of associated orders, linking order numbers to process equipment more directly. Each set of these related order numbers is organized under a master order number that is tied in to the overall engineering and system integration. Using such a scheme an order for a car, for example, might be broken up into order numbers for the engine, the transmission, the chassis, body, interior, etc. and then a master-order number for the assembly, engineering, and instrumentation is assigned to make the whole thing work. EPD uses their cost-buildup tables to assign dollar values to the subsidiary order numbers.

The research and development department designed its own order-entry system on a Macintosh SE computer. Because it was not originally envisioned that R & D would take orders, neither management nor MIS paid any attention to their order processing needs. However, as orders for equipment and for services began to come in, an R & D engineer took it upon himself to set up an order tracking system, using Hypercard from Apple Computer. Later, a consultant was retained to extend and maintain the complex set of Hypercard stacks into a complete order processing system. As of this writing, this order-entry program is undergoing maintenance and is expected to evolve into a very sophisticated and powerful program with a transparent linkage to the System/38.

The variety of order-entry systems presented several problems from the corporate perspective. MIS found it increasingly difficult and costly to support four different programs instead of one. Corporate managers had no single source for data on bookings (orders that have been placed but not delivered). Corporate managers like to follow the total dollar value of bookings very closely. At APVI, a company-wide order summary is produced once a week by the finance department in a very inefficient manner. Printouts are requested from each order-entry system and delivered by intra-company mail. When all the printouts arrive, the relevant numbers are entered into a Lotus 1-2-3 spreadsheet. Finally, a total company-wide summary of bookings is obtained and photocopies of this report are distributed to top managers. By the time the managers receive this report, it is usually out of date. The report loses credibility when it does not include an order that a manager knows has come in.

Another problem arises in the transfer of orders from one division to another. For example, when EPD obtains an order for a plant, it usually transfers a series of orders for pressure vessels to PVD. The transfer is entirely manual, involving data re-entry. More egregious, from an MIS point of view, is that none of the order entry systems, with the possible exception of R & Ds, is sufficiently flexible or user-friendly. They are rigid and unforgiving of errors. Some insist that all fields be filled in before an order can be filed, although in many instances some of the fields are superfluous or inane. MIS has received other complaints from users. For instance, once an order is entered, it is impossible to delete it. Users simply add another order and the system accumulates the bad orders, which, embarrassingly, keep reappearing in all the summary reports. When searching for an old order, the user must remember the exact order number since it is impossible to find an order without an order number.

Many of the orders are repeat orders. Others, from the same customer, vary only slightly from previous orders. Because the systems are not set up to exploit this simplicity in the order- taking process, each order must be keyed in entirely. It is not possible to pull the information from another order from the same customer for the same piece of equipment. Also, errors made in data entry are not easily corrected. When these errors are detected, a new order is entered correctly.

The multiplicity of order-entry systems sometimes results in confusion about part numbers and part names. The same part can be assigned different part numbers and even different names in the four programs. For instance, a "600-pound ASA flange" can be a "600# ASA FL" in another system or a "600# flange" in another. A customer receiving a confirmation for an order that lists a "600# flange" when a previous confirmation had listed a "600# ASA flange" may rightly be concerned about the difference between the two.

What MIS finds most problematic is that the order-entry systems are, by and large, inflexible and not designed to efficiently handle changes to an order. Yet, the nature of the orders processed at APVI is that they undergo continual change. Throughout the lifetime of an order, which can range from a week to ten weeks, the customer may make changes to the design or metallurgy. APVI engineers may substitute, for example, a different type of control valve when availability becomes a problem. Ideally, an order-entry system for such a process would not only allow changes to be made easily but would maintain an audit trail of changes.

The contracts department adds another level of inefficiency. As each order is accepted by Sales, a printout of the order is sent to Contracts. Contracts than makes up the official legal contract between the customer and APVI. The contracts are written on Macintosh computers and the order information is re-keyed from the printout of the order entry system.

MIS to the Rescue

The vice-president of MIS summarized the order-entry situation to the president as "a complete mess" and suggested that MIS be chartered to do a complete overhaul of order processing at APVI to achieve higher efficiency and reduce costs. The users objected to the canned systems and their limitations. However, through the use of these systems, both the users and MIS have learned what the order processing needs of each division are and the pitfalls that need to be avoided. A particular challenge to the new system designer is that many of the staff are used to the Macintosh and expect everything to work as it does in the Macs. It is no longer possible to dictate to users what they can and can't do on a system, since even the most system-illiterate user can use a Mac and develop a certain sense of what he or she can expect from computers. MIS developers are therefore put in the position of having to meet these user expectations. When user expectations are not met, users tend to work around the system.

MIS proposed that APVI should have one integrated order-entry system for the whole company, with all divisions and R & D using this order-entry system. The consolidation of order processing would, it was claimed, result in better company performance at lower cost. Accordingly, MIS submitted a proposal for in-house development of a new order-entry system on the System/38. The proposal by MIS was met with bitter opposition. R & D was pushing its own system. Why, they wanted to know, should the company develop a brand-new order-entry system when they already had one? R & D therefore made a counter proposal — that their Macintosh-based system be modified for company-wide adoption. But MIS prevailed and soon began formal meetings with all users to define the scope and specifications of the new order-entry program.

The overall guidelines for the project developed by MIS were as follows:

1. The new order-entry system would utilize the System/38. The VP of MIS was very concerned about what he called "proliferation of data without integration," and, since the System/38 with MAPICS was the basis of the company's MIS, the order and bookings data rightly belonged as part of the same database. He was absolutely opposed to any notion that the two databases could or should be segregated.

2. The challenge of MIS would be to develop good application software. Since canned order-entry programs had failed at APVI, the new program would be developed in-house. The programming language chosen was RPG-III. The VP had a high regard for his programming staff and for their proficiency in RPG-III. Besides, the staff of fifteen was rather large by industry standards, and there was a danger of cuts in overhead personnel during lean times. Full utilization of the vice president's human resources would ensure their continued survival. The choice of RPG-III was dictated by the hardware environment, since it is the natural language for business software written for the System/38. Cobol code would take too long to develop and maintain and would not allow the ease of report generation that RPG would permit.

3. The dominant objectives of the system design would be to reduce complexity and to achieve a high degree of integration internally and externally. Internal integration is achieved when all data used and generated by the program have one common specification and are consistent. External integration means that the order entry database should be consistent with the main inventory, manufacturing, and accounting data maintained by MAPICS. When the order-entry system needs inventory or accounting data, it should be able to get these data from the main MIS database. Conversely, when order-entry generates data that belong in the main database, it should provide them. However, this push for integration was tempered with the VP's exhortation to "keep it simple." He has made reduction of complexity and the development of a system that is easy to understand, program, change, and use a high priority. In his view, extremely grandiose designs are difficult to maintain, use, or support, since nobody actually understands them and since the complex interaction of the components of a system can turn a minor maintenance task into a nightmare.

4. Integration must be maintained also at the user level. This means that the system must look the same to all users. No matter which division or department is using the system or whether the sales representative, sales administrator, or shipping clerk is looking at the screen, it should

look the same. The commonality of screens and command structure reduces complexity and improves user confidence in the system.

5. The system must be extremely easy to use and must build user-confidence. The design of the user interface and command system must cater to the expectations of the Macintosh users and to users who are considered to be "system illiterate." No training should be necessary for users to begin using the system and it should be robust, that is, at once forgiving of errors and safe from possible damage by inexperienced users.

6. The system must have a high-level query interface so that it can be used by managers in an ad hoc style for DSS.

7. The system must be completed and implemented within 9 months. The fast development cycle requires using a prototyping approach rather than a conventional SDLC. The prototyping stages would start with mock-up of user screens and related commands and help screens, and, with the users' help, would work backwards one step at a time to incorporate the linkage of these screens with the real database.

8. System conversion would follow the parallel scheme. After the 9-month development period, old and new order-entry systems would be run simultaneously for an additional 3 months. After the full one-year period, the old systems would be phased out.

9. The system must meet the needs of the contracts department, as well as those of the three operating divisions and of R & D. In addition, interfaces should be provided for query by customer, corporate managers, and shop foremen. The order-entry system must automatically produce the bookings summary report required by corporate managers.

Case Comments for Solution

Here are some organizational perspectives on the APVI study:

1. R & D and the operating divisions seem to have difficulty understanding the fact that they are there so that the shop will have an adequate workload to justify the fixed investment. R & D's efforts to ignore the rest of the company on the basis of the submersible vehicle and their technical superiority are not organizationally viable. R & D must be made to give up their pet order-entry system and join the rest of the company in bringing about the best possible integrated system. If they have some constructive ideas for the new system, they must communicate these to MIS. Strategic managers must resist being so much in

awe of these white-coated R & D wunderkinds, which allows them to become renegades. It is time for the president of the company to sit down with the VP of MIS and the VP of R & D and firmly lay down the law.

2. The order-entry project obtains a great deal of strength from the support and blessing it receives from top managers, who, after all, approved the project. However, the project did not originate with the managers or with the users of the multiple order-entry systems. Rather, it was MIS that came up with the order-entry project and then tried to sell the idea to top managers first. Only after MIS obtained approval were the users let in on the deal. Thus, although MIS has management support, they can't count on an equal amount of support from users.

3. It is not clear whether the MIS department's concern for the users should be taken seriously. The specific circumstances have other interpretations. The company's income from continued operations is negative, which means that even though cash from investments is available to spend on fixed costs of operations, the net worth of the owners is decreasing. The stockholders must be very concerned. The pressure of such a situation usually pushes managers into drastic cost-cutting measures with fixed overhead costs usually being the first to get the axe. Under these circumstances, one would expect departments such as Contracts and MIS to be cut to the bone. It is possible that the move by MIS is motivated more by these considerations than by user needs and MIS philosophies. The project still appears to have merit because it may actually reduce costs, but it requires careful study by top managers, given the company's financial situation.

4. The VP of MIS is probably being overly inflexible in his approach to the order-entry system. The necessity for managers to provide ideological leadership can easily be taken to excess. Highly opinionated MIS managers who set rigid rules or heuristics as guidelines for a project can stifle creativity and original ideas from their staff. A more open-minded approach, for instance, would allow consideration of a Macintosh-based system that is linked to the System/38 in a distributed processing architecture. The basis for such a system may already exist in the company at R & D, which not only has a running order-entry system but has even achieved a link with the System/38. By the MIS vice-president's own admission, what the users actually want is to use the Macintosh as their workstation. However, he is determined to give them what he thinks they should have. The users will be consulted and their needs determined but only within the constraints he has already established. Although his determination to avoid complexity is

admirable, *complexity* is a vague term that can easily be used to defend what one likes and to attack that with which one is unfamiliar.

System perspectives on the APVI study include the following considerations:

1. *Changes*
   Because of the high degree of change involved, a pure "order-entry" system will fail. The system must therefore be able to deal with change. We must think more in terms of a "bookings maintenance" system rather than just order entry. Prices don't normally change, but quantity, item, and delivery dates are likely to change during the life of the project. The system must be specifically designed to facilitate these changes, to track the changes, and to produce a summary of changes to an order in ad hoc fashion.

2. *Review of old orders*
   Key to this system is the ability to go back into the files and dig up old orders that can be searched, using SQL-type relational algebra or QBE (query by example) by manipulating any field or even partial fields. For instance, it should be possible to call up all orders for a customer by typing in the company name, customer number, or phone number. An effective system of query by partial fields is to display a centered list of orders that meet the criteria entered in the field definition. As each additional character is entered, the list is revised (shortened) dynamically. A "list of orders" should include the order number, date, customer name, and a few characters of the first line item. For frequently ordered items and for large-volume repeat customers, order templates should be set up to expedite this process. Template construction should be easy so that each user can accumulate his or her own library of templates.

3. *Repeat orders*
   The system will be able to accommodate all forms of repeat orders whether a repeat of an order that was placed two years ago or a few weeks ago. Frequently, the only change is the PO number and the ship date; the rest of the order build-up is the same. Therefore, the system will be designed to produce the ordering history of any customer for reference. The operator simply types in a PO number and ship date to a new order form and pulls up a reference order; the rest of the information can then be pulled from the reference order. The ordering history of the customer can also be used as a customer service, since many customers don't have access to this sort of information. The data-entry clerk can look up the information and remind the customer of certain details of the past order, such as unusual shipping instructions or metallurgy.

4. *Error recovery and partial orders*

The system will span all divisions and must be able to handle a variety of different orders. What this translates into is a large number of variables that may possibly overwhelm the data-entry clerk. Two safeguards against this will be built in. First, a hierarchical structure or a menu of order forms will be used to guide the user to the appropriate form. Even then the form may have entries that the user does not need. Therefore, the user will also be allowed to make partial orders. If the user makes errors, error recovery methods will be used to help the user make the correct entries. The error recovery scheme will be used to make all users comfortable with the system. The user interface design will be guided by considerations of the overall user experience, user satisfaction, and development of user confidence.

5. *Acknowledgments and change notices*

The system will be able to show order acknowledgments and change notices on the screen and print them out on local printers. If the customer calls in and wants to change only one item, the system will produce a summary change notice of only the items changed instead of an acknowledgment that is four or five pages long. The system will enable the user to select those items on which he or she wants to give the customer an acknowledgment. As previously noted, the major change items are likely to be item, quantity, and delivery.

6. *Shipping holds and invoices*

Shipping holds can be put on individual line items, tying into the invoicing procedure so that items on shipping hold cannot be invoiced. The database can be separated into two logical databases: a database of orders and a database of shipments. This eliminates picking lists and simplifies the invoicing process, since only the items shipped can be invoiced. The system will bring up every line item on an order and show what is left to be shipped, providing just enough information to the person doing the invoicing. The amount of data displayed is carefully controlled to avoid screen clutter. Mode of shipping, such as truck, air, etc., and ship-to address can be assigned to each line item so that different items can be shipped to different places and by different shippers. This is necessary to meet the complex ordering requirements of EPD.

7. *Error messages*

The system may have up to 100 different error messages. No effort will be made to conserve the number of error messages. Attempting to keep them down to a certain number only results in vague error messages. The wording of error messages is very important and can be changed as the system evolves through the prototyping phase. To avoid performing a recompile procedure each time an error message is changed, these messages will be maintained in a separate file that can be changed using the system editor.

8. *Query by customer*

   A customer query method will be implemented. A customer looking at the screen will see the familiar screen layout but will not be able to change anything and will be restricted to certain screens.

9. *Limitation of access*

   Each user group will be restricted to the data fields that apply to it. This access limitation not only provides data security but also helps simplify the user's view of the database. One of the problems with computerized information systems is that many users are fed too much data. Screens as well as reports are cluttered with numbers just because the capability exists to produce them. However, because of the complexity of the system and the vast differences among the client bases it is to serve, the order entry system will have to appear functionally different to different users and yet maintain the same "look and feel." The person doing the invoicing can see the same screen as the order entry clerk but the only thing he or she is allowed to change is the number to be shipped.

10. *Notes*

    To accommodate the different types of orders that will be handled and the expected changes, the system allows for detailed notes to be tacked on to each order. Like the other fields, these notes are also protected. Anyone can see the notes and add his or her own notes but can't change other users' notes.

11. *Shipping history*

    The system allows the manager to produce a shipping history of a certain line item. This way managers can detect trends and produce ad hoc reports that can be used in managerial decision making.

12. *Credit memos*

    The system is able to generate credit memos for things such as returned material or discounts. Invoices can't be changed but can be voided. Changes are produced on separate documents so that the integrity of the exact audit trail of each order is maintained.

13. *Inquiry and report*

    The key thing about this system is maximum inquiry, which allows users to find orders by customer name, part number, PO number, work order number, order-entry date, order number, or customer number. By using these fields, they can generate lists of orders very quickly. If users are on the phone with customers, they can trace an order all the way through while talking and are also able to bring up an order history of the particular customer and provide details on shipments, dates, and order specifications.

An Integrated System

Figure AP.4 shows a dataflow diagram that integrates the firm's order-entry systems. Note the tie-lines to other programs. Being resident on the System/38, the order-entry system could easily be tied into the MAPICS inventory system and the manufacturing job costing system. The heart of the system is the bookings audit file. The main customer order database generates all the information needed by the divisions. These include standardized bookings history and reports as well as ad hoc inquiry to suit changing and uncommon needs. Invoicing, order acknowledgments, and shipping are all controlled from the main audit file.

Figures AP.5 through 11 show sample screens. These screens and some of the standard reports are used as a basis for designing the system. Figure AP.5, the Bookings Audit File menu, is the starting point for the system and leads the user through the other functional screens. On it are summarized all the salient features of the system. The other screens define these functions in greater detail.

The order entry system was programmed in RPG-III and the implementation was an enormous success. The company was able to cut order processing costs and improve customer service. On a daily basis management at the top level was able to obtain information they never knew existed before. For example, it was very easy for the president to track a botched order through its history and question the people responsible. This sort of information availability increased productivity throughout the operations of the three divisions.

Disclaimer: APVI is a fictitious company. This case is based on information from diverse sources, as well as information that is purely fictional. However, the order entry system described is real, and was designed by Jim Walker.

Figure AP.4
One System for the Whole Company

Order Entry & Invoicing

Figure AP.5
Sample Screen: Bookings Audit File

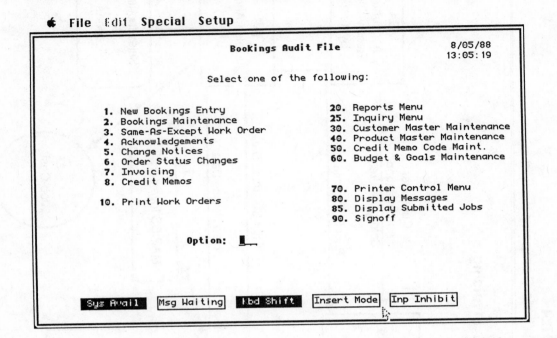

 File Edit Special Setup

```
                    Bookings Audit File              8/05/88
                                                     13:05:19

                 Select one of the following:

     1. New Bookings Entry            20. Reports Menu
     2. Bookings Maintenance          25. Inquiry Menu
     3. Same-As-Except Work Order     30. Customer Master Maintenance
     4. Acknowledgements              40. Product Master Maintenance
     5. Change Notices                50. Credit Memo Code Maint.
     6. Order Status Changes          60. Budget & Goals Maintenance
     7. Invoicing
     8. Credit Memos
                                      70. Printer Control Menu
    10. Print Work Orders             80. Display Messages
                                      85. Display Submitted Jobs
                                      90. Signoff


              Option:  ▌
```

```
 Sys Avail   Msg Waiting   Kbd Shift   Insert Mode   Inp Inhibit
```

Figure AP.6
Sample Screen: Master Search Memo

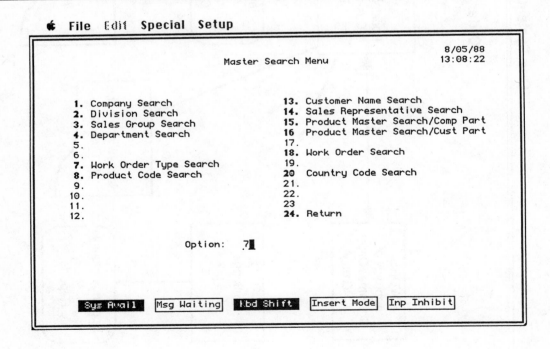

 File Edit Special Setup

```
                                                     8/05/88
                    Master Search Menu               13:08:22

     1. Company Search              13. Customer Name Search
     2. Division Search             14. Sales Representative Search
     3. Sales Group Search          15. Product Master Search/Comp Part
     4. Department Search           16. Product Master Search/Cust Part
     5.                             17.
     6.                             18. Work Order Search
     7. Work Order Type Search      19.
     8. Product Code Search         20  Country Code Search
     9.                             21.
    10.                             22.
    11.                             23
    12.                             24. Return

              Option:   7▌
```

```
 Sys Avail   Msg Waiting   Kbd Shift   Insert Mode   Inp Inhibit
```

Figure AP.7
Sample Screen: Line Item Maintenance

❖ File Edit Special Setup

```
                        Bookings Audit File              8/05/88
                       Line Item Maintenance             14:29:47
                          Page 1 Of 1
         Line Item Number:    910      P.O.#:
         Comp Part Number:  620163           U/M: EA  Prod Code:  DC00
      Customer Part Number:  CUSTOMER PART NUMBER GOES HEREEEEEEEEEEX
         Special Charge?:  N    Supported?:  Y    Ship To?:  N
         Ship Dates - Mfr:          Cust:            Dest:
             Ship Via:  UPS

    Qty: ▌      75    Price:         5.2500   (.4)  Amt:       393.75

              G/G PROFESSIONAL SIZE A _____
  Review      _____
  Mode        _____
              _____
              _____
              _____
              _____
  Cmd05-Audit _____  Cmd07-Header
  Cmd06-Review _____  Cmd08-S.Hist
  Help Key-Help   Cmd02-In Notes   Cmd03-Ex Notes   Cmd04-Search   Cmd09-Calc
                                                                    Cmd24-End
```

[Sys Avail] [Msg Waiting] [Ibd Shift] [Insert Mode] [Inp Inhibit]

Figure AP.8
Sample Screen: Work Order Overview

❖ File Edit Special Setup

```
  BKF7000D                                                8/05/88
  B0F095                    BOOKINGS AUDIT FILE            15:01:41
                           Work Order Overview


              Select one of the following:

              1.   Inquiry By Customer Name
              2.   Inquiry By Customer Part Number
              3.   Inquiry By P.O. Number
              4.   Inquiry By Work Order Number
              5.   Inquiry By Work Order Description


          Option: ▌



                                                      Cmd24-END
```

[Sys Avail] [Msg Waiting] [Ibd Shift] [Insert Mode] [Inp Inhibit]

Figure AP.9
Sample Screen: Invoicing

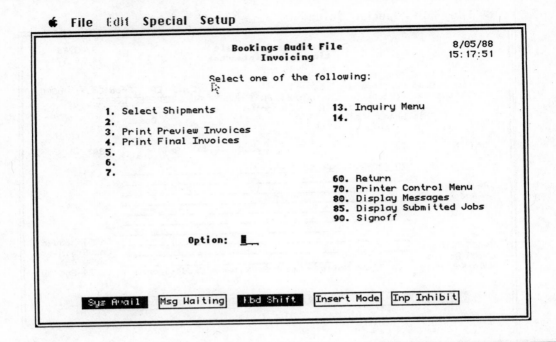

```
  File  Edit  Special  Setup

                    Bookings Audit File          8/05/88
                        Invoicing                15:17:51

                Select one of the following:


      1. Select Shipments          13. Inquiry Menu
      2.                           14.
      3. Print Preview Invoices
      4. Print Final Invoices
      5.
      6.
      7.                           60. Return
                                   70. Printer Control Menu
                                   80. Display Messages
                                   85. Display Submitted Jobs
                                   90. Signoff


              Option:  ▌


      Sys Avail   Msg Waiting   Kbd Shift   Insert Mode   Inp Inhibit
```

Figure AP.10
Sample Screen: Invoicing Line Select

```
  File  Edit  Special  Setup

                    Bookings Audit File          8/05/88
                  Invoicing Line Select          14:58:05

      Line Item Number:    456    P.O.#: . . . . . .
      Comp Part Number:  72120538        Unit Of Measure:  EA
   Customer Part Number:
       Special Charge?:  N   Supported?:  Y   Ship To?:  N
      Ship Dates - Mfr:          Cust: . . . . .   Dest: . . . . .
             Ship Via:  UPS . . . . . . . . . . . . .

  Ship: ▌ . . . . 100    Price: . . . . 750.0000  (.4)  Amt: . . . 75,000.00

        FG GREYHAWK  690043-01 REV.A
        _____
        _____
        _____
        _____
        _____        Cmd07-Add'l
        _____        Cmd08-S.Hist
   Cmd05-Audit                                      Cmd09-Delete
   Cmd06-Review                                     Enter-Update
   Help Key-Help   Cmd02-In Notes  Cmd03-Ex Notes  Cmd04-L Notes  Cmd24-End


      Sys Avail   Msg Waiting   Kbd Shift   Insert Mode   Inp Inhibit
```

PART 3

Cases for Solution

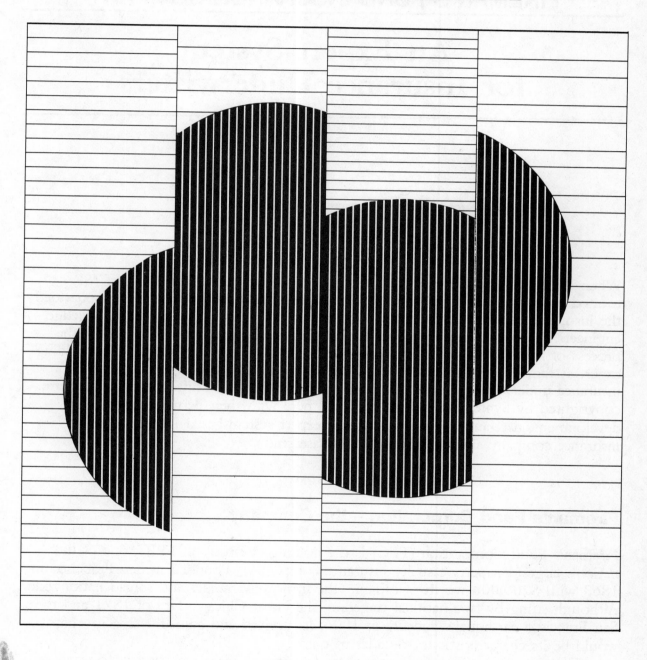

Fireman's
Fund

FIREMAN'S FUND INSURANCE COMPANY

An Expert System for Insurance Underwriters

Scientific discovery is driven by exaggerated expectation.
— Jules Verne

When Fireman's Fund Insurance Company (FFIC) and Syntelligence, Inc. (SI) teamed up to produce a knowledge base for insurance underwriting, FFIC provided the insurance experts and SI contributed the software expertise and the knowledge engineers. (A knowledge engineer is a programmer/analyst who is trained in the process of knowledge acquisition and knowledge representation involved in building expert system knowledge bases.) The result was a successful expert system for insurance underwriting called *Underwriter Adviser* (UA). (Both of these names are copyrighted by Syntelligence, Inc. and used here with their permission.) The development, use, and implications of this expert system-based DSS in a major insurance company are the subject of this case study.

Fireman's Fund Corporation – the Company

Fireman's Fund Corporation (FFC) is the holding company of FFIC, one of the nation's largest property-casualty insurance companies. Founded in San Francisco in 1863 with $200,000 worth of capital, the firm grew rapidly and spread nationwide. Although stung by two national tragedies, the Great Chicago Fire of 1871 and the San Francisco earthquake and fire in 1906, it survived and gained a tenacity that would be its characteristic for decades to come.

The company is organized into three operating divisions according to types of insurance (see Table FF.1). The commercial insurance division is the largest division

Table FF.1
Fireman's Fund Operating Divisions

Division Premiums	Insurance Specialty	% of Total
Commercial	Business insurance General liability Workers compensation Property	More than 50%
Specialty	Specialized policies Entertainment industry Contractors Ship cargo	Approx. 30%
Personal	Home/automobile insurance	Approx. 20%

writing slightly more than half of all the premiums and specializing in business insurance for small and medium-sized companies. Services include general liability, workers' compensation, and property insurance. The specialty insurance division is responsible for about a third of the premiums and writes a variety of unusual insurance policies ranging from entertainment industry risks to contractors and ship cargo. Its underwriting therefore tends to be less routine and more specialized than that of other divisions. The personal insurance division provides home and auto insurance for consumers.

FFC is a substantial enterprise, with 11,600 employees in 49 major offices nationwide. In 1987, it had over $3.9 billion in revenues and showed assets of $9.6 billion. In 1985, when the company was sold to the public by American Express, it issued the largest IPO (initial public offering) in the history of the New York Stock Exchange.

Traditionally, FFIC has been an industry leader in the introduction of high technology, new ideas, and the use of computers in the insurance industry. Today the FFIC headquarters in Novato, California is one of the largest employers of computer professionals in the Bay Area.

A key index of performance of insurance companies is the payout ratio, the number of dollars' worth of claims paid out for every $100 worth of premiums collected. Contrary to popular belief, this amount is frequently greater than $100; that is, the company actually loses money in insurance underwriting but may still show a profit as long as returns from investment of premiums exceed the payout loss. Ratios as high as $105 can indicate reasonable performance, but ratios of $120 or more are clear signs of problems that are usually to be found in bad underwriting and/or bad pricing. In 1987, for instance, the commercial insurance division of FFC showed a ratio of $109.6. The key insurance function controlling this ratio is underwriting.

To fulfill part of its corporate charter to "become a model of excellence within the industry," FFIC has decided that it must offer the "highest-caliber underwriting" in the nation. This is the story of how a company that has always sought innovative and technological solutions to old insurance problems is applying the emerging technology of artificial intelligence to the old art of underwriting to achieve its corporate goal of excellence.

The U.S. Insurance Industry

More than 3000 insurance companies in the U.S. together write over $300 billion of net premiums per year. Of this sum, more than half comes from property and casualty underwriting. In 1986, the net premium written for commercial property/general liability was over $40 billion and that for workers' compensation exceeded $20 billion.

The insurance business is cyclical in nature and goes through periods of net losses in excess of premiums to the tune of $10 to $20 billion per year. Although these losses may be compensated for to some extent by investment income, they point to a malaise in the industry and offer opportunities for dramatic competitive advantage for any insurance company that can make significant improvements in the risk-assessment and underwriting skills of the staff as a whole.

A major consumer of information technology, the insurance business is data- and information-intensive by its very nature and has been an early adopter of transaction processing and information reporting systems. The industry spends over 5 percent of its gross revenues on information technology, a figure that is increasing as maturing technology offers innovative solutions and conveniences to insurers. The point is that the industry has clearly embraced computer technology and easily accepts computer solutions to insurance problems.

The Property/Casualty Underwriter

A good underwriter will generate profits of more than a quarter of a million dollars per year for the company (Lisa Howard, "Bad Staffing Devastates Bottom Line," *National Underwriter,* March 23, 1987) while poor underwriting can cause an equal amount in losses. Yet, the typical frontline underwriter is in his or her twenties, has about 2 years' experience with the firm, is paid about one-tenth of the profits he generates, is likely to leave the firm within the next 2 years, and spends 80 percent of his or her time pushing paper and looking up information in company manuals.

The property-casualty underwriter's job is essentially to assess, by combining computed quantitative factors and subjective qualitative factors, the exposure or risk in writing a policy. Even a routine renewal can take hours to classify and complex issues can require days of research and analysis (see Figure FF.1).

The underwriter must determine whether to issue or renew a policy, the amount of coverage, and the premium to charge. The process begins with the initial communication with the client. The nature of the business and type of coverage desired are evaluated from the position of the insurer's current company objectives. These factors are evaluated to determine the desirability of the business according to current company standards. The results are used in the first decision level — whether the company is interested in issuing or renewing this policy.

Following this initial evaluation, the underwriter asks a series of specific questions to assess the riskiness of the policy, regardless of whether it is a new issue or a renewal. Many of these questions are standardized for the type of policy being written. Some of the responses are subjected to quantitative analysis while others can be evaluated only subjectively. Depending on the answers, the underwriter asks new questions to pursue specific details.

Response to these questions are used to establish line-by-line and class exposures, as well as the risk quality, and the most important risk factors. An

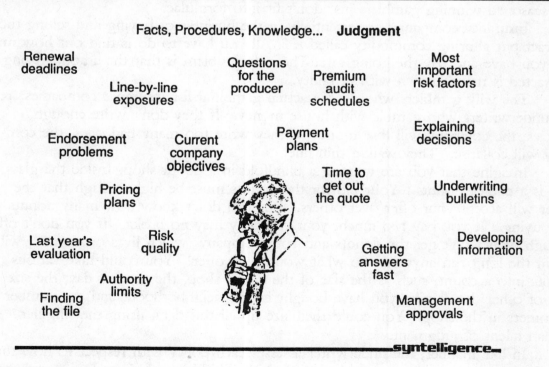

Figure FF.1
The Underwriter's Challenge

Facts, Procedures, Knowledge... **Judgment**

Renewal deadlines

Line-by-line exposures

Questions for the producer

Premium audit schedules

Most important risk factors

Endorsement problems

Current company objectives

Payment plans

Explaining decisions

Pricing plans

Time to get out the quote

Underwriting bulletins

Last year's evaluation

Risk quality

Developing information

Authority limits

Getting answers fast

Finding the file

Management approvals

syntelligence

evaluation of overall risk is used to produce the premium schedule and the payment plan.

In case of a renewal, the underwriter must first find the file and review last year's evaluation and renewal deadlines. Work must be done within authority limits and follow all procedures outlined in company underwriting bulletins pertaining to the type and class of risk. The underwriter must strive for an exhaustive initial interview to keep the need for follow-up questions to a minimum. He or she must also follow premium audit schedules, explain all decisions, obtain management approval if needed, and get quotes out quickly. And typically, the underwriter must do all this under a tight schedule and a heavy workload, with little room for error.

The company procedures, policy, schedules, and bulletins the underwriter must follow are kept in several large binders. He or she must refer to these and to the customer file at all stages of the risk evaluation.

The Underwriter as an Expert

Insurance is like gambling — a very calculated sort of gambling, but gambling nevertheless. Although calculations of probability are necessary, they are not sufficient. Additional subjective factors that cannot be directly modeled using equations or statistics must be taken into account. Certain methods and heuristics of wily and seasoned winning gamblers just don't fit into formulae.

Insurance companies are essentially in the business of buying and selling the abstract but alluring commodity called *risk*. All you have to do is find out how much risk you have and pay the going rate. The only problem is that the amount being transacted is never known with certainty.

The wily gamblers who do the actual gambling for insurance companies are the underwriters who gamble with house money. If they don't write enough policies, the company will lose money; if they write too many bad ones, the company will collapse. They walk a thin line.

Imagine that you are wearing a blindfold in a donut shop. Inside the glass case is a pile of donuts. Your bid for the donuts must be high enough that the baker will accept your offer over others. But you don't know how many donuts you are buying. If you pay too much, your company may go broke. If you don't offer enough, you won't get the donuts and your company (which lives on donuts) will die in the long run anyway. So what would you offer? You could take various factors into account, such as the size of the donut shop, the time of day, the size and cost of other donut piles you have bought in this neighborhood, and the number of customers in the shop. You could then size up all this data, using the singular human talent of judgment.

In like manner, the underwriter assesses each policy with respect to how much risk the company is taking on, whether the risk should be taken, and, if so, what the required benefits to the company must be in terms of premiums to offset this risk.

In such semi-structured problem situations of a highly specific nature, certain people are successful in their resolution while others are not. Let us call the successful problem solver an *expert* within the domain of the specific problem that he or she is able to solve. The expert has specialized knowledge, past experience with similar problems, and a set of special rules by which he or she plays the game. Experts also fail sometimes but are normally able to solve the problem with a higher degree of success than those who are not experts. On the average, the expert wins.

The insurance underwriter fits this description of an expert with the additional hazard that a single bad decision can be associated with catastrophic costs. Yet the underwriter must play in a highly competitive environment and write as many policies as possible.

Expert Systems: Computer-Aided Decision Support

The tenet of expert systems (ESs) is that experts are expert only in a highly specialized field. Each field is characterized by a body of specific facts or knowledge about the subject matter and a set of heuristics or rules by which these facts are combined to arrive at one of a specified set of conclusions. In this sense, the underwriter is an expert in risk assessment, for which there is an associated body of knowledge and heuristics. If empirically extracted, such a body of knowledge could largely mimic the experts successful problem-solving style, even though no equation could be written to model it. The mimic could then be used to aid nonexperts in making the same sort of decisions with a higher degree of success than they could otherwise achieve. Such a mimic is called an *expert system*.

ESs are best applied in problem-solving situations requiring repeated use of an intricate and complex set of facts and rules in a highly specific problem domain. Insurance underwriting is such an activity and therefore a candidate for the application of ESs.

ES software technology has been written about since the late 1960s but has remained a curiosity of researchers and academics in the medical sciences for more than a decade. The computer explosion of the 1980s created an environment in which the technology could finally be commercialized in the business world to serve as a computer-aided decision support tool.

The roots of ESs are in medical diagnosis procedures and, to this day, ESs can best be understood in those terms: record all the symptoms, see what fits, and come up with the most likely diagnosis. The application of this simple diagnostic construct in business problem solving has enormous potential. It can enhance the competitive advantage of businesses that rely on experts to solve semi-structured problems in which the consequences of a single bad decision are enormous.

A question often raised is "Why do we need an ES if we already have good underwriters (the actual experts)?" Clearly, expert systems improve the efficiency, productivity, and consistency of knowledge workers by acting as a decision support system (see Table FF.2). The issue with real experts is that they are human and as such have bad days, moods, other commitments or priorities and tend to be less consistent than machines. Specifically in the field of underwriting, in which disastrous consequences can result from one bad decision, there is a need to supply the underwriter with a mechanical aid that will be thorough, relentless, and consistent in its pursuit of the recommended decision according to the rules of risk assessment. Thus, one reason for developing an ES is to provide a way of capturing and replaying an expert's good days for reference.

But a more important reason is that there aren't enough experts to go around. The use of ESs enables underwriters who are spread out over vast distances to benefit directly from the experience, knowledge, and expertise of the company. The quality and consistency of underwriting in general can be expected to go up while the costs of training go down; that is, valuable and costly expertise can be canned and made available to knowledge workers wholesale. In the old days, before music could be recorded, the only way to hear an expert performance of Mozart's Violin Concerto No. 25 was to attend a rare live performance by a chamber or symphony orchestra. Today, we just flick a disk into the CD player anytime we feel like it. In like manner, the goal of ESs is to make specific expertise available on a large scale.

Finally, building an ES forces us to draw information from disparate sources and to formalize a body of expert knowledge. The formalization process involves accumulating and organizing knowledge in a way that forces the experts to resolve conflicts and gaps consistently. From this process a new synthesized knowledge base evolves.

Essentially, an ES is a computer program consisting of a knowledge base, an inference engine, and a user interface. Such a system allows the user to operate a large base of inferential building blocks, each of which can take this form: "IF x is true, THEN y is true (or false)." The knowledge base consists of a list of all possible observations about the problem, a list of rules by which the observations can lead to conclusions, and a list of all possible conclusions.

An important attribute of ESs is the so-called *explain reasoning feature*. They must be able to explain the decisions being recommended at each stage, that is, to list the rules used to arrive at each stage of the logical process. ESs do not act as

---

Table FF.2
ES Requirements That Are Crucial to the Underwriting Process

Captures judgment and knowledge
Combines quantitative and qualitative information
Handles inexact information
Copes with missing information
Deals with inconsistencies

(Courtesy of Syntelligence)

---

decision makers but as advisers. If the process is not intuitive to the decision maker, he or she must be able to trace the explanation for each conclusion stepwise and backwards until satisfied.

ESs can be classified according to the type of application and end user for which they are targeted. The three categories are advisers, controllers, and trainers. Advisers do not take action but assist human experts. Controllers are usually prevalent in factory automation/process control applications, where they are expected to make decisions and take appropriate action. Trainer-type systems are normally intended for use in familiarizing lower-level experts with problem-solving techniques and training them. This system of classification is based on intent. In fact, ESs often serve in more than one capacity, since systems designed to advise may easily be used to train, as we will see in this case.

The AI R & D Group at Fireman's Fund

An insurance company operates by taking on risk for a fee (premium) and then investing these fees in the financial market. Both activities, risk assessment of insurance policies and risk and returns assessment of portfolios of financial instruments, are unstructured problems requiring experts. The effectiveness of these experts is a critical success factor that affects the performance of the company. FFIC recognized early in the evolution of AI technology that AI in general and ESs in particular could be a determinant in the competitive advantage of insurance companies. These new tools were changing the way insurance companies could carry out such key activities as risk analysis and portfolio selection.

Accordingly, and in keeping with the nature of FFC to take advantage of technology and the corporate charter of seeking excellence in underwriting, FFIC established a research and development group within the information systems organization reporting to the vice-president of commercial systems. The organization chart showing the structure of information systems and that of the artificial intelligence group are shown in Figures FF.2 and FF.3 respectively.

The AI group immediately went to work on several key projects, one of which was the development of an ES for underwriting. The objective of the group was primarily exploratory: to stay abreast of what was going on in the field of AI and to identify opportunities. The AI group was relatively small and without a heavyweight budget or staff. The most effective strategy was therefore to seek out active developers and engage them in symbiotic partnerships. It was in this disposition that the FFCs AI department entered into an agreement with Syntelligence, Inc. to develop a knowledge base for an underwriting ES.

Figure FF.2
Organizational Structure of Fireman's Fund
Insurance Company IS Group

```
                                              ┌─────────────────┐
                                              │  Vice President │
                                              │  Personal Lines │
                                              └─────────────────┘
                                              ┌─────────────────┐
                                              │  Vice President │
                                              │ Second Data Ctr/│
                                              │  Data Security  │
                                              └─────────────────┘

┌─────────────────┐                           ┌─────────────────┐
│  Vice President │                           │  Vice President │
│ Personal Systems/│                          │  PALS/Migration │
│ Info. Processing│                           └─────────────────┘
│     Systems     │
└─────────────────┘         ┌─────────────────┐
                            │  Vice President │
┌─────────────────┐         │   Information   │
│  Vice President │         │    Resources    │
│   Controllers   │         └─────────────────┘
└─────────────────┘
┌─────────────────┐                           ┌─────────────────┐
│  Vice President │                           │  Vice President │
│  PALS/Migration │                           │ Processing Svcs.│
│ Plnng. Corporate│                           │      Dept.      │
│    Utilities    │                           └─────────────────┘
└─────────────────┘
┌─────────────────┐         ┌─────────────────┐
│  Vice President │         │  Vice President │
│  Claims Systems/│         │   Comm. Ins.    │
│  Design Review  │         │     Systems     │
└─────────────────┘         └─────────────────┘
┌─────────────────┐         ┌─────────────────┐
│ Vice Chairman & │         │  Vice President │
│ Chief Financial │         │ Processing Svcs.│
│     Officer     │         │      Dept.      │
└─────────────────┘         └─────────────────┘
┌─────────────────┐         ┌─────────────────┐
│ Sr. Vice Pres.  │         │  Vice President │
│  Comm. Systems/ │         │      MARS/      │
│ Corp. Systems   │         │    Data Base    │
│     Devel.      │         └─────────────────┘
└─────────────────┘
┌─────────────────┐         ┌─────────────────┐
│  Vice President │         │  Vice President │
│  Spec. Systems/ │         │ Corporate/Fin.  │
│ Office Sys./    │         │     Systems     │
│ Wrkstations/    │         └─────────────────┘
│   Telecomm.     │
└─────────────────┘
                            ┌─────────────────┐
                            │  Vice President │
                            │ Corporate/Fin.  │
                            │     Systems     │
                            └─────────────────┘
```

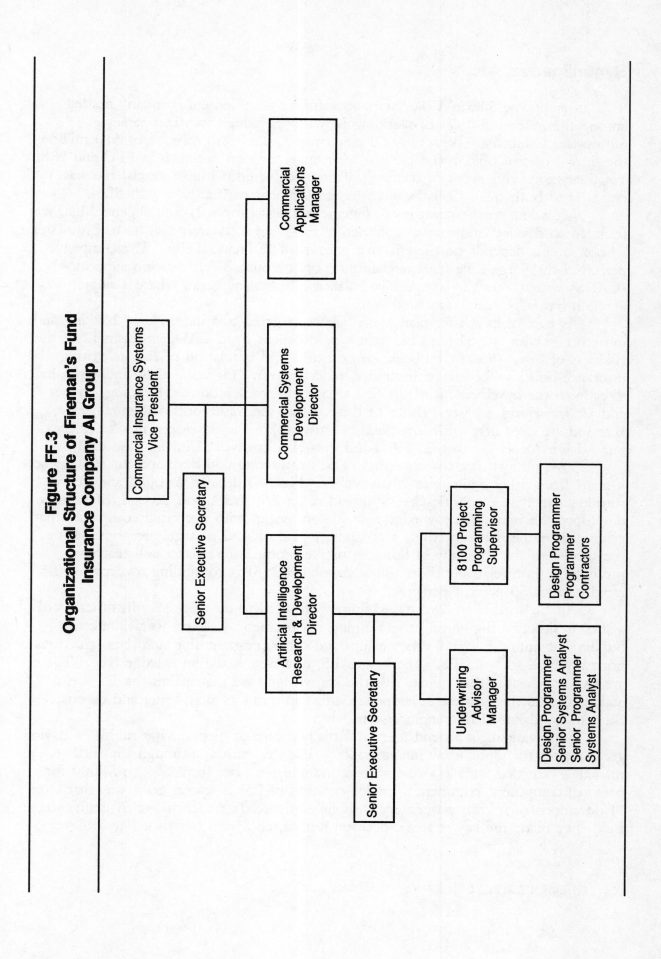

**Figure FF.3
Organizational Structure of Fireman's Fund
Insurance Company AI Group**

Syntelligence, Inc.

SI is an archetype Silicon Valley start-up software development company nestled among the miles and miles of sparkling new low-rise, high-tech companies in Sunnyvale, California. With only 70 employees and a 1988 revenue of $10 million, the firm is microscopic in comparison with huge corporations such as FFC and IBM. Yet their pioneering work in commercializing ES for estimating financial risk has encouraged both these Goliaths to form development partnerships with SI.

According to the company's strategic business proposal, Syntelligence, Inc. was founded to develop and market commercial ES-based software products to businesses whose success depends on the effective assessment of financial risk. The company perceived that large-scale commercialization of computer-aided decision support (CADS) would alter the competitive balance in those industries where a single decision has large costs associated with it.

As part of its master plan Syntelligence targeted two industries — banking and insurance — with critical functions that would benefit from CADS; assessment of the riskiness of loans (for use by bank loan officers) and evaluation of risk in writing insurance policies (for use by insurance underwriters). Targeting these industries led directly to the development of SIs first two commercial products, Lending Adviser and Underwriting Adviser. (Both of these names are trademarks of Syntelligence, Inc. and are used here with their kind permission.) The development of Underwriting Adviser (or UA) involved FFIC and thus also involves SI in this case study.

Two noteworthy characteristics of SI's marketing and development strategy set it apart from other companies in the Valley. First, SI decided to build and deliver turn-key expertise — specific CADS instead of an ES "shell"; and, second, SI initially developed the required knowledge base in partnership with operating companies that possessed the needed expertise. The strategy paid off and is largely responsible for the success of the company in bringing usable products to market and reaching profitability in a relatively short time. As of 1988, SI is continuing to grow at the rapid pace of 50 percent per year.

An ES shell is an "expertless" framework used to develop ES. In other words, a shell is simply a high-level programming environment designed to facilitate the building of multiple logical relationships and other programming and data structures normally used to build ES. The key to ES, however, is the knowledge base. There are two reasons for this. First, it is the knowledge base that makes the ES useful and that takes the greatest development effort in terms of skill, time, and expense. Second, good knowledge engineers are rare.

Supplying shells to end users is actually a case of "first catch a rabbit" — having great recipes for rabbit stew but no rabbit. For this reason, although the shell market is crowded with low-cost software ranging in price from $99 to $3000 for personal computers, commercial implementation of ESs is scarce. So it was that after SI developed their own proprietary shell called Syntel (a trademark of Syntelligence, Inc.) they made the key strategic decision not to sell Syntel but to use it to develop application-specific and ready-made solutions to business problems that could be commercialized.

Syntel was developed using LISP, a popular AI language and the Xerox 1186. This obscure computer was chosen because it had been specifically designed for AI development. However, it was not intended to be the target vehicle. Since most of the insurance industry computers were IBM mainframe users, it was decided that the knowledge base and inference engine would be developed on the Xerox for each application and then ported to an IBM mainframe such as the 3090 or 4381. The user interface would utilize a PC environment, usually regarded as the most user friendly of all computer environments. This arrangement places the big number crunching parts of the program on the mainframe and uses the PC effectively as a gateway to the mainframe resident routines as well as to the MIS databases of the insurance company.

The development took 150 man-years — or approximately 100 people working for long hours for a year and a half at a Silicon Valley pace. Start-up software companies usually face an enormous hurdle — the difficulty of surviving the initial development phase when there is no revenue. In addition, the lack of in-house knowledge of underwriting made it imperative and crucial for SI to seek development partnerships with insurance companies such as FFIC. The success of this strategy and the use of IBM mainframes for commercial implementations of ES have led to a cooperative marketing agreement with IBM under the computer maker's IMAP arrangement (Industry Marketing Assistance Program).

Costs and Benefits to Both Parties

In August of 1985, the AI research and development departments of FFIC and SI entered into a joint development program. Their objective was to come up with an ES for commercial property/casualty underwriting. Due to the anticipated massive scale of the knowledge base that would be required for underwriting the wide variety of insurance under this category, it was decided that the initial effort would be directed toward the very specific domain of workers' compensation.

Among the principal guidelines of the effort were the following axioms: First, the system would be designed only as an adviser to underwriters in the field and not as a decision maker; that is, the underwriter, not UA, would make the final decision. This approach eased considerably the tightness of the validity specs but escalated the importance of the show-reasoning capabilities. It was decided for this reason to include an "override" feature with comments to allow the underwriter to disagree with UA and to record the disagreement along with reasons for it.

Second, although the system would be designed as an adviser, it would also be used to reduce overall training costs for new underwriters. Use of the system by field underwriters, it was felt, would accelerate the learning curve. This benefit was expected to be an indirect result of making constant use of an expert consultant rather than of any specific user interface for training purposes.

FFIC expected three distinct benefits from the system (see Table FF.3). First, in keeping with the promise of its corporate charter, the system was expected to "improve the quality of underwriting," resulting in fewer errors and oversights, along with smaller tolerances in contingency margins. Thus, fewer bad risks would be taken, while good business would be competitively quoted. This benefit would be possible because the ES would be thorough and exhaustive in its analysis and consistent in its recommendations, even when used by users with a wide range of expertise and experience in underwriting.

The second benefit anticipated by FFIC relates to the productivity of underwriters; that is, it was expected that they would write more premiums per week than otherwise. Underwriters normally spend hours or even days looking through FFIC underwriting bulletins and customer files, performing computations on a calculator, and looking up tables in manuals. The ES was expected to substantially automate this process.

Table FF.3
Benefits Offered by the Underwriting Adviser System

Underwriting quality
    Improves quality and accuracy
    Highlights problems
    Reduces errors and oversights
    Guides each evaluation for consistency
    Presents guidelines in context
    Applies new guidelines
    Improves control of pricing adjustments
    Collects data for analysis

Productivity
    Speeds initial review
    Minimizes manual look-up time
    Reduces uncertainties
    Eliminates time to organize renewal file
    Speeds authorization reviews and home office referrals
    Provides automatic documentation
    Reduces senior underwriters' time to assist others

Training and professional development
    Reduces classroom time
    Speeds transition out of training
    Strengthens on-the-job training
    Supports professional growth and cross-training

(Courtesy of Syntelligence)

This aspect of UA has significance from an academic point of view that sets it apart from pure ES technology. The system would not only be an expert but also an information server, performing the task of an ad hoc information reporting system (IRS) by pulling up customer files, reference files, and relevant quotes and comments automatically for perusal by the underwriter and/or direct use by UA. (It should be mentioned here that within the UA context, "reporting" refers to the output of UA. These outputs are designed for statistical purposes, management review, and for use by other systems. Data about individual risks presented to the underwriter are not considered to be "reports" per se.)

The third benefit FFIC expected from the project was shorter training time, and therefore lowered training costs, for new underwriters. Not only would the system speed up and automate training but the underwriters might need less training. This reduction in training costs was used in the cost/benefit analysis to justify the system.

As part of the agreement, FFIC agreed to pay most of the costs in advance of delivery to assist SI in its development efforts. Other costs incurred by FFIC would include time charged to the project by five full-time analysts and one part-time supervisor for the duration of the project; the time and effort of the expert underwriters, who would be interviewed by SI knowledge engineers; the cost of the Xerox 1186 development systems; the cost of any hardware modifications or upgrades required on the IBM mainframe and peripherals; and the consulting fees to Syntelligence.

Some of these costs may need explanation. Although the software development would be performed by SI, the testing, validation, implementation, and training were to be handled by FFIC's AI group, hence the personnel costs. The cost of several Xerox 1186 machines at $25,000 each exceeded $100,000, but was a necessary expense since the knowledge base would be built using a prototyping development cycle. During the development, FFIC's 1186 would mirror the development system at SI. Upon first-pass completion, the system would be initially tested on the 1186 at FFIC. Only upon completion and final debug would the program be ported over to the IBM host. The consulting fees should be budgeted because once the product is turned over to FFIC, all subsequent services in terms of enhancements, training, customization, etc., are provided by SI at an hourly fee. These services were anticipated, since an examination of SI's financial statement shows that a significant portion of the firm's earnings are derived from such services.

The benefits to SI of this arrangement are obvious. Knowledge engineers had no underwriting expertise but wished to market an expert system for underwriting. FFIC would provide the expert underwriters to define the rules of underwriting, and SI would provide the knowledge engineers to draw out the rules from the underwriters and then encode them into the knowledge base. SI would be gaining the knowledge required to build the system. The financial benefit to them would be equal to the present value of future cash flows generated by the sale of UA to other insurance companies. The principal cost would be the 150 person-years of development time required to build the system.

Underwriter Advisor: Development and Implementation

The project got underway in the fall of 1985. During the next 3 months the technicians from SI picked the brains of a few chosen experts in workers' compensation underwriting at FFIC. By following case examples and using tactical questioning the technicians extracted the knowledge of workers' compensation underwriting; that is, the three lists of the knowledge engineer, consisting of a list of all possible conclusions, a list of facts used by the experts, and a list of rules used to arrive at one of the conclusions from a given set of facts was constructed.

When Syntelligence first decided to build expert systems for financial risk assessment, they evaluated various commercial ES generators or shells, of which there are many on the market. However, none of these was found to be adequate from a standpoint of assessing financial risk. An important requirement was that the knowledge base to be developed on the Xerox could later be ported to the IBM mainframe. No shell was available that would support this software transfer and this was another reason that shells could not be used. Shells are usually specific to a certain kind of knowledge base and ES design. Although they make the development of a distinctive kind of knowledge base easier and quicker, they limit developers who use other designs.

SI identified the following requirements of the system that would dictate the choice of the shell and inference engine used. The system must be able to assimilate and evaluate numbers and subjective data on a common basis. Because of its role strictly as adviser, it must allow the user to control the decision-making process. At each point in the process, the user must be able to replace UA's judgment with his or her own. Also, at each stage the system must be able to explain not only the decision but the rules it used to arrive at the decision. Both the data and the rules in underwriting are subject to uncertainty, which may at times lead to contradictions that are resolved using probability. Thus, the rules would be constructed to assign probabilities to each decision node. Lastly, the system must be able to function with incomplete data. The shell and inference engine used in the development must be capable of building the system in this manner.

Normally, an ES user interface (dialog subsystem) uses a question-answer format, with each question usually based on the previous answer. As part of the SI design specification, however, it was decided that the user interface must resemble the forms underwriters normally use and follow the paper-work production workflow familiar to underwriters. The objectives were to minimize logical errors that might occur when deviating from a tried and true system and to reduce the trauma of conversion and enhance acceptability by underwriters. If the input screens are the same as the forms now being used, then the user interface will be familiar to the underwriters. This will make it easier to get them to use the new system. The conversion process will be hampered if the underwriters have to learn a completely new method of entering and reviewing data. The new method will have a longer learning curve and will be more prone to input errors. This decision to use existing forms as entry screens placed an additional rigid and nonconventional condition on the shell or development tools to be used. ESs normally use a formless question-answer format to collect data.

In view of all these conditions, no ES shell was found suitable. SI thus decided to write their own shell and inference engine — Syntel, designed specifically for developing ES for financial risk assessment. Not only the ES but the development platform itself is problem domain-specific.

Because of the power and extreme customization of Syntel, SI was able to produce the initial version of the UA knowledge base on the Xerox 1186 in just 10 months. On a hot summer day in Novato in June 1986, SI delivered the first prototype of the Workers' Compensation knowledge base to FFIC. The AI group of FFIC had already acquired the Xerox computer and was able to bring up the prototype almost immediately.

The knowledge base, inference engine, and the dialog subsystem were all resident on the Xerox prototype machine. For the run-time IBM version of the system, SI developed a user interface on the IBM PC that was identical to that of the Xerox prototype. The user interface is mouse driven and uses windows and pull-down menus and represents one of the first uses of such devices in an ES dialog subsystem. This scheme was designed to take advantage of the user friendly aspects of the PC with which many underwriters are expected to be familiar. (See Figures FF.4 through FF.9 on pages 64-66.) Another advantage of the PC interface is that it can be retained when the system is transferred to the production processor. Additionally, the use of the PC to carry out the user dialog, validate data, and preprocess the input will unload the main production processor. Many of the user query, data collection, and data validation functions of the front-end would otherwise be performed by the mainframe host and tie up badly needed CPU cycles. This is a critical consideration, since ESs are usually storage and CPU "hogs." The link between the PC and the main processor is transparent to the user, who feels that he or she is using PC software and who boots up from a PC disk. The program auto-executes and automatically establishes the mainframe link.

The KB (knowledge base) developed on the Xerox evolved into the first KB that was delivered to FFIC. The Xerox is used at SI as the development environment for all UA KB's. However, the FFIC run-time environment is the IBM 3090 with MVS/XA CICS. Therefore, after development, the KB are ported to the IBM mainframe.

In September of 1986, the AI group approved the prototype and SI delivered Release 1 of the working version for the IBM MVS/XA CICS. The artificial intelligence group of FFC took over at this point and carried out a thorough and intensive program of testing and validation. The validation process was carried out by AI analysts in concert with the expert underwriters who participated in the development of the knowledge base. The sensitive and critical nature of the application made this an important phase of the development process. It took over six months to complete.

Figure FF.4
File Cover Sheet

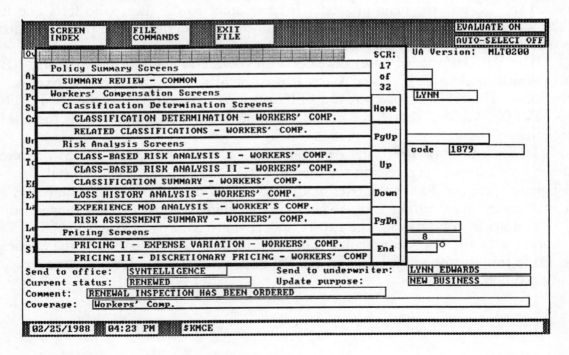

SCREEN INDEX	FILE COMMANDS	EXIT FILE		EVALUATE ON AUTO-SELECT OFF

Overview   FILE COVER SHEET   UA Version: MLT0200

Applicant/insured: ABC COMPUTER INC
Description of operations: ELECTRONIC EQUIPMENT MFG
Policy No.:   WC 123 672   Policy modifier: RENEWAL
Submission No.:   WG # 278
Cross reference: CPP 345 709 AND UEL 335 127

Underwriting office: WESTERN   Underwriter: GRANT
Producer name: WESTERN GENERAL   Pr. code   1879
Total estimated annual policy premium: $163,000.00

Effective date: 06/01/1988   Submission date: 03/01/1988
Expiration date: 06/01/1989   Next review date: 05/01/1988
Last access date   02/16/1988   Action date: 04/10/1988

Legal structure: CORPORATION   D & B rating:
Year business started: 1980   Years in business   8
SIC code: 3573   SIC description ELECTRONIC EQP MFG

Send to office: SYNTELLIGENCE   Send to underwriter: LYNN EDWARDS
Current status: RENEWED   Update purpose: NEW BUSINESS
Comment: RENEWAL INSPECTION HAS BEEN ORDERED
Coverage: Workers' Comp.

02/19/1988   01:05 PM $KMCE

Figure FF.5
Pop-up Menu of Screens with Mouse-Driven Scroll Commands

SCREEN INDEX	FILE COMMANDS	EXIT FILE		EVALUATE ON AUTO-SELECT OFF

SCR: 17 of 32   UA Version: MLT0200

Policy Summary Screens
  SUMMARY REVIEW - COMMON   Home
Workers' Compensation Screens
  Classification Determination Screens
    CLASSIFICATION DETERMINATION - WORKERS' COMP.   PgUp
    RELATED CLASSIFICATIONS - WORKERS' COMP.
  Risk Analysis Screens
    CLASS-BASED RISK ANALYSIS I - WORKERS' COMP.
    CLASS-BASED RISK ANALYSIS II - WORKERS' COMP.   Up
    CLASSIFICATION SUMMARY - WORKERS' COMP.
    LOSS HISTORY ANALYSIS - WORKERS' COMP.   Down
    EXPERIENCE MOD ANALYSIS - WORKER'S COMP.
    RISK ASSESSMENT SUMMARY - WORKERS' COMP.   PgDn
  Pricing Screens
    PRICING I - EXPENSE VARIATION - WORKERS' COMP.   End
    PRICING II - DISCRETIONARY PRICING - WORKERS' COMP

LYNN

code   1879

8

Send to office: SYNTELLIGENCE   Send to underwriter: LYNN EDWARDS
Current status: RENEWED   Update purpose: NEW BUSINESS
Comment: RENEWAL INSPECTION HAS BEEN ORDERED
Coverage: Workers' Comp.

02/25/1988   04:23 PM $KMCE

Figure FF.6
A Sample UA Screen

```
┌──────────┬──────────┬──────────┐                    ┌─────────────────┐
│ SCREEN   │ FILE     │ EXIT     │                    │ EVALUATE ON     │
│ INDEX    │ COMMANDS │ FILE     │                    ├─────────────────┤
└──────────┴──────────┴──────────┘                    │ AUTO-SELECT OFF │
                                                       └─────────────────┘
┌────────┐
│Overview│         INITIAL ASSESSMENT - WORKERS' COMPENSATION
└────────┘
Applicant/insured:  [ABC COMPUTER INC                              ]
Description of operations:  [ELECTRONIC EQUIPMENT MFG              ]
Total standard premium  [$122,599]    Weighted avg. exp mod   [0.53]
D & B rating:  [        ]
----------------------------------------------------------------------
Producer name:  [WESTERN GENERAL            ]     Phone  [(408) 867-5588]
Overall producer assessment  -▨▨▨▨▨▨▨▨▨▨▨▨ ▨▨▨▨+
----------------------------------------------------------------------
Total states  [  2  ]   Total locations  [  2  ]
  Loc#  Class#   Code    Subcode         Phraseology          Auth.   Premium(%)
                                   (click on box to select)
  [1]   [3]     [3681]    [2]    [INSTRUMENT MFG.-PROFESS▶]    [3]     [89.3%]
  [1]   [2]     [8810]    [1]    [CLERICAL OFFICE EMPLOYE▶]    [3]     [5.4%]
  [1]   [1]     [8742]    [1]    [SALESPERSONS, COLLECTOR▶]    [3]     [2.7%]
  [2]   [1]     [8742]    [E]    [SALESPERSONS OUTSIDE   ]     [3]     [1.0%]
----------------------------------------------------------------------
Aggregate loss ratio  [12.6%]     Preliminary L/R assessment  -▨▨▨▨▨▨▨▨▨▨▨▨ ▨▨▨▨+ A

Recommendation  [Underwriting judgment is necessary using the following screens:]
         [Mngt/Financial | Loss History | Class-Based | Class-Sum]
                 Initial assessment  -▨▨▨▨▨▨▨▨▨▨▨▨ ▨▨▨▨+
┌───────────┬──────────┬──────────────────────────────────────────┐
│02/19/1988 │ 02:05 PM │ $KMCE                                     │
└───────────┴──────────┴──────────────────────────────────────────┘
```

Figure FF.7
UA Screen Showing Details of Financial Analysis

```
┌──────────┬──────────┬──────────┐                    ┌─────────────────┐
│ SCREEN   │ FILE     │ EXIT     │                    │ EVALUATE ON     │
│ INDEX    │ COMMANDS │ FILE     │                    ├─────────────────┤
└──────────┴──────────┴──────────┘                    │ AUTO-SELECT OFF │
                                                       └─────────────────┘
┌────────┐
│Overview│          DETAILED FINANCIAL ANALYSIS - COMMON
└────────┘   DETAILED FINANCIAL ANALYSIS IS RECOMMENDED FOR THIS INSURED.

D & B rating:              [        3        ] A
Financial report source:   [FINANCIAL STATEMENT]

SIC code:  [3599]          SIC description  [ELECTRONIC EQP MFG    ]

Total assets:        [$17,906,600.00]
Current assets:      [$13,301,500.00]   Short term solvency  [2ND QUARTILE]
Current liabilities: [$5,519,300.00]
Total liabilities:   [$6,855,300.00]    Long term solvency   [2ND QUARTILE]
Net worth:           [$11,051,300.00]
Profit:              [$5,035,000.00]    Profitability        [1ST QUARTILE]
Net sales:           [$23,589,500.00]   Efficiency           [4TH QUARTILE]
Net working capital  [$7,782,200.00]
Financial audit type: [OPINION UNQUALIFIED]

                              ┌──────────┬──────────┐
Quantitative financial assessme│ CLARIFY  │ FOOTNOTE │
                              ├──────────┴──────────┤
   Overall financial assessment│ OVERRIDE │         │
      Overall management/financi│         │SHOW REASONING│ ▨+
----------------------------------------------------------------------
       Associated Screen ===               NALYSIS - COMMON
┌───────────┬──────────┬──────────────────────────────────────────┐
│02/26/1988 │ 11:33 AM │ $KMCE                                     │
└───────────┴──────────┴──────────────────────────────────────────┘
```

Figure FF.8
UA Screen Showing Pop-up "Clarify" Menu

```
┌─────────────┬─────────────┬─────────────┬────────────────────────────┐
│ SCREEN      │ FILE        │ EXIT        │              EVALUATE ON   │
│ INDEX       │ COMMANDS    │ FILE        │              AUTO-SELECT OFF│
├─────────────┴─────────────┴─────────────┴────────────────────────────┤
│ Overview                                                             │
│            CLASS-BASED RISK ANALYSIS I - WORKERS' COMPENSATION       │
│ Premises no.:    1       2100 ONE TECHNOLOGY DRIVE, SAN JOSE, CALIFORNIA 95133 │
│ Class                                                               │
│         ┌──────────────────────────────────────────────┬─────────┐  │
│ Phrase  │                                              │  CLOSE   │  │
│ Author  │                     CLARIFY                  └─────────┘  │
│ Age of  │ Material handling/overexertion: . . . . . . . . . . . . │
│ What i  │                                                          │ S ? │
│ Workpl  │ Material handling and overexertion are the largest single sources of │
│   Hsk   │ workers' compensation losses nationwide.                 │
│ Materi  │                                                          │
│   Weig  │ Evaluation signs to use in addition to the factors displayed and their │
│ Employe │ clarify text include the following: . Claims caused by lifting, picking │
│ Turno   │ up, carrying, pushing, pulling, twisting, over-exertion, deadlines, heat │
│ Equipme │ exhaustion . Injuries to back, stomach (hernia) . New location, product │
│ Haz Eq  │ or process . Employees with prior or recurring back strains . Contracts │
│ Wage l  │ or agreements to unload within premises of others (e.g. teamsters have │
│ Wage Le │ a "curb delivery" restriction)                           │
│ Vehicles:└──────────────────────────────────────────────────────────┘
│ MVR-3 yrs │ Selection │ Veh Type │ Radius │ Maint │ Auto Ins. │     │
│                                          Class assessment  -▓▓▓▓▓▓▓▓▓▓▓▓+│
│              Associated Screen ===>   CLASS-BASED RISK ANALYSIS II - WORKERS' COMP. │
├──────────────┬──────────────┬─────────────────────────────────────────┤
│ 02/26/1988   │ 02:09 PM     │ $KMCE                                   │
└──────────────┴──────────────┴─────────────────────────────────────────┘
```

Figure FF.9
Risk Assessment Summary

```
┌─────────────┬─────────────┬─────────────┬────────────────────────────┐
│ SCREEN      │ FILE        │ EXIT        │              EVALUATE ON   │
│ INDEX       │ COMMANDS    │ FILE        │              AUTO-SELECT OFF│
├─────────────┴─────────────┴─────────────┴────────────────────────────┤
│ Overview                                                             │
│              RISK ASSESSMENT SUMMARY - WORKERS' COMPENSATION          │
│                                                                     │
│ Applicant/insured:  │ABC COMPUTER INC                            │   │
│                                                                     │
│ Description of operations:  │ELECTRONIC EQUIPMENT MFG              │  │
│                                                                     │
│ Producer name:  │WESTERN GENERAL                                 │   │
│                                                                     │
│ Total standard premium   │  $122,599  │   Weighted avg. exp mod  │ 0.53 │ │
│                                                                     │
│                                                                     │
│          Final all class assessment      -▓▓▓▓▓▓▓▓▓▓▓▓+ A          │
│          Loss history assessment         -▓▓▓▓▓▓▓▓▓▓▓▓+ A          │
│          Overall management/financial assessment  -▓▓▓▓▓▓▓▓▓▓+     │
│          Overall producer assessment     -▓▓▓▓▓▓▓▓▓▓+              │
│                                                                     │
│ Summary risk assessment  -▓▓▓▓▓▓▓▓▓▓+                              │
│                                                                     │
│                                                                     │
│ Recommendation │Underwriting judgment is necessary using the following screens: │
│                        │  Class-Based  │                            │
│                                                                     │
├──────────────┬──────────────┬─────────────────────────────────────────┤
│ 02/23/1988   │ 02:55 PM     │ $KMCE                                   │
└──────────────┴──────────────┴─────────────────────────────────────────┘
```

The system was still not deemed ready for full implementation, however. The conversion would be phased in one branch at a time through a series of successful pilot tests. In April of 1987, FFIC began these pilot tests at two branches in California. The cautious, controlled release of UA by the AI group was necessary partly because of the concern over what some perceive as its "heavy, almost batch-like performance." This turned out to be the major implementation problem.

The knowledge base was big and logic intensive. The problem was exacerbated by the use of one of FFIC's main production machines that is also used for corporate MIS services. Applications of such magnitude would normally be run on a batch-processing basis. Operation on an interactive basis posed some problems relative to resource usage and response time.

As a partial remedy, the AI group performed several tuning operations to streamline resource usage by UA, identifying certain key operations of UA that caused a majority of the excessive resource usage. Some of these were rectified by SI greatly enhancing product performance. AI decided that they could live with the others by drawing up procedures and training the underwriters in efficient use of the system and in avoiding the CPU-intensive transactions of UA.

These results were encouraging. By June of 1987, the AI group of FFIC assumed full responsibility for the knowledge base (SI continued to be responsible for the inference engine) and decided to move ahead from pilot tests into limited conversions. Use of UA was limited to cases involving $25,000 and above to control CPU usage.

Operational UA for Workers' Compensation

By February of 1988, eleven FFIC branch offices in California were using UA in pilot testing. The implementation was successful in several ways. First, the expected improvements in underwriting had clearly been achieved. UA, it was found, provides correct and consistent guidelines for evaluating risks in workers' compensation underwriting. The desired increase in productivity had also been achieved. A case that formerly might have taken a day to complete could be finished in an hour or less, and the job would be performed more thoroughly and with a much lower chance of error. The most promising achievement has been in the proficiency of UA in helping less experienced underwriters write risks that would have been unquestionably beyond their expertise without the help of UA. This achievement underscores the real promise of ESs, that of making expert knowledge widely available.

As an added bonus, many underwriters took to the new system. In MIS jargon, the system was accepted at the user level. A high level of user acceptance is evidence of a good user interface, proper implementation and training, and a usable system that gives useful results.

But did the system improve the quality of underwriting? This was the principal concern of management (recall the corporate charter to "improve underwriting"). One of the big reasons for the UA project was to take a step in that direction. However, now it seemed unclear what "improve underwriting" meant and exactly how to go about measuring such an improvement. Ultimately, what must be measured is the effect in improving the expense ratio or reducing the loss ratio. To make this measurement directly will require a carefully controlled experiment over a sufficiently long time. In the meantime, UA's performance is being closely monitored to accumulate more factual evidence of benefits to the workers' compensation line. In any case, the question of improvement will not be answered for a few years. If there is indeed an improvement, a gradual recovery can be expected in the expense ratio for workers' compensation. Presumably, management could then pass final judgment on UA and decide whether to expand its usage into the other lines of commercial property/casualty insurance underwriting.

Beyond Workers' Compensation: "To Explore Strange New Worlds"

FFIC managers decided to also investigate expansion of UA into a yet undetermined second line of insurance.

The AI group began preparation for moving into a second line by installing the generic knowledge base for General Liability (supplied by Syntelligence, Inc.) on the in-house Xerox 1186 ES prototype environment. AI would have to come up to speed on the General Liability system and test, validate, and check performance. The group must then demonstrate the system to the FFIC underwriters and managers and make modifications as necessary to customize the decision rules for adherence to FFIC procedures.

Since the development partnership with SI had ended, the AI group was really on their own in this new adventure. The first obstacle they had to overcome was learning Syntel. Since the knowledge base was encoded in a vendor-developed language, the AI programmers had to first learn the new language so that they could continue to develop and maintain the knowledge base. An additional difficulty the AI programmers had to face (one that relates to both the Workers' Compensation and the General Liability knowledge bases) was the lack of "hooks." Without hooks or exits for calling other applications from UA, it became difficult to integrate UA into the general production environment of the MIS. Subsequently, SI provided the hooks and interfaces to FFIC files and other programs.

Knowledge bases coded in strict production rules are relatively easy to change, especially when a good screen-oriented rule editor is available with the development system. But UA was not based on strict production rules. It used a connectionist network to tie together a large number of relations. Although this scheme allows greater complexity and improves performance (both of which are important in this application), we have to pay the piper when it comes to maintenance. As the AI group found out, simple modifications to the knowledge base required complex and intricate changes to the network. Changes can be complicated because the domain is complicated.

However, once the AI programmers became comfortable with Syntel, they found it an extremely powerful and a highly customized tool for risk assessment applications.

"To Boldly Go Where No Man Has Gone Before"

It is the nature of exploratory projects to accumulate peripheral benefits in terms of knowledge and experience about something new, thereby adding a new dimension to the firm's total technological know-how. So it was that this probe into ES has served to build the first layer of FFIC expertise not only about this emerging field but also about development and implementation of such systems.

The use of a prototype machine: Was it a good idea to use the Xerox 1186 as a prototype and then transfer the knowledge base to the IBM? This special purpose computer costs about $25,000 and has absolutely no application beyond the ES prototype development. Besides, the software transfer to the production platform consumes time and resources. During production tests, quick fixes are impossible, since all fixes have to loop back to the Xerox, the only environment in which changes can be made.

Picking the experts: It is usually acknowledged that ESs are very problem domain-specific. However, they may be even more domain-specific than we think. FFIC recommends that when picking experts for knowledge extraction, the individuals must be selected from the exact environment in which the machine will be installed; otherwise, according to Murphy's Law, some consideration will be overlooked that plays a role in that specific environment but not in others. The knowledge base built by interviewing home office underwriters ran into problems at branch offices. The procedures are sufficiently different that the knowledge base had to be modified for installation at branch office locations.

What's the difference between an *analyst* and a *knowledge engineer*? Without direct experience with ESs, one may tend to disavow knowledge engineers. They are, after all, just interviewers and we already have interviewers, only we call them analysts. But an analyst is trained to follow only the physical process and identify data flows. Although he or she has interviewing and communication skills, the analyst can only follow the process but is unable to discover it. A knowledge engineer must discover, understand, mimic, and document the expert's cognitive and decision-making processes without being an expert himself or herself. He or she does not know anything about the subject matter, but by starting from an example, can trace the decision process to track and code ALL the factors that are taken into account and the manner in which they are taken into account. Clearly and undeniably, this is the single most important and critical process in ES development. It is recommended that companies wishing to implement expert systems train their AI analysts in the knowledge-acquisition process.

Validating rules with test cases: The development cycle can be accelerated if the rules are validated as they are extracted in the knowledge-acquisition process. This can be accomplished by using a test case during the interview. As rules are extracted they are tested in the test case to ascertain that they will lead to the correct decision, or at least to a decision that the expert agrees with. This additional effort will assure greater conformity between the expert's and the knowledge engineer's notion of each decision rule. The same test case can be used to validate the knowledge base, once encoded.

The show-reasoning capability is essential: It is only after using an expert system that one appreciates the value of the show-reasoning feature. The inference engine must be able to provide the user with the rules and facts used to reach each stage of the decision. Only then can the underwriter be in a position to accept or override advice that is inconsistent with his or her judgment. As an extra benefit, the documentation of these overrides eventually leads to system refinement. This feature is useful to system developers, since the debugging procedure is greatly aided by the ability to see what the program is doing. The explanations provided must be clear and must be easily understood by the users for whom the system is intended.

ESs eat CPUs for breakfast: Without direct experience with ES, one is likely to underestimate hardware resource requirements. Knowledge bases require very large storage areas, and inference engines can be very CPU-intensive compared to transaction processing systems most MIS departments are used to. The use of the general purpose corporate MIS hardware may not be appropriate. When the ES, which is by nature interactive, runs, it could compromise system performance in other areas. Normally, an MIS manager will not allow an application of this size to run in interactive mode. This aspect of ES must be clearly thought out before installation of ES on a production scale.

Case Study Questions

1. What were some of the business priorities of FFIC that led to its participation in the UA knowledge base development? What organizational aspects would you credit for the success of the UA implementation at FFIC?

2. Since the most important ingredient of UA is the experts' knowledge, which FFIC already possessed, how has the company benefitted from the partnership with SI? Assuming that FFIC has a sophisticated computing staff and facility, compare the partnership option with an all in-house development option using a commercial shell. Would your analysis and decision be different for the next ES project at FFIC?

3. The literature refers to "integrating ES" with MIS and DSS systems. What special aspects of the FFIC system shows this sort of integration? If asked by top managers to enhance the integration, what steps might you take?

4. The conversion to UA has followed a very gradual and careful sequence of phases and stages. Initially, only the workers' compensation insurance was converted, and then only one office at a time. What are some reasons for following such a slow and careful inplementation and conversion phase?

5. In the future, as FFIC begins to convert more and more of their underwriting to expert systems, what changes would be needed organizationally? In the hardware environment?

6. "Underwriting expert systems will eventually lower insurance premiums for most FFIC customers." Support this statement. Refute this statement.

7. If you were a competitor of FFIC, what would you want to know about the UA system? What would your response be? Why?

8. The case shows that the UA implementation has become hardware bound. Although the system is useful and the underwriters will use it, the conversion is severely limited by the capacity of the 3090. What would you do as the manager of the AI group? As VP of the Commercial Insurance Systems division? What implementation scenario can you project with no hardware change?

9. Assume the role of manager of AI. Based on the experience with UA, write a memo to the VP of systems describing your plans for the future.

10. What were some development and implementation problems with UA? Were any of these related to the type of agreement that FFIC made with the knowledge base developer? In hindsight, how would you want to structure this agreement differently?

TAYLOR-DUNN CORPORATION

Staying Abreast
of New Technology

The Company

Taylor-Dunn Corporation is a privately held manufacturer of electrically powered industrial vehicles (see Figure TD.1) used in warehouses and factories for moving people, parts, or inventory around (models B2-38, B2-48, B2-5x). Some models such as the R3-80 and R6-80 are used on university campuses and in parking lots. Although the company specializes in electrical units, it also manufactures small gasoline-powered vehicles.

Founded in 1949, the company has been very successful over the years and has established itself as a major supplier of specialty industrial vehicles worldwide from the factory and corporate headquarters in Anaheim, California. The company is considered to be conservative and stable in a mature industry. President and CEO R. Davis Taylor is the son of the founder.

The recent entry of the Japanese into the market has posed new challenges to the firm, which reacted by beefing up its engineering capabilities through the use of new technology. In so doing, the company was forced to take risks and to deal with the cutting edge of new computer-aided design and manufacturing technology.

Taylor-Dunn is now fully automated and it uses CAD for all engineering drawings, CAM and robotics for vehicle manufacturing on the shop floor, and a sophisticated MRP (Material Resource Planning) system to control the flow of materials through the manufacturing process. The company has been an industry leader and continues to innovate with new products and features and to impress customers and competitors alike with the high degree of quality and reliability of its products.

1978 – In the Beginning There Was the IBM System/3

In 1978, Taylor-Dunn had approximately 300 employees operating in two shifts, with sales of about $15 million. The company was running all DP (MIS) functions on an IBM System/3. The system was completely batch-oriented and used keypunched-card decks as input and line-printer reports as output. The system did not have multi-user terminal access capability. The turnaround cycle for making a batch run and producing production reports was two days.

This simple transaction processing system was used to record all orders, invoices, and purchases, and to track inventory. It also performed the basic accounting functions of payroll, accounts payable, accounts receivable, and general ledger. The DP department consisted of about five persons, including programmers, operators, and keypunch data entry clerks.

The transactions were recorded manually on paper and later keypunched up for the computer. At some predetermined time, the cards were fed to the computer and a run was made. Because of lag time between transactions and data processing, the computer's inventory file was inaccurate at any given time, which made planning the manufacturing cycle extremely difficult. At the time Taylor-Dunn was manufacturing ten industrial models and two golf-cart models of electric vehicles. Assembly of these vehicles required more than 9000 components, each with an assigned part number. Production planning was done on a weekly basis and required accurate data on part availability. However, the computer printouts could be as much as several days out of date. To be safe, the company had to sacrifice cost-efficiency and carry excess inventory.

In 1978 the company organization was restructured and an executive management committee, consisting of all the vice-presidents and group managers, was formed. One of the first items on its agenda was the inventory problem. The limitations in planning and computer operations were identified and the committee undertook a search for a solution. At the time, MRP was being introduced as the best planning tool for a manufacturing environment. It was decided that the committee would investigate MRP as a possible solution for the inventory and production planning problem.

1980 – MRP and the IBM System/34

In 1980, the company signed on to be a pilot location for the new MRP program from DATA-3 Systems. The MRP system was new and complex, with volumes of documentation. A major part of the implementation process included extensive training for DP personnel as well as end users. Because Taylor-Dunn was not familiar with MRP systems, a consultant was hired to assist with DATA-3 implementation of MRP.

Since the DATA-3 software required an IBM System/34 minicomputer (predecessor of the System/36 and 38), a System/34 machine was leased from IBM. Even though a consultant was retained and a proven MRP system was procured, the implementation took much longer than expected and was more expensive than budgeted. The expense, including man-hours, was in excess of $500,000 over the implementation period.

The System/34 and the MRP program gave Taylor-Dunn a multiple-terminal input capability throughout the plant for the first time. Twenty CRT terminals and several high-speed printers were installed at various locations throughout the company, including DP, accounting, engineering, and production. As data were entered at any CRT, the MRP database was immediately updated and the information instantly available to any other CRT user through screen inquiry. The information obtained by inquiry could also be printed out. Essentially, the production and inventory systems went on an OLTP (online transaction processing) system.

However, the system was difficult to learn and use and did not immediately yield the data integrity that was sought. After much biting of fingernails and gnashing of teeth, and many trying hours of hard work, data integrity was eventually improved. As a result, inventory accuracy reached the 95 percent level, which means that if the computer indicated a component was in inventory, 95 percent of the time it was; the computer was wrong only 5 percent of the time.

An unexpected cost savings was realized in DP manpower. In the old system, all transactions were made on paper and then keypunched into the computer. Essentially, each transaction was being recorded twice. In the new system direct screen entry of data supplanted much of the paperwork and the keypunch operation became redundant. As a result, the data processing group was reduced slightly to four members — three programmers and one operator.

The end result could only be described as immensely successful in terms of user and management acceptance and achievement of a high degree of data integrity. One of the determinants of a successful implementation is usage: are the people using the system or are they working around it? The IBM system turned out to be a winner in this category. Employees found the system so useful that usage began to climb, although this implementation success brought with it its own problem. As more people began taking advantage of the system's capabilities, and with managers making increased demands of the system, increased usage overloaded the system's response capability and the system speed slowed. Within one year, system response had reached an unacceptable level and Taylor-Dunn decided to upgrade to more powerful hardware using current technology.

1981 – The IBM System/38 Versus the HP 3000

The hardware upgrade was constrained by compatibility with the DATA-3 software. The new hardware environment would have to support a System/34 version of RPG, the language in which DATA-3 was written and the language that in-house programmers could use to write custom patches. Further, DATA-3 would have to support that hardware environment. The budget constraint limited the search to minicomputers, since multimillion-dollar investments in mainframes was completely out of the question for a company of this size. Given these constraints and the current technology of the time, the search for new hardware narrowed to two, the System/38 and the HP 3000.

Taylor-Dunn's DP staff felt that the System/38 was too new and without a track record that could be checked for reliability. DATA-3 and RPG were supported by both hardware environments, but while the System/38 version had already been released, the HP 3000 version was still in the oven. The HP 3000 was particularly attractive because it was being marketed specifically as a canned MIS for small manufacturers and seemed to have a good track record in manufacturing firms similar to Taylor-Dunn. After careful comparison and much deliberation, Taylor-Dunn decided to go with the HP. Hewlett-Packard sales staff assured Taylor-Dunn that the System/34 software would run on the HP version of RPG with only minor modification. Further, it was felt that having two different machines would reduce vendor lock-in. An HP 3000 was purchased in 1981 and installed to run parallel with the System/34. The two machines together would give Taylor-Dunn the MIS hardware horsepower mandated by heavy usage of the DATA-3 system.

The Engineering Department Gets Involved – the HP 9845

Since Taylor-Dunn was in the business of designing and manufacturing electric vehicles, the company had a competent staff of electrical engineers. Management decided, therefore, that the engineering department would oversee all technical aspects of the HP 3000 installation except for software. Bob Cammack was engineering manager at the time and dutifully undertook the installation project in close cooperation with HP personnel. Cammack saw this project as a magnificent opportunity to add technical computing capability to the engineering department, which had no computers at the time.

At that time HP was marketing a small desktop computer, dubbed the HP 9845 and being billed as an *Engineering Workstation* strictly on the basis of high-resolution graphics capability and computing power that exceeded that of most microcomputers of the time such as CP/M and Apple II computers. The HP 9845 was packaged with a BASIC interpreter containing high-level graphics commands but there was no other software. It was also claimed that the 9845 could be connected to the 3000 in a distributed processing workstation architecture, but no specific software was available that could achieve such connectivity. It appears that HP imagined that the engineering- and graphics-oriented BASIC interpreter would be sufficient and that engineers would simply write their own software in BASIC. This turned out to be a simplistic and overly optimistic assumption and the 9845 was later dropped from HP's product line.

Cammack had for some time been actively looking for some computing capability for the engineering department, particularly with respect to graphics and for floating-point computational power for performing engineering computations. The HP staff demonstrated the 9845 to Cammack, who was impressed with the graphics potential and the "benefits" that HP claimed this machine would offer. He outlined these benefits in a memo on May 14, 1981 (see Figures TD.2 and TD.3) and, with the help of HP staff, persuaded the company to add the HP 9845 to the purchase.

As it turned out, the benefits shown in the May 14 memo were grossly overstated. The severity of this overestimation became more apparent with time. In particular, the claim that the capability provided "would be equivalent to adding another engineer to the department" turned out to be entirely inaccurate. Although the idea of a technical workstation in engineering that could later be connected to the HP 3000 was attractive, such a connection was in fact never realized.

Figure TD.2
Memo Outlining the Benefits of HP 9845

May 14, 1981

Hewlett Packard 9845 Computer

Some Notable Quotes:

"Leadtime conventionally would be about four months. Our new system does it in one week."

"Typically, it would take a week for us to design one part. Now it takes an hour. So we are going into 15 or 20 times as many design alternatives to optimize the product."

"What has been said about the front-end load of CAD/CAM is true. The payoff will come tomorrow, but the commitment and the planning has to take place today."

"Our business is so competitive that there no longer is a question about whether to use CAD/CAM or not, the questions are which system and how soon."

Engineering Analysis: The acquisition of the model 9845 with proper peripherals will increase the capabilities of engineering tremendously. The graphic and numerical processing of the machine will accelerate the work effort in engineering and would be equivalent initially to adding another engineer to the department. Long term, it would be equivalent to more, since it will be capable of performing work in minutes that would take a group of engineers months to complete.

From a products viewpoint, this will translate into quicker design turnaround, better design solutions and better results at manufacture. Vehicles will be lighter, less expensive, and fit together.

Capabilities:
Numerical analysis
Engineering programming with HP BASIC & FORTRAN
Graphics analysis
Drawing generation
Fit analysis
Test data accumulation and analysis

Also:
NC tape generation
Machine control
Financial and business analysis
Project-program management

Figure TD.3
Justification for CAD System for Engineering Department

HP 9845 Package for Engineering

Description	Price	PMMC
Hardware		
Standard system 9845 B Option 150	24,500	106
187, 146 BYTES R/W Memory		
Standard Language Processor		
Standard Monochromatic CRT		
Graphics Package		
Second Tape Cartridge Drive		
Thermal Printer (Option 60)		
Keyboard (Option 800)		
Utilities Library 09845-10200 Included		
Graphics Plotter 9872 C (Color)	5,300	35
HP-1B Interface 98034 A OPT 445	525	3
9111 A Graphics Tablet	2,050	
Software		
09845-10540 Graphics Presentations	750	
09845-10050 Graphics 2-D	500	
TOTALS	$33,625	$144/mo

This system will provide the Engineering Department with a useful amount of equipment. It will allow a tremendous increase in engineering capabilities and will be equivalent to adding an engineer to the staff. I do not propose that we connect the 9845 B to the HP 3000 at this time. After some experience has been gained in use and application, we can spend a small amount of money to achieve the connection. In the early stages this will prevent contamination of the HP 3000 by Engineering.

Bob Cammack

Bob Cammack
Manager, Product Engineering

BC/lh

The purchase price of the HP 9845 was $33,625, including some software. This did not include any CAD software but did include a digitizer and plotter to give "CAD capabilities." All you had to do was write your own CAD software, using their enhanced BASIC. Clearly, this was not a realistic position. However, the marginal cost to Taylor-Dunn of adding the 9845 to the purchase was virtually nil because of a peculiar HP discount structure. The purchase of the 9845 increased the "total memory" purchased and qualified Taylor-Dunn for a bigger discount on the entire order, including the HP 3000. This also made the justification very easy, BUT the engineering budget was charged $33,625, the full-value purchase price of the 9845. The savings realized by the discount were ascribed solely to the HP 3000 in the budgets.

The HP 9845 was received in September 1981. The machine failed as an engineering workstation and was turned into a laboratory data logger with the additional purchase in October of a data-acquisition unit, which cost about $5,000 and allowed interfacing with laboratory experiments.

IBM System/38 to the Rescue

In the meantime, the HP 3000 conversion was not going well. Beleaguered with software problems and poor performance from the new machine, DP had become disenchanted. By the end of 1982 it became apparent that the HP 3000 conversion was not going to work. The interface between the engineering HP 9845 and HP 3000 became inconsequential. The use of the HP 3000 as a multi-user CAD system was evaluated but rejected because the software alone would cost $200,000 and severe performance degradations were expected.

By this time the IBM System/38 had entrenched itself into the MIS market for small-scale manufacturers and had gained a reputation for reliability and software support. In 1983, Taylor-Dunn leased an IBM System/38 and upgraded the software. The System/38 experience at Taylor-Dunn was similar to that with the System/34, with the implementation a total success. The system worked flawlessly and gained a high degree of user confidence. The machine is still in use in 1988 after a number of upgrades and continues to be the MIS workhorse at Taylor-Dunn.

It is interesting to note that the System/36 and the System/38 have been exceptionally successful products for IBM. Users tend to develop an almost irrational attachment to these machines. Interestingly, when IBM finally came up with a new model in this category (the AS/400) and even promised software compatibility with the System/3x computers, many users refused to part with the 3x systems. Currently, IBM is trying to kill the product but sales continue at a rapid pace and are, in effect, suffocating the AS/400 market.

Today, the IBM System/38 provides total company support in all areas except engineering design and drafting. There are 25,000 part numbers and associated records for the company, which now has sales of about $20,000,000 and a total workforce of 220. With increased system sophistication and reliability, the DP staff has shrunk even further, to only two programmers. Since the System/38 is simple to operate, the programmers also double as operators during the day, and there is a part-time night operator. The MIS functions have become routine and fewer programming changes are needed for normal operation.

The HP 9845 has been decommissioned and has little or no resale value. Although used primarily as an engineering calculator and word processor, it probably provided value to the company at least as a teaching tool to help the engineering staff become more familiar with desktop computers. Although no savings were realized, the HP 9845 prepared the department for the progression into desktop CAD.

Engineering Functions at Taylor-Dunn

There are two engineering centers at Taylor-Dunn. Most of the engineering design work is carried out by the engineering department, while additional engineering groups under manufacturing produce specs for custom carts and perform vehicle servicing.

The engineering department consists of

2 staff engineers
2 draftsmen (one is a trainee)
1 secretary
1 lab technician
1 technical administrator/writer
1 manager/vice-president

The primary function of the engineering department is to design new products and produce engineering specifications for product revisions. In addition, the department is responsible for preparing all maintenance manuals and technical documents.

The Specials group operates within the manufacturing department and is responsible for design and specifications of custom one-of-a-kind options requested by specific customers on large orders. In 1982, this group consisted of

1 manager/engineer
1 designer
1 planner (part-time)
1 floor engineer/technician

The service and warranty group also works under manufacturing and consists of

1 warranty administrator
1 shop clerk (part-time)

The Need for CAD

In July 1982, Cammack was promoted to vice-president of engineering. As one of his first major decisions in his new position of authority, Bob identified CAD as one of his top priorities. The options available to him were constrained by the limited availability of funding as well as by the extent of CAD technology at the time.

The HP 9845 was no longer an option. During the first six months of use, it had become clear that the HP 9845 had limited capabilities in the area of CAD. The single station was being shared by three engineers, each of whom had to do his own programming, since packaged programs were limited and expensive. The machine was being used as an expensive calculator and laboratory datalogger. Later, at an additional expense of $2,000, Bob added a printer and word-processing software to the 9845 to realize additional usage, but its CAD capabilities were abandoned. Bob decided that he was back to square one in terms of computerizing engineering drafting and design at Taylor-Dunn.

Several CAD systems were available for mainframes, such as CADAM from IBM and systems from Intergraph and Computervision. These systems cost in the $1 million range and were not economically feasible. Cammack reviewed the least expensive functional systems available. The one that seemed best and that had the largest user base was the BRUNIG CAD system. A complete system was $65,000, and an upgrade was $50,000. At wages of $20,000/year for graduating engineers in 1982, Cammack could not justify the capital expenditure based on cost savings.

Without automation, engineering design had long life cycles. New products had a three-year cycle time and product revisions took eighteen months to complete on the average (see Figure TD.4). These long cycle times created a severe competitive disadvantage. The technical handicap was particularly egregious at a time when the Japanese (Yamaha) were entering the golf-cart market in the US.

In 1982, the department had two new products and three product-revision projects underway, and the schedule resulted in completion of one new product item and one revision each year. Documentation was about 80 percent complete on each item, with shortcuts taken in drawings. Drawings of similar parts were photocopied, the copies were marked up in red pencil to denote the changes, and these marked-up photocopies were then released as final production drawings. (The stoic engineers were turning over in their graves.) Many of the drawings in maintenance manuals were pre-1974 designs, with only the part numbers changed. In short, the production work of the engineering department was in a deplorable situation, mostly because of the inability to produce and change engineering drawings quickly.

The previous vice-president had been relieved in 1981 for this reason and the output of the engineering department had not improved during the previous five years. In 1982, the business climate for Taylor-Dunn products was depressed and getting worse. As sales dropped slightly below $15,000,000 for the year and were headed lower, the heavy expenses and disappointment with the HP 3000 squeezed budget allowances. Finally, with the entry of Yamaha into the golf-cart market and declining margins on the TEE-BIRD product line of golf carts, Taylor-Dunn decided

Figure TD.4
Engineering Design Cycle

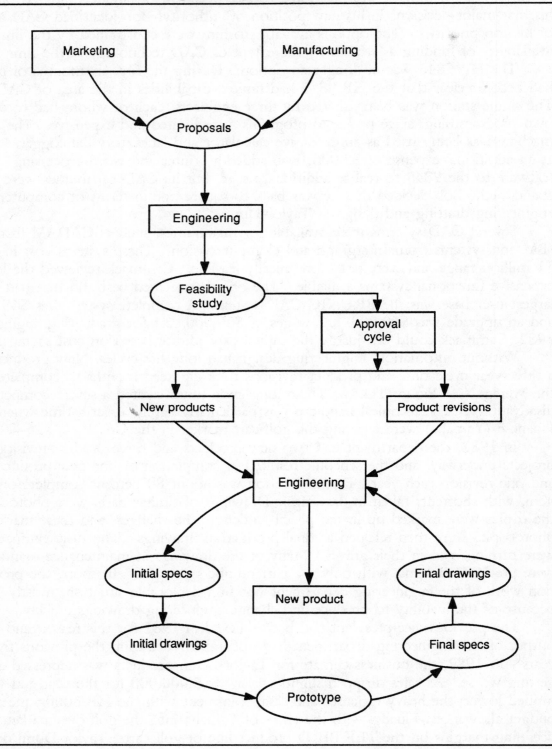

to surrender the golf-cart market to the Japanese. Production of TEE-BIRD golf carts was discontinued.

The cancellation of the TEE-BIRD product line created an additional urgency for the engineering department. The company needed more new products to fill the void. Bringing a brand-new product to the production floor would require an extended design cycle. Bob Cammack needed to hire new engineers and draftsmen and accelerate engineering output, but engineering was "overhead" and overhead budgets were tight because the lower sales volume generated a smaller contribution margin. Thus, while the engineering group wanted to expand, the financial group recommended cutting costs as a means of financial survival.

The compromise reached between engineering and finance was a variant of "voodoo economics." Engineering could spend more if they spent less; that is, they would be allowed to invest in new technology if the investment resulted in lower operating cost with a payback of one year. The funds available were limited, but Cammack had essentially won the battle for CAD and set out to search for appropriate, available, and affordable technology that would bring CAD capability to his designers. The decision had been made to invest in CAD.

The Search for CAD

In November and December of 1982, Cammack attended numerous engineering shows and conferences in Anaheim and Los Angeles to look for solutions. The idea of computer design was intriguing and the more he saw of what was possible, the more convinced he became that the answer to Taylor-Dunn's engineering productivity problems lay in CAD. At the time, Cammack was 34, vice-president, computer-literate, confident, and highly motivated. He knew that his new ideas were about to turn the company around.

In his technology search, Cammack discovered other low-cost CAD systems in the market, some even lower in cost than BRUNIG. Most of the systems available cost more than $35,000. The low-cost machines required keystroke input and seemed slower than pencil drawing in the show demonstrations. More practical machines were $100,000 and more. However, at the NCGA show in Anaheim, Cammack spotted a small sign, about 6 inches by 8 inches, that said, "Computer Graphics for under $10,000." The booth was small and plain, with computers that were small and unknown to Bob Cammack at the time. The person staffing the booth was unimpressive, didn't want to talk about the machine mechanics, and did not have a complete system for sale. When pressed, he gave Cammack a phone number in Sausalito, California, where the CAD system could be purchased. Despite the lack of salesmanship, support literature, and information, Cammack was keenly interested because the machines were displaying real mechanical drawings and making real plots on paper. At $10,000, the system was quite impressive. The possibility of a one-year payback at one-half the cost of an engineer's wages was alluring.

The source for computers running this AutoCAD (trademark of Autodesk, Inc.) software was a small company called MOMS Computing in Sausalito. If these machines actually worked as they apparently did at the show, Cammack knew he had found the answer to Taylor-Dunn's problems. He set out for Sausalito to investigate these computers and found the company was housed in old army barracks at Fort Cronkite, on the oceanfront. The location had a wonderful view but was unimpressive as a place of business. Inside the shop were numerous machines in various stages of assembly and testing. A demonstration was attempted, using a unit being prepared for shipment (later discovered to be serial number 1). The demonstration did not go smoothly, since the equipment was not set up for customer manipulation. There were four malfunctions during the demo and no plotter was available, so the final product could not be evaluated. Nevertheless, there was paper proof of the plotting ability, and the features described were far above those of any other equipment Cammack had viewed in the under-$50,000 price range.

The estimated lease cost of the MOMS machine was $250/month, which compared most favorably with the salary of $1900/month for a draftsman. (See Figure TD.5 for a detailed cost/benefit analysis.) Cammack decided that the venture was worth the gamble, especially since the amount of money involved in obtaining a single test unit was small and the potential rewards immense. A verbal commitment was obtained to purchase the first unit. Because Taylor-Dunn needed additional output but didn't have money to waste, the executive group was willing to go along with the suggestion, but only after a great deal of responsibility for the installation was placed directly on the new VP of engineering. For Taylor-Dunn, and for Cammack personally, this would be a make-or-break venture. The order was placed on February 18, 1983.

The MOMS AutoCAD System

This unit may have been one of the first CAD systems shipped by MOMS. However, the machine operated perfectly when first set up, although it lacked adequate documentation, especially on the operating system. To learn this operating system took the staff some time. They made several mistakes, one of which resulted in inadvertent erasure of some disks. But on the whole, the implementation was successful and actual drawings were soon being produced on the new machine.

The machine was placed in a central location where it would be accessible to all draftsmen and engineers. Although the system gained a remarkable degree of acceptance from the more curious members of the design staff, it was ignored by those who were more resistant to change. To Bob's surprise, age was not a factor in accepting the system, which was soon being monopolized by a few staff members.

The quality of output was four to five times better than that produced manually by trainee draftsmen and engineers, but the increase in productivity was not yet apparent. The actual drawing time was shorter, but there was considerable time

Figure TD.5
Cost/Benefit Analysis of MOMS CAD System

Cost Analysis

Basic System with D-Size Plotter   11,400
         Tax & Shipping   1,100
         $12,500

Lease Cost $\frac{12,500}{1000}$ x 25 = $ 312/mo

Second System with Size Plotter, No Digitizer   9,600
         Tax & Shipping   960
         $10,560

Lease Cost $\frac{10,560}{1000}$ x 25 = $ 264/mo

Third System & Up, No Plotter   8,600
         Tax & Shipping   860
         $ 9,460

Lease Cost $\frac{9,460}{1000}$ x 25 = $ 236/mo

Current Draftsman Cost = $23,000/year = $1916/mo

30% Improvement @ $1916/mo = $575/mo

Drafting Extraneous Workload That Cannot Be Scheduled

Est Hours	Savings	Item
200	50	Excess Inventory Revisions (Scrap)
300	30	RPC Preparation
50	–	Code 4/Deletes
150	50	1210B Manual
50	30	1210B Options/Prod Stds
100	60	380R Options/Prod Stds
400	200	Gas Car Documentation
200	100	380R Manual
500	200	Model SS Upgrade
600	250	1248B Revisions
900	300	Pkgs Requiring Update 1200+ Qty
30	–	Delete MS 8200
200	50	Misc Product Part Revisions 140 Qty
40	10	Eliminate 1438C Tiller Steering
50	10	Revise for New Batlok
20	2	Pwr-tron Std on C
40	10	Model C Dual Fork
100	50	Pt Replacement Parts
3,930	1,402	

Savings 1,402 hours x $10/hr = $14,020

Additional Work Includes:
Pwr-tron Designs	Employee Suggestions
1210B/380R Designs	Misc Prod Requests

Figure TD.5 Continued

Examples of Results:

1. Improved Quality
   Examples: Kit Instructions

2. Time Factor
   Example: Revision to SS & C Frame for Power-tron Required
               10 Engineering Man-Hours, Draftsmen Booked-up
   Also: Incomplete Documentation in Shop ~ 5 hours for Prod Std on Stake Sides, Ring Term
            on Charger Recep

3. New Capabilities:
   Example: Manual Isometrics
               MHI Vechicle Drawings
               Reqd 12-16 Hours – Still Not Perfect
   Higher Quality and Speed Could Be Achieved with $12-14/Hr Draftsman (Vs Current $9)
   Current Budget Reserve = $2,800
   Current Draftsman Loss = $2,200

wasted as people vied with each other for the opportunity to use the MOMS machine.

It become clear that the real gains in productivity would be realized during drawing alteration, once most of the standard drawings had been entered into the computer. It was also obvious that immediate savings were possible if people didn't have to stand in line to use the CAD system. With no improvement in department output but with many examples of clear and beautiful drawings, another justification was prepared to add two more machines (see Figure TD.5), one for a draftsman and the other for an engineer. The proposal was for a $575/month lease cost for 5 years. (It turned out that, because of technological obsolescence, the machine life was actually about four years.) If the machines provided a 15 percent increase in efficiency, the department savings would be about equal to one-third the cost of a draftsman. The machines were ordered in May 1983. The units received were serial numbers 7 and 10.

During the remainder of 1983, the MOMS machines performed much better than expected. The plotter output and consistent quality of the drawings made an impression on manufacturing. Although the increase in output was difficult to measure as being one-third or any other fraction of the cost of hiring a draftsman, real improvements in quality and productivity were obvious. For example, turn-around on drawing changes started to be measured in hours instead of days. The potential was enormous.

Complete Conversion

During 1983, the company's sales, still stinging from the loss of the TEE-BIRD, slumped even further as a result of a stagnating economy. When a number of the engineering staff left the company and replacements were hired, the new engineers were screened to ensure that they would be open to the idea of computer-aided drafting. A restructuring of engineering functions within the company followed. The Specials group was transferred back to the product-engineering department from manufacturing, and demands were made on the group to provide more detailed documentation and to make it consistent with the MRP system. In addition, warranty responsibilities were assigned to engineering.

With all this extra work and responsibility, Bob decided to take the plunge and purchase CAD stations for all the engineers. The success of word processing on the HP 9845 resulted in a desire to put word processing at everyone's desk. The data processing group, which had shrunk to two programmers and a night operator, was not prepared to implement word processing. Neither were they interested in developing a tracking system for warranty claims.

Consequently, on the strength of success of the MOMS computers (which resulted in the introduction of two new vehicles from engineering design in a two-year period) and the persuasive charm of the VP, authorization was obtained for more MOMS systems. Orders were placed in April 1984 for additional, higher-speed computer stations and multiuser word-processing system from MOMS Computing. WordStar was selected as the word-processing program, and word-processing terminals were installed by engineering in different departments. Bob wrote the programs in dBASE II to track and analyze warranties. The program Supercalc/2 was made available on every computer for parts-lists/generation, scheduling, cost analysis, and other purposes. An investment of $3,000 was made in special desks to hold the computer stations, and all the drafting boards were removed from the department. By virtue of its experience with computers, engineering was in fact now performing some MIS functions with respect to office automation, warranty tracking, and parts-list maintenance.

In September 1984, the original computers were upgraded to 16-bit processors (Intel 80286/287) and the larger hard-disk capacity (50 megabytes) of the new machines. Additional machines were purchased in October to get the Specials engineering function online with CAD. By this time, the total monthly lease costs had grown to $4,000/month, but the project completion rate was double the amount before computerization. The department had added only one person as a design engineer, and the quality of output was estimated to be four times better than previously. The technical writing became more precise and accurate, and revision turnaround improved dramatically.

The overall evaluation of the MOMS computers was quite favorable. The improvement factor in engineering quality and productivity was about 50 percent, far better than most other companies were reporting. The primary difference was the total commitment to CAD and the complete conversion Bob had achieved (see

Figure TD.6
CAD Drawing of a Vechicle

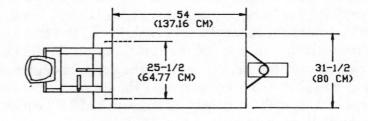
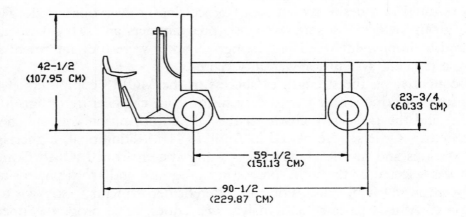

Figure TD.6 for an example of a CAD drawing). There was a "willingness" of all staff members to use the machines, since they had no choice. The machines were extremely easy to use and the training time required was minimal, even for the fresh college graduates Taylor-Dunn hired.

The advantages of the engineering systems were numerous. First, with independent workstations, the 12 computers running simultaneously did not interfere with the company's System/38. At the same time, the multiplicity of units meant that they were not subject to system-wide shutdowns. And, with four plotters and two printers to share, the group had ready access to output devices. The overall reliability of the system instilled confidence in the users.

At the same time, there were numerous drawbacks to the approach taken. First, while the use of independent workstations made the machines safe from system-wide failure, the data processing group did not understand these systems and could provide no support because they had been completely excluded from the entire process. In a curious twist of organizational evolution, the engineering department became the department with computer experts. With the passage of time, DP became defined more and more as the keepers of the System/38, with all other MIS functions being relegated to engineering. The evolution had begun with CAD and taken the natural progression to word processing, warranty tracking, parts-list maintenance, and finally to company-wide responsibility for PC specifications, office automation, and networking.

Dealing with Death and Obsolescence

In the meantime, some technological shifts that were to have a significant effect at Taylor-Dunn were in the wind. The MOMS systems were S-100 machines that operated under the Turbodos operating system. With the introduction of the IBM PC in 1981 and its increasing sophistication and popularity in the next several years, the S-100 market atrophied. Autodesk shifted its emphasis to the IBM and eventually dropped S-100 support altogether. Taylor-Dunn was left with CAD stations that could not make use of the latest versions of AutoCAD.

To make matters worse, one of the biggest fears in doing business with a small startup company came to pass. MOMS Computing did not survive, and continued maintenance and support of the hardware became a concern. Taylor-Dunn ended up purchasing numerous pieces of equipment from the bankruptcy sale to keep a good parts supply for its equipment. With the loss of MOMS service, the engineering department had to become its own programming and repair department, not a bad circumstance for a company such as Taylor-Dunn, which happened to have technically competent electrical and electronics engineers on the staff. However, it might not have been practical at other companies.

Today, the department consists of

4	design engineers
2	draftsmen
1	lab technician
1	warranty administrator
1	secretary
1	technical administrator/writer
1	vice president
1	engineer, Specials
1	clerical support person
1	floor engineer
1	manager, Specials
1	warranty administrator

The entire staff is computer-literate, since just about every facet of the work is computerized. Word processing, data processing, analysis, and drawing are all performed on computers.

Conversion to New Technology

In February 1988, all the CAD computers were upgraded to IBM AT-compatible machines. The CPU, graphics display controller, and keyboard were replaced, but much of the peripheral devices could be retained and used in the IBM environment. A mouse was added to replace the digitizer for those wishing more table space. The plotters and printers were retained for use with the new equipment. The old machines were decommissioned at a residual value of zero dollars and the new equipment was placed on a three-year lease (its expected life).

Data conversion from Turbodos 8-inch disks to PC DOS 5¼ inch disks is still being completed. The cost of converting the 250 megabytes or so of drawings and data is estimated at $5,000, with the new IBM equipment costing $50,000. Since the installation of the new equipment, the database has grown to 400 megabytes.

With regard to the TEE-BIRD, the company has decided to stop fighting Yamaha and profit from its success. Taylor-Dunn now distributes Yamaha golf carts in the Southern California region. The number of Taylor-Dunn vehicles has grown to fourteen, which the firm manufactures and distributes nationwide and to many customers overseas. Sales have recovered and are in excess of $20,000,000/year. The next projected step in CAD is the introduction of higher-powered workstations similar to those manufactured by Sun Microsystems. The expected price drop of these machines in 1990 should be consistent with the department's operating goals and budgets.

Case Study Questions

1. Taylor-Dunn has shown a propensity toward adoption of new technology. What are some of the reasons that TD had to follow such a risky policy? What were some of the risks they took in using new technology? What were some of the problems they encountered? How would you rate this policy in retrospect?

2. The TD case shows that the MIS or accounting function may not be the major information technology area of the firm. Does this pose any problems to MIS designers? To MIS managers? How did this situation arise at TD and under what conditions could it have been avoided?

3. Give an account of the gradual reduction in the size of the MIS staff with time. What are some reasons for this decline?

4. What was the "inventory problem" at TD? What role did it play in the evolving use of computer technology at TD? What effect, if any, did it have on the their eventual adoption of CAD? How could the MIS department have handled the problem differently? With what result?

5. TD went against the tide in changing vendors when they went with the HP 3000. Events showed that they would have been better off if they had stayed with IBM. Analyze and justify the decision to go with HP. Under what conditions might they have chosen to go with IBM?

6. As we have seen with respect to MOMS Computing, one of the biggest dangers of procuring systems components from small startup companies is that they may collapse and therefore not be able to provide continued support. To what extent has this affected TD? What precautions, if any, did they take against this possibility? How did they cope with it when it happened? What advantages or perceived benefits caused TD to take this risk? Provide arguments to support this decision. Provide some arguments against this decision. If you were a TD manager would this cause you to make some new policy regarding this situation?

7. Describe the evolution of CAD at TD from a SDLC or prototyping standpoint. What benefits of CAD were realized at TD? What are some of the problems of implementing CAD and how were these addressed at TD? What were the rationale and benefits of combining word processing and CAD?

8. Perform a cost/benefit analysis for CAD implementation at TD.

BECHTEL POWER CORPORATION

Strategic Information System for Executives

Logic only gives a man what he needs. But magic gives him what he wants.
— Tom Robbins, *Another Roadside Attraction*

Bechtel Power – The Company

Bechtel Power Corporation is a large multinational engineering and construction company headquartered in San Francisco, with regional offices in Houston and London, as well as in Canada, the Middle East, the Far East, and other parts of the world. Bechtel is one of the largest privately held companies in the country. Because the firm is not public, information about the company's finances and activities are not readily available.

Bechtel's forte and primary product is good, solid engineering and a project management system that is the envy of the industry. The strength of the company lies in its technical expertise and its proven ability to manage very large projects. To achieve this reputation – to be able to harness and direct the efforts of thousands of engineers working on multibillion dollar projects on a global scale, Bechtel has had to rely heavily on information technology. For this reason the company's information systems group plays a key role in Bechtel's success strategy.

Bechtel started life as a mule train supplying goods to the railways at the turn of the century. The company took on bigger and bigger projects until, by the thirties, it had built the Hoover Dam and the Bay Bridge across San Francisco Bay. Bechtel soon gained a reputation as a manager of mega-projects and in the next several decades built many large hydroelectric, nuclear, and conventional electric power generating plants around the world. The company has diversified and is very active in mining and mineral processing, oil and gas field development, pipelining, oil refining, civil and structural projects, and chemical plants.

Bechtel has more than 17,000 employees worldwide. Their largest centers are in San Francisco, London, and the Middle East. In San Francisco, the company is spread out among five buildings, including three skyscrapers in the financial district. The information services group operates out of one of these buildings and coordinates the information flow worldwide.

One of the critical success factors in Bechtel's strategic plan is to provide financial and support services to its clients. In this way, the company hopes to use the breadth of its engineering know-how and financial strength to provide a full project management service from conceptual designs and feasibility studies to putting together the financing package, and the more traditional functions of design, construction, and startup. This capability clearly differentiates Bechtel from the competition and creates new projects where none existed before, but the information needs of such a venture are new and unmapped and present special challenges to the MIS/DSS groups of the firm.

The Problem

In the late 1970s Bechtel was at the height of its power and success, having built a pipeline clear across Alaska, produced the first commercial-grade oil pumped from sand in the Canadian tundra, and built cities out of the desert in Arabia. With more than $5 billion worth of work on the books and offices in San Francisco, Houston, and London brimming with busy engineers, Bechtel was mobilized for full participation in the energy boom.

Unfortunately almost overnight, news of the accident at the Three Mile Island nuclear power plant conspired with falling oil prices to take the steam out of this boom. As a result, more than $20 billion worth of construction in nuclear power plants, offshore platforms, oil refineries, coal gasification plants, and natural gas processing plants were taken off the drawing board. Bechtel, having gone to considerable effort to build an image as a manager of mega-projects, suddenly found itself with no mega-projects to manage. To survive, Bechtel would have to redefine itself — take a fresh look at its resources and find new markets for services it could provide. The firm needed a new strategic plan with a 7- to 10-year horizon into the future. Bechtel decided to reexamine its company structure and its business philosophy.

This decline in energy-related construction was compounded by the fact that the engineering and construction marketplace is dynamic: a moving target driven by global economic and political events to a far greater degree than what American business could comprehend or deal with in the short term. To endure, Bechtel would have to be flexible, roll with the punches, and become a moving target itself.

Adapting to a Changing Market

Bechtel's plan was the essence of simplicity. First, since the firm was fatter than the market could feed, it would have to shed some weight. Self-examination revealed a huge underbelly that had quietly accumulated during boom times.

Management acted quickly and decisively. Some offices were virtually shut down, and the San Francisco and London offices were trimmed to the bone. As projects wound down, extraneous engineers and project staff were not reassigned but furloughed. Second, the company decided to streamline administrative costs by reorganizing under fewer corporations and divisions. Some divisions were eliminated while others were merged. For example, research and engineering (R & E) was absorbed by Bechtel National Inc. The outcome was a simpler organization with fewer lines of command, one that was more flexible and adaptive to rapid changes.

Third, since there were no billion-dollar projects, the company would pursue smaller, million-dollar contracts. It was thought that the company was now leaner and meaner and could be profitable in small jobs. However, to maintain a comparable work load, the firm would have to carry a large number of projects at any given time. Project organization, engineering, accounting, and administration must be rethought. The mega-project formula was no longer applicable and would result in an unwieldy and unprofitable operation.

And fourth, in order to bid, obtain, and manage a large number of small and diverse projects — and be profitable doing so — Bechtel must develop an "edge." This edge would be provided by information technology. Being lean and mean would require Bechtel to do more jobs with fewer people. The information services (IS) group was to play a key role in making this possible through information productivity tools.

Changing Information Needs

In this new scenario of business at Bechtel, corporate executives are required to be more flexible, react more quickly, and deal with a much larger mass of data than before. The information system must provide managers with a clear view of a more complicated picture and assist them in accomplishing the following:

1. React faster to internal and external events.
2. Detect problems much earlier than they could using existing information systems.
3. Devise alternative strategies on a much shorter decision cycle than traditional Bechtel methodologies would allow.
4. Take corrective action "on the fly."

As Bechtel executives have adjusted to the demands of the new marketplace, their information needs have changed. The astute IS group was aware of the disparity between the information needed and that which they were able to provide. IS therefore instituted a program of systems analysis and design to define and meet this new challenge.

Bechtel has an enormous amount of data, both internal and external, on its battery of Univac 1100/90 and IBM 3090 mainframes, as well as in a number of IBM System/38 and System/36 computers used for project management and on thousands of PCs company-wide. Since the late seventies, Bechtel has enhanced its engineering design capabilities by the addition of Intergraph CAD systems and VAX minicomputers. Data comes from project monitoring systems, corporate accounting systems, and marketing and engineering databases. Strategic information is obtained from service bureaus and other outside sources. Currently, the MIS department is the "keeper" of the data and provides some of this information in summary report format to managers on a periodic basis. The MIS department also controls the data and computing resources used by the projects.

At Bechtel each project team is spun off into a semiautonomous task force and cost center with its own line of command from the project manager down to staff engineers, draftsmen, and manual field workers (see Figure B.1). A project may include hundreds of engineering personnel and thousands of field workers with a budget of millions or even billions of dollars. The project management plugs into the Bechtel infrastructure for all services, including information services. A project may last from several months to several years. As the project winds down, the ranks are thinned as personnel, equipment, and services are reassigned to other projects. At the conclusion of a project, the project team is dissolved. At any given moment there may be hundreds of projects ongoing worldwide.

From an MIS perspective, the greatest demand for data and services comes from transient managers and temporary needs in the shifting sands of projects, which grow, generate unique information requirements, and then disappear. MIS involvement includes initial hardware and software setup and ongoing support during all phases of the project. Project management needs include scheduling, inventory, purchasing and vendor control, personnel time and job cost control, and engineering design needs, including CAD and CAE. A combination of dedicated minicomputers, micros, and special access to the corporate Univacs is used to satisfy these needs according to project size and location.

Although this approach worked with the large and slow mega-projects, information communicated through the traditional process is inadequate and untimely and will not meet the demands of the new organizational objectives.

Another problem is the report format being used. Cumbersome and large printouts on computer paper, requiring managers to turn through page after page of numbers and cryptic descriptors, are a hindrance to managerial effectiveness. A big problem with the report format is that there is simply too much data presented — an excess of detail that obfuscates rather than informs, intimidates rather than supports,

Figure B.1
Project Teams and Their Relationship to the Corporation

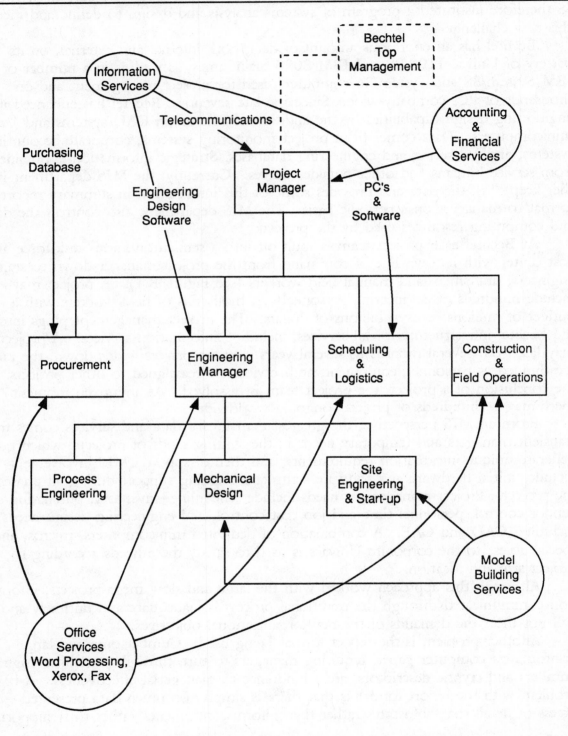

hides rather than reveals. You just cannot put a 500-page computer printout on a busy executive's desk and actually expect it to be read.

But the real fly in the ointment is this: Although you can't encumber executives with detailed data in the report, specific details must be accessible to them when they want them.

For example, suppose that on a "Project Costs To Date" report, you provide the manager with total, budgeted, unused, and percentage used of engineering hours, overheads applied, direct materials, and construction labor man-hours on a week-by-week basis. Invariably, one of these weeks, the project manager will ask for the number of engineers who were charging time to the project or for a breakdown of man-hours by plant number, the amount of overhead charged, or some other data that are not in your report.

The traditional approach has been to add that information to the report in the next revision cycle. If this process is allowed to continue, the report grows in each cycle, carrying with it every piece of data ever requested. Before long, a simple report balloons into one of those dreaded "books" that nobody dares to open. This is what happened not only at Bechtel but in most information reporting systems.

Bechtel MIS identified this problem and decided that the traditional approach just would not work in the new business format. The challenge was to devise an information system that would keep report formats simple and yet allow immediate access to specific data on a per request basis.

A Strategic Information System to Meet the Challenge

Bechtel needed a strategic information system (SIS). Such an information system must meet the challenge of data access described above and, even more important in light of Bechtel's new business philosophy, it must be adaptive like a DSS; that is, the SIS must be responsive to changes in market directions and corporate strategy.

Most information systems are built with critical mass and inertia. Once an MIS gets rolling, it can take on a life of its own and require the business organization to adapt to it in strange ways. For example, at a well-known trailer rental facility, if an additional cash deposit is assessed after an initial deposit has been made, the transaction is handled in the following manner: First, the original deposit ticket is voided and the deposit money is physically returned to the customer. Then, a new transaction entry showing the higher deposit amount is made and the money is received from the customer before a printout of the new deposit ticket is made. The reason for this procedure is that the transaction processing system (TPS) does not allow any changes to a transaction once it has been entered into the computer. In this case, the way this company conducts its business must adapt to the way the TPS works.

This situation had to be avoided in the new SIS design, which would have to be flexible and changeable. Flexibility would have to be built into the design so that the system and its report format automatically changed as the firm's information needs and business strategy changed.

Another primary design criterion was that the new SIS present a user interface to the executives that was consistent with the way managers actually ran the business. Further, the system would have to make sense to managers and the operation of the system must be intuitive. It would take into account not only the managers' information needs and the type of decisions they made, but also their cognitive styles and the way they made decisions. In this respect, the SIS design would be required to follow systems analysis methods normally used for decision support systems (DSSs).

Reliance on such methods was a bold and clear departure from traditional system design, in which the emphasis is only on what data the managers need. Such systems are characterized by inadequate concern for the way in which the data are to be presented. In the data-oriented environment, programmers may write programs and documentation that are so technical they can be understood only by other programmers. Users, for whom the programs are apparently intended, may find these programs perplexing and the documentation incomprehensible. As a result, they may feel insecure, intimidated, and confused, and therefore refuse to use the system. Programmers may then label these users as "naive," "novice," "computer-illiterate," or "lay," and may admonish them to consult the user manual or to take extensive training.

Managers and executives are normally hindered from participating in training programs because of their busy schedules. To be successful, an information system meant to be used directly by executives must incorporate a different design philosophy, one in which managers are not made to feel as if they are novices or illiterates. If they cannot use a system that was supposedly designed for them, then it is the programmer who is the novice.

The IS group at Bechtel understood the necessity to follow such a philosophy if their new SIS was to be successful.

The Options

Two possible approaches to the system design could be taken to meet the criteria set out for the SIS.

1. *Use the current information system and write customized programs to meet individual needs on a piecemeal basis.* This alternative required MIS to build up a large staff of experienced programmer-analysts responsible for working closely with Bechtel executives to identify and respond to their specific needs. They would generate on a very quick turnaround custom in-house programs to solve information problems as they arose.

However, the MIS backlog would have to remain low to sustain the fast turnaround.

2. *Replace the current information reporting system with an executive information system (EIS).* The EIS would be designed to feed critical business information directly to Bechtel executives. The presentation would utilize online terminals. The primary reports would be highly visual in nature, consisting of text and graphics images, and "live" in that they would be tied into large databases containing detailed information. A query system would allow the executive to access deeper and deeper levels of detail on any item of interest. The report formats would be consistent corporate-wide but would address a broad range of problems and information types. This option required development of a new system with associated high costs, long development life cycle, commitment of funds, and the trauma of change.

Bechtel's Decision

Bechtel's MIS group decided that the objectives of the new SIS could best be realized with the implementation of a new and flexible EIS. A crucial specification was that the system be responsive to changing management information needs and business styles. However, the standard by which this system was to be measured was the extent to which managers could and would use the system; that is, the degree to which the user interface was intuitive and flexible would make or break the system, regardless of the amount of sheer data it could churn out. Clearly, this was a significant system development project for MIS to undertake.

In skeleton format, the system envisaged would have the following logical design features and capabilities: From a programmer's point of view, it was principally a "data server" that tied together several diverse databases, automatically extracting and delivering pertinent information from them and hiding system complexities from the user.

Three primary types of databases (see Table B.1) would be used by the EIS: The corporate database is the primary store of the firm's business records. It includes financial, accounting, human resources, facilities, and administrative data and is maintained on the IBM mainframe in San Francisco. The primary users of this data are top-level strategic managers, as well as accountants and financial managers. The data include records of all financial transactions, assets, liabilities, and information. Detailed information on all salaried personnel, in addition to payroll and benefits information, includes technical background, capabilities, and current assignment.

The second type of database, the project database is the meat of Bechtel's business. Data on all projects, past and present, are available on the project computers (System/36, System/38, and IBM PC AT, PS/2). Project data include

Table B.1
Three Types of Databases Used by the Bechtel EIS

Type	Contents	Users
Corporate (IBM mainframe)	Business records	Managers Accounting personnel
Project (System/36, System/38, IBM PC AT, PS/2, and IBM mainframe)	Project data	Project and department managers
External	Online data services	Investment managers

construction details, costs, man-hours, schedules, project personnel assignments, and profitability analysis. These data are also stored in summary format on the IBM mainframe.

The final type of database includes external databases and services. External online services such as The Source, CompuServe, Dow-Jones, and others provide needed data about Bechtel's business environment. Bechtel executives use these services to keep track of changes and trends in the marketplace, and to glean insights from competitor activities.

Relevant data from all these sources would be extracted and maintained in a central database, using a software package called *Command Center*. This program was to be the main engine of the new EIS.

Report Formats

Good MIS design practice is to start with the reports that will be needed and work backwards to specify a system that would be able to produce them.

The EIS would use a combination of mainframe and microcomputer technology, utilizing the best features of each to maintain large databases and present on-screen information to executives in a familiar and user-friendly PC environment.

Three types of reports would be presented as shown in Table B.2.

The first type, standard reports with "drill-down," are highly summarized graphics-oriented reports designed to fit easily and clearly on one PC screen. The amount of data reported on the main report screen is minimized. Thus, data to be presented are chosen carefully, based on the criteria of revealing various aspects of the operation. Once the report is structured, the user can change it and ask for new types of data to be included (as before). The difference is that this time any new data requested are included only at the expense of other pieces of data.

Table B.2
Three Types of Report Formats

Type	Description
Standard reports with "drill down" capability	Graphics-oriented summaries with pyramidal structure
Trends and patterns	Comparison reports utilized in decision making and forecasting
Exception	Customized extracts of specified data retrieved on the basis of preset trigger points

These reports have a pyramidal structure and sit on top of layers of detail. The drill down feature permits the user to dig below the summary report for specific details. Because the dig is very precise, it does not yield mountains of data but only the specific data requested.

The second report facility, trends and patterns, yields data in a manner that facilitates the types of comparisons managers utilize when making strategic decisions. A comparison of current information can be made with historical data to expose exceptions and changes that a manager wishes to highlight. This comparison can be made numerically in absolute numbers and in terms of percentages. Various kinds of graphical and iconic devices are also used in this comparison process. Pie charts, bar charts, and line graphs with shaded areas are used on a high-resolution color monitor to accent the trends and changes in data.

The comparison report also helps managers gain new heuristic insights into the patterns of performance and the relationship of these patterns to current performance. These insights help managers develop a clearer view of changes in business activity with time and external events. As a result, managers play a more informed role in forecasting activities. Whenever special mathematical procedures and models are used, explanatory notes are made available to inform managers of the exact procedures used and assumptions made in arriving at the results being displayed.

Exception reports, the third type of report format, is based on a set of predetermined trigger points or benchmarks of performance. A manager can use this report writer to search through the entire EIS database. The report is an extraction of all data items specified that exceed the maximum variances the manager wishes to examine. A standard set of trigger points provided as a default can be changed for a particular search. In this manner, executives can do what they have wanted to do for a long time: produce custom exception reports that give them the information that is appropriate for the particular decisions at hand. In this way, thousands of pages of data (remember the "book"?) can be distilled to a screen or two of highly visual and relevant information. This feature alone was expected to greatly increase Bechtel managers' ability to identify priority problems and opportunities at a speed and effectiveness never before possible.

The User Interface

The digging process and the entire user interface were designed to be uncomplicated, permissive, and tolerant. Cryptic error messages were replaced with helpful suggestions. For example, the system did not use error messages such as these:

> Fatal Error 0762: EOF Encountered or Inconsistent Data Type
> Error in command syntax
> File error: File not found
> Error: Incomplete file spec

The word "error" is best not used at all. It is a holdover from the "arrogance of perspective," the notion that "programmers don't make mistakes, only 'computer-illiterate' users do." Good software development targets the end user very carefully when designing the dialogue subsystem. This approach is particularly crucial in this case because the users were company executives who were not expected to be computer-literate and who were short on time and patience.

Training has been traditionally overused by MIS professionals to compensate for poor programming. However, these executives did not have time to be trained or to read mountains of documentation, so the program must appeal to the managers' intuition or it would not be used.

The type of error messages used was based on a format similar to the following examples:

> You are asking me to compare Employee Name with Employee Numbers. I assume that you want to compare names. Do you wish to (P)roceed on this assumption or (C)hange your command?

> The command I am trying to perform is "PRONT." This is not a command I know. I assume you mean "PRINT." Do you wish to (P)roceed, (C)hange your command, (D)efine the command PRONT, or do something (E)lse?

The users of the EIS would primarily be extracting data, i.e, giving commands rather than typing in data. This is important to note because managers might not know how to type, might not want to sit at a terminal and type, and might not have the time to do a lot of typing. It was essential, therefore, that the amount of keyboarding be kept to the bare minimum. The dialogue designer had to be sensitive to the number of keystrokes required to perform simple functions.

Consequently, the "command line" approach of operation must be discarded and a comprehensive menu selection method devised to issue all commands to the EIS. The menu selection method could use arrow keys or a mouse to point to commands and a hierarchy of menus. Whenever keywords, field names, report types, number formats, dates or other data must be typed in as arguments to a command, a window should be used to present as many options as possible so that the user can select one of these by pointing.

In the case where the data to be typed are not listed, then keyboarding by executives is required. However, in such cases, the data typed in must be automatically added to the appropriate list for future selection. However, it is felt that the commands and application-specific keywords used by managers will fall within a small, repetitive set and the constant addition of new keywords will not engender large, unmanageable lists.

Inasmuch as managers are expected to repeat the same sequence of commands on a recurring basis, a macro facility was made available to automate routine tasks. (A macro is a group of discrete commands that can be executed in sequence with a single command. A system that incorporates a macro facility allows users to generate macros as they work.) The macro generation itself needed to be automated so that no special knowledge was needed to create them. Many macro generators provide a record facility so that keystrokes are automatically saved into a macro. This feature can be improved even further by offering "macros by hindsight"; that is, record all keystrokes in a buffer and at any point give the user the option of creating a macro of what he or she has just done. This is the way people work; i.e., they typically do not think of creating macros until they have already done the task stepwise. It is the job of the system designer to understand this and adapt the system design to conform to the user. If this facet of the design fails, the system will fail because the users will simply not use it.

Executives rarely need precise numbers. Rather, they need to see the big picture encompassing a lot of numbers. A very effective way of rendering data in this manner is to use graphics. The user interface and reporting structure should utilize graphics, charts, icons, and pictures to a high degree so that the executive may visualize trends and changes, and spot danger signals and opportunities. High-resolution color graphics should be used to make the charts appealing as well as clear in what they depict.

Although voice input is still embryonic in its development and cumbersome to use, it might be suitable for this application. Some voice input CAD systems have had a limited degree of success. The current state of this technology should be investigated for possible application in this case.

The ideal workstation that could offer the features outlined is the personal computer. Both the IBM PS/2 and the Apple Macintosh have features that could be used to build the dialogue system envisioned. In addition, user-friendly software is plentiful and inexpensive. For example, either Lotus 1-2-3 or Microsoft Excel could be used as a frontend (i.e., a computer program used to simplify or streamline access to another program) to the EIS. The microcomputers would be networked and connected to the mainframe, using a high-speed synchronous line so that the corporate data can be rapidly accessed as necessary. Bechtel MIS personnel would be required to build the necessary software interfaces (both the mainframe-resident portion and the PC-resident portion) to achieve the PC-mainframe connectivity. The connectivity must be seamless: i.e., it must hide the technology from the user and be completely transparent.

The Case Against EIS

The EIS design, despite its advantages, creates a broader philosophical dilemma that must be addressed. Many would claim that it is perverse and narrow-minded to tie down executives to computer terminals, since they are very special people with unique intuitive and heuristic characteristics that make them the successful business people and managers that they are. They see the "big pictures"; they arrange and rearrange gigantic corporate jigsaw puzzles; they take short cuts; they act on instinct; they take risks, weigh opportunities and hunches, and make decisions in ways that no sequential von Neumann processor or programmer could comprehend. Have systems designers become so enamored of their creations that they would propose to turn these executives into machine operators? The proponents of such ideas would claim that the only "human interface" for executives is another human. It is the lower echelon of technicians who should process the data that machines can provide. Executives are at their best when talking eyeball-to-eyeball, not eyeball-to-screen display. Computers are marvelous machines, but putting them (in their current form) on executives' desks may be an entirely wrong application.

Case Study Questions

1. Bechtel's MIS department had two options: write custom programs or develop EIS. They chose the EIS option. As MIS manager, write a memo to top managers describing and supporting this decision. As an executive manager, what questions would you want to ask the MIS manager about this plan?

2. Top executives would never use a computer terminal. Computers make typists out of managers. Managers are communicators not computer operators." What is your response to these comments? Are they justified? Why or why not?

3. One of the key factors stressed in Bechtel's EIS implementation is flexibility. What are the hardware and software implications of this requirement? What determines whether a system is flexible or inflexible? What aspects of the Bechtel EIS design address the flexibility issue?

4. The Bechtel EIS design incorporates ad hoc queries to the corporate database, as well as the use of graphics displays and mathematical models. How does this design fit the usual textbook taxonomy of a DSS? How would the redefinition of the project as a DSS affect its design and implementation?

5. "Training has been traditionally overused by MIS professionals to compensate for poor programming." What are the pros and cons of this statement? Based on the case study, is there any evidence of such "overuse" at Bechtel? Why is the issue of training particularly important in the EIS design?

6. One of the maxims of MIS is that projects must originate with and have the full support of management; that is, projects initiated by MIS and forced onto the organization without management support are not likely to succeed. How do you perceive the Bechtel EIS project in this respect? What aspects of the project would tend to ensure its success? As an MIS manager, what are your concerns?

7. Assume that you are a systems analyst on the EIS project. Your boss asks you to investigate the use of voice input in the EIS. What actions would you take? Write a memo to your boss with your recommendations.

8. In what ways could ES technology be used in the EIS?

9. By comparing the EIS option to the custom report option, show that "The Case Against EIS," on page 106, has no merit because of cost considerations and Bechtel's business situation.

Integrating Customer Support with Call Logging

A High-Tech Company and Its Product

In a rural industrial park set among chicken farms, dairies, and wineries in Sonoma County, California, Compumotor is quietly building technological leadership in high-technology components for process automation and robotics. With their new microstepping technology and PC interface, this small company is gaining a reputation as a major manufacturer and innovator in motion-control technology. The product line includes stepper motors, AC and DC servo motors, linear step motors, and a new product created by Compumotor called *Compumotor Plus*.

Stepper motors play a key role in the field of motion control in robotics and industrial process automation. The read/write heads of the disk drive in your computer are moved back and forth over the platter by such a motor. These motors, unlike the ones you get from Sears to run your water pump or air compressor, don't spin. Instead, every time they receive a pulse of electricity, they turn by a very precise amount (normally 1.8 degrees) and stop. By the right combination of pulses, the motor can be made to turn by any exact amount in either direction. Since the pulses can be sent by a computer through a controller board, stepper motors have paved the way for computer control of motion.

Much of the movement of industrial robots, such as those of the articulated manipulator arms, are performed by these devices. So are movements in valve stems, cutting machinery, metering pumps, wafer handlers, and other control elements in process automation. Other applications include x-y plotters, instrumentation, aircraft, machine tools, and laser optics.

There are three important aspects of this product that relate to our case problem. First, the product is normally not used directly by end users but is incorporated into a machine or tool put together by someone else. These manufacturers of machinery or instrumentation are called OEMs, original equipment manufacturers, and constitute the major customer group for Compumotor. The OEMs are normally very sophisticated in terms of stepper motor technology. Even in end-user purchases the motors are used by a sophisticated machine builder and incorporated into larger systems.

Second, even though Compumotor's customers are technically knowledgeable in the application of stepper motors, as a result of the highly technical nature of the product, customers must be provided a great deal of technical support in key situations that are important from a marketing viewpoint. Technical support is most important when existing customers are developing new products or trying to troubleshoot problems that may be related to malfunction of the stepper motor. Another important situation requiring technical support is that of new customers who are unfamiliar with the product and who require assistance in integrating the Compumotor stepper motors into their products.

Third, Compumotor products incorporate technological innovations with which many design engineers are not familiar. For instance, the company's motors divide the 1.8 degrees motion (a step), into 125 microsteps. Through the use of microstepping, Compumotor is able to offer enhanced positioning accuracy, smoothness, and range of speeds. When OEM engineers specify stepper motors, they have to consider torque, speed, accuracy, acceleration, deceleration, heat dissipation, control logic, and other factors. If the engineers are not familiar with microstepping technology, they will require a great deal of assistance in selecting a motor for an application from the large number of models offered by Compumotor. This requirement dictates a high degree of technical support at the engineer-to-engineer level to sustain sales. Engineers who do not understand the product will not use it, and those who apply it incorrectly will cause the product to develop a bad reputation.

Technical Support as a Marketing Strategy

Because of the importance of technical support in maintaining and extending current markets and in developing new markets, the marketing department of Compumotor maintains a technical support center staffed with five "application engineers" and an assistant. Engineers are used in this capacity because support involving a high level of technical expertise must be provided to other engineers. The information needed by the OEMs requires detailed knowledge about the product, its maintenance, and its application.

An additional use of the technical support center is to handle initial queries about the product from prospective customers. Prospects who respond to Compumotor ads are usually engineers who call or write for technical information regarding specific applications or for details of the microstepping technology. Compumotor believes that they would not stand a good chance of "changing prospects into customers" if they did not provide a technically knowledgeable staff to respond to these queries. In terms of sheer volume, this function — providing technical information to prospective customers — has become the prominent activity of the support center.

The support mechanism spans various modes of communication. The support center, or the applications engineering department (AED), as it is called, offers regularly scheduled customer training workshops and seminars, publishes a technical newsletter, and answers questions on the telephone. The telephone is the dominant and critical mechanism. It consumes most of the time and effort of the AED, is an area in which they gain maximum effectiveness, and presents a significant challenge in information management and control, as we shall see in this case study.

The Applications Engineering Department: Telephone Support

The AED maintains a toll-free 800 number for customer support calls. These calls are taken by the assistant and routed to the application engineers, all of whom occupy a circle of cubicles in one corner of the building. Thus, if needed, call handling can be determined by direct conversation while the customer is on hold.

In rare cases, an application is handled completely in one call, the customer asks a simple question, the support engineer provides the answer, and the call ends with no further follow-up activities needed to handle the inquiry. In most cases, however, each new call is the start of a complex series of activities, follow-up calls, promises, and obligations that normally involve several application engineers and even other departments in the company. If a call is not a new call, it is simply part of this process.

Over 25 different products supported by the AED include not only stepper motors but also logic control boards for various computers, including the IBM PC. The control boards act as intelligent interfaces between computers and the stepper motors. Although the PC interface represents only a small segment of the Compumotor product line, the popularity of the PC has helped increase sales of the PC-based products by an order of magnitude, resulting not only in an increased number of calls to the AED but a new group of customers.

Because these users are not as technically sophisticated as the traditional OEMs and are setting up complex motion devices running off their PCs, an increased level of support must be provided to them. Support is also provided to Compumotor's own field service personnel, as well as to distributors and salespeople in the field.

The AED not only provides product information to prospects and customers but is also a valuable source of information for the company. It is a critical component in the feedback loop connecting the company's decision makers to the marketplace they serve. The AED obtains three types of market information: product defects, new prospects, and new application and design ideas. Calls involving product defects are attributable to failure of a product to perform to specification. These must be technically identified, documented, and reported to production and quality control for corrective action. Frequently, AED and marketing may be involved in tracking the corrective action to verify that the defect has been corrected. Two types of corrective action are taken: The defective units in the field must be repaired, and the design, manufacturing, or quality-control process must be changed to avoid defects in future batches. Equipment may be repaired at the factory or sometimes in the field by technically sophisticated customers under the direction of AED engineers.

New prospect calls made to Compumotor on the 800 number in response to advertisements and promotions are taken by AED. The AED engineers ascertain customers' technical needs, mail them the proper information sheets, qualify customers, and sell the appropriate Compumotor device to solve customers' motion-control problems. The names and addresses of prospects who have called, have been qualified by AED, and have had their needs defined, become very valuable sales information. The data are passed on to the sales department, which will pursue the sale. Such sales are usually not piece sales but large contracts since, over a period of time, these customers will purchase a large number of the device that they choose.

Innovative customers will frequently report new applications they have found or design modifications they have performed that would increase the market base, the performance, or the versatility of a Compumotor product. Even if an attempt to match a given application with a Compumotor device proves futile, the AED engineer may be able to identify a need for a new device or modification. This information is directed to research and development and to production for possible action but normally does not involve the AED any further.

AED Inputs and Outputs: A Complex Tangle

To summarize, AED supports many different products and many different kinds of calls from many different kinds of callers, requiring various processing methods and final disposition. These tasks must be carried out with extreme care and precision since the company's sales and product integrity are on the line.

Working in AED is also a thankless job. Tasks carried out perfectly may go unnoticed while a miss may rock the organization with accusations and vitriol. A miss can occur when (1) technical literature is promised but not mailed, (2) a technical solution is proposed but fails, (3) a customer calls repeatedly but each time is put on indefinite hold and never reaches an application engineer, and (4) a customer is given incorrect technical information.

The Manual Method and Its Pitfalls: Handling Incoming Calls

The manual method is completely paperwork-oriented with no mechanism to integrate the efforts of the five engineers, or to make connections between similar calls or calls from the same customer. An incoming call is handled in the following manner. If the caller asks for an engineer by name, then the call router (the assistant) will route the call accordingly unless the engineer is busy. In that case, she makes some queries to categorize the call and routes it to an appropriate engineer. If all the engineers are busy and she determines that it is a routine request for product literature, she will handle the call. If not, she takes the customer's name and phone number and adds them to the stack of call return requests. When an application engineer is free, he checks this stack for calls to return.

When a call is taken, the taker, be it application engineer or assistant, fills out a customer call report form. The diagram in Figure C.1 outlines the call handling process. The call taker fills in the date and his or her name and then, before addressing the needs of the caller, asks the caller for his name, company name, address, and phone number, writes this information on the form, and classifies the caller as a prospect, customer, distributor, or field service engineer while the caller waits.

The call taker then tries to determine the Compumotor product (model number) to which the call relates and fills in that information on the form. He or she is now ready to be responsive to the caller's problems.

In the ensuing conversation, the AED engineer handling the call discusses the caller's application, problems, and needs, and may suggest specific remedies or make promises of certain information or remedies for the future. At the conclusion of the call, he enters this information onto the form and files it under either "completed" or "pending."

In the example shown in Figure C.2, the call related to product Model PK2. The customer wanted to know whether he could draw some power from the PK2 5-volt power supply to run an LED display. He was told that he should use an external power supply and the matter was closed.

In making this determination, the application engineer may have had to look through technical specifications, consult with R & D and design engineers, or make calculations and engineering judgments. In the manual system the results of this effort are not shared with the other application engineers or recorded in a manner that would allow them to be retrieved when AED was faced with a similar situation. Thus, if a similar call were to come in the next day and be taken by a different engineer, he might repeat this procedure and might even reach an inconsistent conclusion.

The failure of the manual system is even more apparent when the call requires follow-through. If the response requires shipping out a manual or a part, then the AED engineer must make sure that it gets shipped that day, possibly by Federal Express. Promises not kept can create very irate customers out of perfectly good ones. The customers themselves may be sitting on critical shipments of equipment to end-users. Tens of thousands of dollars may be at risk in each phone call.

Figure C.1
Call Handling in AED

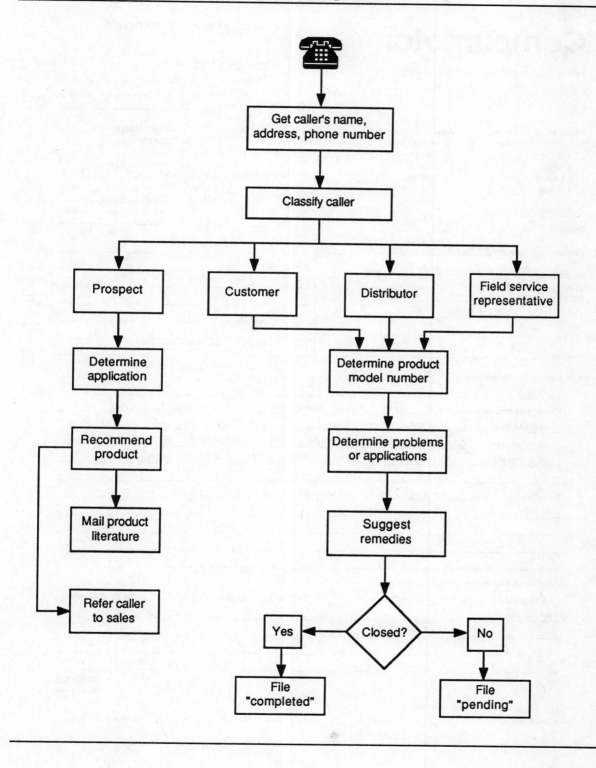

Figure C.2
Completed CCR Form

Compumotor

1179 N. McDowell Blvd., Petaluma CA 94952

CUSTOMER CALL REPORT

Compumotor Information

C² Personnel: Melody

FAE/REP Name:

Date Lit. Sent:

Application Resolved	App. Eng. Handled	Type of Customer	Customer Needs
☒ 1st Call	☒ Immediately	☐ Prospect	☐ Catalog
☐ 1 Hour	☐ 1 Hour	☒ Customer	☐ Linear Cat.
☐ 4 Hour	☐ 4 Hour	☐ Rep/Dist.	☐ Spaulding Cat.
☐ 24 Hour	☐ 24 Hour	☐ C² Field Person	☐ PKS Cat.
☐ 1 Week			☐ Attached
			☐
			☐
			☐

Customer Information

Date: 7/18/88

Person Contacted: Howard Heid

Company: Metro Metal & Design

Address 2313 So. Train St.
Charlotte, N.C.

Tel. No. (704) 334-9871

– Customer Call Back Status –			
Init.	Date	Time	Action
Attempts to return call were unsuccessful. Customer information placed in FAE V.M.B.			☐

Compumotor products: PK2

Customer problem/application: Tie LED across power supply and ground. Wanted to know if could tie to power supply of PK2 — NO. Needed 5V external supply and resister between.

Solution: Use external supply & resister.

Additional comments/action required:

☐ Voice Mail ☐ ECR ☐ Manual change ☐ FAE, message in

Parker

White: Regional Mgr. Yellow: REO Pink: C² Rep/FAE Goldenrod: Lit. Request

The customer may report a hardware "bug" that is new to the AED engineer, who may then have to run a simulated bug test so that he can analyze the customer's problem and propose solutions. Many such diverse activities are carried out as part of the support process. The manual system is not conducive to coordination of these activities.

The system provides no verifiable way to track a call from its reception to completion when the activities may require several days, many phone calls, and diverse activities on the part of the AED engineer handling the call. In general, the lack of proper filing and retrieval of call data, information sharing between engineers, and a consistent and cohesive response from this group sabotages the effectiveness of the AED.

The problems with the manual system can be summarized as follows:

1. The system does not automatically create a central and shared "bug" list and "fix" list so that the group can work as a unit and respond to customers in an efficient and consistent manner. A bug reported to one engineer may be unknown to another, at least while the customer is on the phone, and bug fixes engineered by one engineer may not be immediately available to another. Therefore, when another engineer is faced with a similar problem, he would repeat the entire problem-solving process. This approach causes delays, inefficiency, and inconsistency in response.

2. Customer names and addresses are repeatedly requested and entered into the call report form. A customer should never have to give his name and address more than once.

3. Research and engineering work done by one engineer for a given customer are not available to a second engineer, should he have to take the next call from the same customer. Consequently, the second AED engineer may unwittingly start anew. The system allows two engineers to work on the same problem independently, almost in a Mutt-and-Jeff fashion.

4. When problem resolution requires several calls, more than one AED engineer may become involved with the same problem. When this happens, the customer must brief each new AED engineer on the problem and outline the history of the case, since there is no ready reference file of cases that an engineer may refer to while on the phone. This problem is not only a source of inefficiency but one that breeds inconsistency in response and frustration for customers.

5. The system does not automatically generate a history of product problems, making it virtually impossible to detect trends in product

quality and performance. The information gathered by AED is potentially of great value to R & D and production but is not available in a way in which it can be used.

6. AED engineers make promises to customers that may involve (1) calling them back with information, (2) shipping out technical documentation or product literature, or (3) shipping out repaired or replacement parts by Federal Express. Frequently during busy periods, these promises tend to become lost in the paperwork and are not kept.

7. Field service personnel are not always apprised of customer calls. Consequently, they may not always know that a customer has been calling the AED directly. This situation can happen either because the CCR (customer call report) has not been processed or because the call was not properly recorded. The effectiveness of the field service personnel is compromised if they are not working in concert with AED, since their functions are similar with respect to the customer.

AED Engineers Take Charge: The Genesis of End-User Computing

Both the marketing department and the AED recognized that they had an information problem that had jeopardized the effectiveness of the AED. However, the levels of responsibilities had not been clearly delineated. The AED engineers claimed that they needed some sort of computerized system to keep track of the myriad of information they dealt with. There were no computer professionals in the department but some of the engineers were familiar with PCs and felt early on that some sort of dBASE file could be created to save the data they generated. However, no one had a clear idea of exactly how this would work.

The Compumotor MIS department operated as an arm of the accounting department. They used the ASK manufacturing system software package running on an HP 3000 minicomputer to track inventories, manufacturing costs, and perform all accounting functions including production reports, cost of goods manufactured, cost of goods sold, income statements, inventory of goods on hand, etc. The MIS department saw their role in most part as the "keeper" of the ASK system. It is for this reason that MIS did not take an active role in the information problems of the AED.

With MIS out of the loop, it was left to aggressive and creative AED engineers to "push" for "a system." The push consisted in approaching their bosses in marketing to allocate funds for hardware — IBM PCs. Because of the general feeling at the time that PCs tend to "alleviate business problems," it was decided that a good start would be to install a PC on each AED engineer's desk. Further, it was obvious that the PCs should be networked, since one of the key objectives of this plan was to enhance information sharing between the engineers. This effort by the AED engineers, although informal at inception, soon became an activity of the department and was referred to as the "network project," a reference to the plan to network the PCs that would be procured.

However, in their efforts to secure management approval for the "network project," the AED engineers discovered that the costs were tangible but the benefits were intangible, fuzzy, unstructured, and ill-defined. They were stumped on the very first phase of obtaining management approval. The cost/benefit analysis or the financial feasibility study attempted by the engineers optimistically identified many benefits of the system but could not convince managers of the dollar worth of these benefits. Because the AED engineers felt overworked and strained by their jobs and believed that the PCs would alleviate this stress, they viewed management's disinterest in the network project as insensitivity to their plight.

The AED is not a profit center. When management decision-making processes utilize efficiency, cost minimization, and profit maximization in the short run as the basis of evaluation, capital is unlikely to be allocated for such an activity.

The perceived benefits became the foundation of the first level of specs for the network system. Essentially, the benefits consisted of removing the deficiencies of the present system in terms of communication between engineers and of building an information base from which repetitive data could be retrieved and used, and trends identified. The structure of the database is shown in schematic form in Figure C.3. The objectives of the system were enumerated as follows:

1. The system must obviate asking for the customer name and address at each call. The name and address of the callers will be added to a database on the first call by the assistant. The caller will be assigned a reference number (customer number). On future calls, if the caller can identify his or her customer number, the name and address can be automatically extracted. Benefit: reduction in call time and caller frustration.

   Because the MIS department also maintains customer, field service engineer, and distributor databases, the data compiled by AED would parallel the MIS data. Assigning customers two different numbers might be confusing, although this is not very likely, since the customer numbers assigned by MIS are used mostly on accounting documents such as invoices and statements. The customers' engineers who call presumably do not deal with these sorts of documents. In the system as implemented, the customer number is not necessary, since the company name, city, or person's name can be used to pull the customer file.

2. When an engineer takes a call, he will be able to access all information about previous calls made by the same customer, regardless of which AED engineer took the previous call or calls. He will therefore not

Figure C.3
Schematic of Database Design

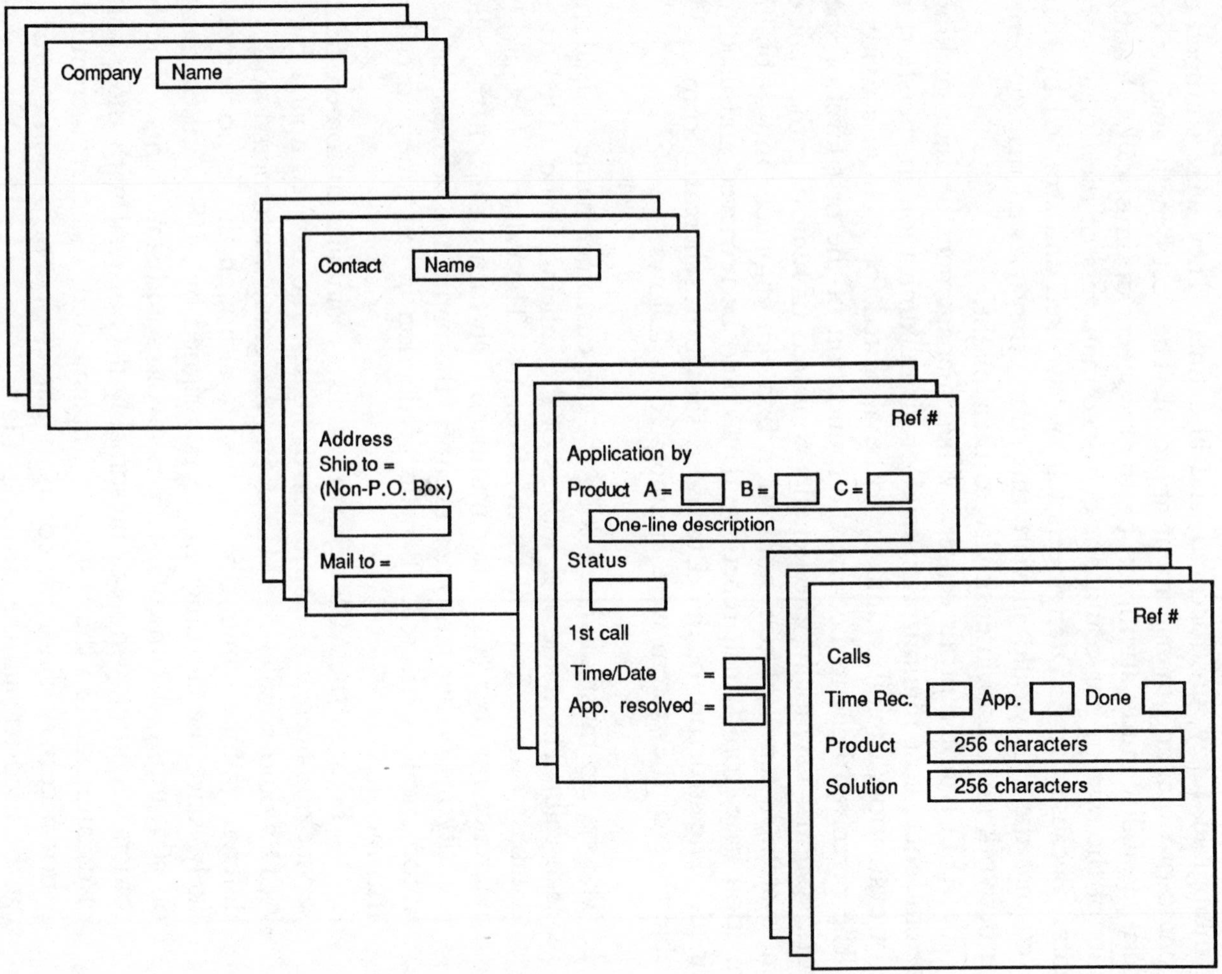

Company | Name

Contact | Name

Address
Ship to =
(Non-P.O. Box)

Mail to =

Ref #

Application by

Product A =   B =   C =

One-line description

Status

1st call

Time/Date   =
App. resolved =

Ref #

Calls

Time Rec.   App.   Done

Product   256 characters

Solution   256 characters

need to ask the customer to repeat the information and bring him "up to speed" on his problem. Further, by having a case history of this customer's problem on the screen, the engineer can be more effective in diagnosing and solving the problem. Benefit: increased effectiveness and less time per call.

3. At the end of the day, the AED engineers can meet and review all unresolved problems on the screen and share their technical know-how. Benefit: better and more consistent service to customers.

4. Both the AED and the engineering design department can use this system to identify product trends. This will be possible because the problems reported by customers and validated by AED will be cross-referenced by product model number. A review of the bug history of each product can be used in design modifications that would eliminate recurring problems. Benefit: improved product quality.

5. The system will be able to produce a summary of shipments promised by the AED engineers. The AED assistant can run this list and ship out the promised items in an orderly manner. The system will automatically generate the shipping labels. Benefit: time savings in shipping promised items and little chance of forgetting to ship promised items.

6. The system will generate periodic reports of calls and problems by region. These reports will be mailed to the respective regional field service personnel, who will use this information to streamline and focus their service activities. Benefit: increased effectiveness of field service personnel.

7. The system will be used by the manager in charge of AED as an aid to evaluation and control of AED personnel. A periodic report of activity and successful problem resolution broken down by AED personnel will allow the manager to identify areas of improvement in setting goals (see Figure C.4).

The estimated financial value of the project to Compumotor was identified in terms of efficiency and effectiveness. AED estimated that the value of time saved in phone conversations and in making promised shipments would amount to $50 per day. The improved effectiveness of the AED, the field service personnel, and of engineering were considered to be of much larger financial value, but no basis was easily found for a hard and fast dollar figure.

The cost of the system was estimated to be $15,000 with an initial outlay of $2000 to have the CCR software developed by an outside consultant. The initial development process was expected to take about 2 months. Once the program is

Figure C.4
Report of AED Activity

Summary Totals Report: Application Engineer...All   From 05/02/88 to 05/06/88

	/02 Mon	/03 Tue	/04 Wed	/05 Thu	/06 Fri	Week	Jan	Feb	Mar	Apr	May	Jun	Jul	Aug	Sep	Oct	Nov	Dec	Year	Call %
Total Calls	81	93	97	99	101	471	0	0	0	0	471	0	0	0	0	0	0	0	471	100.00
Calls	10	3	7	7	15	42	0	0	0	0	42	0	0	0	0	0	0	0	42	8.92
FAE Calls	14	16	15	11	8	64	0	0	0	0	64	0	0	0	0	0	0	0	64	13.59
EMP Calls	0	1	0	0	0	1	0	0	0	0	1	0	0	0	0	0	0	0	1	0.21
DIS Calls	17	24	26	20	15	102	0	0	0	0	102	0	0	0	0	0	0	0	102	21.66
CUS Calls	33	32	38	43	55	201	0	0	0	0	201	0	0	0	0	0	0	0	201	42.68
VEN Calls	0	2	2	2	0	6	0	0	0	0	6	0	0	0	0	0	0	0	6	1.27
PRO Calls	6	13	7	15	6	47	0	0	0	0	47	0	0	0	0	0	0	0	47	9.98
REP Calls	1	2	2	1	2	8	0	0	0	0	8	0	0	0	0	0	0	0	8	1.70
Calls for ACR	8	2	1	5	9	25	0	0	0	0	25	0	0	0	0	0	0	0	25	5.31
Calls for MYC	20	0	5	7	46	78	0	0	0	0	78	0	0	0	0	0	0	0	78	16.56
Calls for JBD	14	18	24	16	12	84	0	0	0	0	84	0	0	0	0	0	0	0	84	17.83
Calls for JCB	0	21	17	17	0	55	0	0	0	0	55	0	0	0	0	0	0	0	55	11.68
Calls for DOC	8	17	22	19	17	83	0	0	0	0	83	0	0	0	0	0	0	0	83	17.62
Calls for LLL	31	35	28	35	17	146	0	0	0	0	146	0	0	0	0	0	0	0	146	31.00
Handled Immed	12	15	8	11	5	51	0	0	0	0	51	0	0	0	0	0	0	0	51	10.83
Handled in 1 hr	56	57	44	44	69	270	0	0	0	0	270	0	0	0	0	0	0	0	270	57.32
Handled in 4 hr	8	15	33	26	13	95	0	0	0	0	95	0	0	0	0	0	0	0	95	20.17
Handled in 24 hr	3	5	5	14	6	33	0	0	0	0	33	0	0	0	0	0	0	0	33	7.01
Handled 24 hr+	2	1	7	4	8	22	0	0	0	0	22	0	0	0	0	0	0	0	22	4.67
Resolved in 1 hr	65	65	46	47	69	292	0	0	0	0	292	0	0	0	0	0	0	0	292	62.00
Resolved in 4 hr	9	16	33	26	14	98	0	0	0	0	98	0	0	0	0	0	0	0	98	20.81
Resolved in 24 hr	3	6	8	15	6	38	0	0	0	0	38	0	0	0	0	0	0	0	38	8.07
Resolved 24 hr+	2	5	8	9	11	35	0	0	0	0	35	0	0	0	0	0	0	0	35	7.43

DIS = distributors   CUS = customers   VEN = vendors   REP = manufacturers' representatives   FAE = field application engineers
EMP = employees   PRO = prospect

ready for an on-site test, an additional $12,000 would be needed to acquire five PCs, the necessary networking hardware and software, and the database environment specified by the developer (assumed to be dBASE III). After two months of operation, an additional software will be developed to link the CCR system with Compumotor's main MIS (the ASK system on the HP 3000). This link is needed so that AED engineers can view customer RMAs (returned material authorizations), which are used by the MIS to track all defective items that are returned for repair. This development was also expected to take two months.

In this cost-estimation scenario, the CCR software development was assumed to be complete at delivery. No funds were allocated for debug, enhancements, and training after the trial implementation. However, as system development follows a prototyping path, the iterative changes to the software can be a significant cost factor. It is not uncommon in end-user/prototyping developments for development and debug to drag on for months and incur huge expenses that easily dwarf the hardware costs.

The Development Process

The AED engineers viewed the development of the system in three phases: CCR software development (by consultant), system implementation, and system enhancement. They estimated that problem definition and systems analysis would take two weeks. The system design and implementation would then follow.

This is a good application of *end-user computing,* a term referring to situations in which the end user (or the final user) is directly involved in the system development process. However, this practice is becoming so common that this term may be dropped from MIS terminology.

An additional aspect of this development process was that it employed many of the attributes of prototyping. This is normally the case with end-user computing systems. Prototyping can be categorized into two broad groups: those in which the prototype evolves into the system itself ("keep") and those in which the prototype is used only in development ("throw away"). In the second kind, when the system development is complete, a new system is implemented and the development system is never used in the actual application. The CCR development was the "keep" or evolutionary kind. This development path has many pitfalls usually related to a growth path through unforeseen problems and changes.

Another way to look at prototyping methods is to classify them according to the development path chosen. One type will proceed by first dividing the system into logical components and then develop these one at a time. The other method looks at the whole system but proceeds by solving the simplest problem statement first and then modifying the system by adding successive layers of complexity.

In the first phase of development, a dBASE III programmer whom AED had already contacted would write the software on his development system (see Table

C.1). Initially, the program would not have network support but would be designed to run on stand-alone computers only. This caveat was necessary since the developer did not have access to a network. The network support was to be added after hardware implementation.

When the software was "ready," the development would advance to the next phase, when the hardware would be acquired and installed in the AED and the network would be brought online. The developer would then install the CCR software and develop the enhancements necessary for network/multiuser support. Hardware acquisition would include purchase of five IBM PCs or PS/2s, one 60-megabyte hard disk, networking hardware and software, and a printer. The IBM PC-compatible hardware environment was dictated by several factors: (a) Compumotor is a manufacturer of IBM PC add-on boards for stepper motor control and as such possesses a great deal of familiarity and technical sophistication with the machine. (b) The company had already selected a developer, and the PC was the developer's hardware environment. (c) But the most important criterion was critical mass and momentum. "Computer" and "IBM PC" were synonymous. Once the decision was made that computers were needed, it was assumed that these would be IBM PCs. Alternatives were not investigated.

The final phase would not begin until the system as installed had run for two months so that it would be mostly bug-free. At that time, further programming would be requisitioned to make a data link between the network and the HP 3000 of the MIS department. The technical details of this link were not defined. The MIS department was not involved in the project and their analysis of this link was not available. However, it was assumed that such a link was possible because other PCs in the company could communicate with the HP.

Table C.1
Compumotor CCR System: Phases of Development

Phase	Development Tasks Performed
Software development	Writing of software by dBASE III programmer/consultant
System implementation	Acquisition and installation of hardware; installation of CCR software; development of enhancements for network/multiuser support
System enhancement	Creation of data link between network and HP 3000 in MIS departments following installation and debug

---

Successful End-User Development: A Stellar Experience

Management finally approved the project after some attrition and the system soon became a success story. The greatly increased effectiveness, efficiency, and morale of the AED was very apparent. The HP 3000 link was never achieved and was soon abandoned. Although the software debug and enhancements began to chew up large sums of money well beyond the budgeted amount, management put up few barriers once the value of the system was demonstrated. In fact, they became actively involved and made suggestions of their own about possible extensions for the future. The Compumotor CCR is a stellar example of a successful end-user development project that is more complex and sophisticated than most end-user systems.

Application of AI Technology

A possible extension of the idea of automating customer support is the use of expert system technology to capture the expertise of the application engineers, to provide sharing of expertise between application engineers, and to formalize the experience acquisition process in general. With such a system, the facts and reasoning necessary to answer a majority of user queries could be coded into a knowledge base that would serve as an inventory of the reasoning used by the application engineers to solve specific problems.

Initially, this knowledge base would be used to support the application engineers themselves, affording them an easy way to access their combined experience. The formalization of the experience acquisition process would reduce the learning curve and enhance the effectiveness of the engineers. In the long run, the use of the expert system could be extended. During busy periods nonengineering personnel such as salesmen and secretaries could provide a first level of support to callers and obtain relevant information to facilitate further support by the application engineers.

Ultimately, the expert system could be made directly accessible by customers via modem link. In some cases, the customer might be able to achieve problem resolution by using the expert system. In other cases, the details of the problem would be captured by the expert system and placed in an electronic in-box for resolution by the application engineers. In either case, the call would be logged into the CCR for future reference by application engineers.

Such a system should be able to "learn," that is, be able to add new rules or modify old rules during normal usage. Customer support is dynamic in nature. Although the bulk of the problems are repetitive, new products, new applications, new situations, and just plain customer "ingenuity" constantly challenge the engineers with new problem situations. As each new problem area is encountered, researched, and resolved, the new reasoning would be added to the knowledge base for future reference by all the application engineers. The ideal system must allow such additions to the rule-base by its expert users.

Application of Hypercard Technology

An alternate method of accumulating the experience of the application engineers for easy retrieval is by the use of Hypercard (a trademark of Apple Computer, Inc.) or similar software. Hypercard, available for the Macintosh line of computers from Apple Computer, is an object-oriented programming environment that allows even novice programmers to store highly interconnected numeric, text, and graphical data. The data structure uses the *stack* metaphor and is free-form in nature compared to the restrictions of traditional database environments. In this metaphor, data are stored in *cards,* which are arranged in *stacks.* Cards and stacks can be logically connected by using *buttons.*

This environment can be used to store customer support data so that cases can be interconnected, based on a variety of criteria such as product and part number, customer number, problem type, resolution type, and so on. A database of all product and part numbers may include a stack of drawing details. These drawings could serve as one of the take-off points for the system with part numbers being connected to customer stacks and problem stacks. But because of the free-form structure of Hypercard, any stack can serve as a starting point, so that the search could begin from customer lists, problem lists, or even from a given application engineer.

The system is mouse-driven and uses a graphical user interface based on icons, windows, and pull-down menus. The extreme user friendliness of the system facilitates use by computer novices even in fairly sophisticated applications. This means that not only would application engineers be able to use the stacks to retrieve information, they would find it just as easy to update the system with new information. Besides, the development and prototyping period would be short and inexpensive because much of the programming could be done by the application engineers themselves.

All commands are issued by clicking the mouse. In a typical interchange, the user might bring up a stack of standard drawings and click his or her way to the part (card) wanted. Then a click on the portion of interest would bring up a card with drawing details of that area. A click on a specific portion of the card could bring up a stack of related problems, which in turn would guide the user to related customers, solutions, application engineers, and other drawings and parts. The complete integration of graphical data with more traditional forms of fields of databases creates a unique information base capability for engineering applications.

Case Study Questions

1. Since the CCR system already knows the customers, phone numbers, could the additional expense of installing a computerized dialing feature be justified? What hardware components and software modifications would be required to accommodate this feature?

2. To what extent does the system development approach outlined use the SDLC method? To what extent does it resemble prototyping?

3. Using the information provided in the case study and figures cited in current computer magazines, make a budget estimate of the system configuration and cost.

4. Computer systems are frequently used as a substitute for good management practice. However, the astute MIS professional can separate procedural aspects from those that are informational in MIS problems. To what extent could the technical support problems have been solved by redesigning the manual system?

5. The MIS department was not involved in the project. What problems, if any, has this created? How could these problems have been avoided?

6. Whereas profit centers can justify investment by showing increased profits, cost centers must show reduced costs. Since the application engineering department is not a profit center or an investment center but a cost center, it is difficult to justify a capital expenditure for AED based only on its own turf. How could a broader view of the benefits help in the cost justification process?

7. Draw a system diagram to define the role of AED and the staff's interactions with customers and other departments (such as engineering) at Compumotor.

8. Develop a logical design for the proposed system. Identify new problems created by this system.

9. Propose an alternate physical design. On what basis are proposals to be compared?

10. Develop software specs for outside consultants and terms under which the software development should take place.

11. Identify project benefits and perform a cost/benefit analysis.

12. Are there any training considerations? If so, what are they? How are these to be treated?

TYSON FOODS, INC.

Drawing the Line Between Maintenance and Development

The baby boomers have been a marketing phenomenon and we never tire of analyzing their enormous impact on the American consumer market as they age and go through the system, creating a huge lump on the normal curve. Among other things good and bad, they awakened the nation's consciousness of health and "natural foods" and raised the general level of awareness of food quality, cholesterol, preservatives, additives, and nutritional values.

In this light, beef and "red meats" did not fare well against "white meats" such as chicken. And so it was that America's love affair with beef was abated and the decades of the seventies and eighties saw the ascendance of the lowly chicken. Whereas in 1960, the per capita consumption of beef was approximately twice that of chicken, by 1986 chicken had broken even. By 1990 chicken is expected to overtake beef and become America's favorite meat.

Simultaneously with the change to white meat, the American consumer began to show an increasing preference for gourmet frozen dinners suitable for quick home meals.

As with any change, these market transformations provided a fertile opportunity for those companies in the food service industry with the vision, the courage, and the resources to react swiftly and take competitive advantage of the situation. The company that has most successfully exploited these changes is Tyson Foods, Inc., of Springdale, Arkansas.

At the Right Place at the Right Time

Although Chairman and CEO Don Tyson modestly claims that his company was simply at the right place at the right time, the meteoric rise of the firm provides many lessons to the student of business management. What was a medium-sized regional chicken producer tucked away in the Ozarks is today the world's largest producer of poultry products. While students of marketing and finance may study how such growth comes about, we will concern ourselves with how an organization is reshaped as it grows. When the growth extends across multiple levels of operation, management information system (MIS) needs must be reevaluated and the MIS system must be redesigned.

In less than a decade, sales have increased more than tenfold to about $2 billion. Sales and operating income continue to grow at the rapid rate of about 20 percent a year. Much of this growth has been brought about by acquisitions, both horizontal (other poultry producers) and vertical (poultry feed production, further processing of meats). The company has strengthened its market position and growth curve by expanding into new markets such as "value added" or "further processed" food, including patties, chunks, frozen dinners, and semi-prepared meals. This market now accounts for about 70 percent of sales. Tyson is equally aggressive in the retail market (with 45 percent of sales) and the food service market (with 55 percent of sales).

Tyson is not only a very large market but a very profitable one. The company has benefitted enormously from its strategy of targeting the processed food market. As a result of this strategy, Tyson now generates more than two-thirds of its revenue from "value-enhanced" poultry products. Its basic standard product, fresh packaged chickens for supermarkets, accounts for less than a quarter of the total dollar value of sales. This trend is expected to continue, shrinking the ratio of fresh chicken to processed foods sales and fueling further growth in revenue, profits, and market share.

Because of its sheer size, Tyson has the opportunity to lower production costs and become entrenched in its market share. Vertical integration, which has paid handsome dividends in terms of production efficiency and cost control, has been the cornerstone of Tyson's successful strategy of maintaining its growth rate. Expansion into vertical markets has occurred in both directions. The elemental raw material in poultry production is chicken feed (chicken is essentially biologically processed chicken feed). Tyson's vertical expansion now allows it to produce all of its chicken feed so that the company can control quality, cost, and formulation of the feed to maximize profits. In the other direction, Tyson has expanded into several marketing channels. With its fleet of 500 trucks, Tyson could otherwise be a major trucking company. The firm's expansion into frozen and prepared foods has allowed it to compete in specific market segments instead of simply being a raw material supplier to these markets.

The Tyson strategy that has yielded the greatest degree of success is summed up by CEO Don Tyson as "segmentation, concentration, and domination." This approach is exemplified by Tyson's entry into the fast-foods market. Chicken meat with the bone removed (deboned chicken) and the cavernous market for this product in fast foods and elsewhere were visions of Don Tyson 11 years ago. Tyson produced a specialty product for this market segment and now dominates it with an 80 percent market share. In similar fashion, the company has been able to address and control other niche markets such as Rock Cornish game hens, TV dinners, and IQF (individually quick-frozen) chicken.

Tyson's growth has been market-driven. Currently, demand outstrips production capacity and workers are putting in long hours to keep up with orders. Tyson has responded by accelerating construction of new production facilities and by attempting to increase its production base by acquisition of other poultry producers. Expansion projects recently completed and put into service include the 200,000 square-foot freezer and warehouse at Russellville, Arkansas, for military and export products, and an automated chicken processing plant in Rogers, Arkansas, that can process 64 chickens per minute. Innovation has also increased production. In the Rogers plant, the time required to debone a chicken has been reduced by cooking the bird prior to the deboning process.

Tyson has recently made a bid to acquire Holly Farms of Memphis, Tennessee. If this acquisition goes through, Tyson will double in size to a $4 billion company almost overnight. Whether or not the bid for Holly is successful, it simply points to Tyson's continued emphasis on growth not only by segmentation, concentration, and domination, but also by acquisition. The message for organizational planners is this: Tyson is still growing and the most explosive growth may be just around the corner.

The big market Tyson is stalking is clearly "further processed chicken," a market that is estimated to increase from about 18 percent to 40 percent of the poultry industry's output in the next 7 years. Tyson intends not only to stay abreast of this growth but to increase market share. This objective then must be the basis for projecting growth and future MIS needs.

Here a Cluck, There a Cluck...

It is hard to imagine anything more incongruous than the Tyson corporate headquarters in Springdale, where what appears to be a large and efficient Silicon Valley office building seems to have been transplanted onto the serene farmlands and rolling hills of northwest Arkansas. From this modern complex, the corporation operates its giant chicken empire consisting of over 25,000 employees working in over 32 fully integrated plants located throughout Arkansas and in nine other states in the southwest and southeast regions of the United States. The company controls every phase of production from feed mills to hatcheries, growing farms, meat processing plants, production of specialty value-enhanced products, and storage and transportation to markets, producing more than 14 million pounds of chicken per week in over a hundred different product lines. These products are sold nationwide to a variety of different markets including retail supermarkets, fast-food chains, the U.S. military, and large institutions. The company has even begun exporting chicken to Japan under an agreement with the C. Itoh trading company.

Although the truck fleet (like the firm's large feed plant at Pottsville, Arkansas) is centralized, the functional Tyson architecture is that of a cellular production network. Each cell is a semi-autonomous and self-sufficient production unit that normally controls its own entire production process. This production structure includes feed, hatcheries, production, and packaging operations. These production cells and contract growers are spread out over the south and the southwest, a layout that presents special challenges to the design and operation of an effective MIS.

It is significant and consequential that Tyson is not a holding company or some gigantic mutual fund of operations but an actual producer of poultry. The distributed production structure is used only to gain control and flexibility of operations.

Tyson's production scheme uses three types of operations: the production complexes, contract growers, and processing plants. The production is distributed in the sense that these operations are spread over a wide region.

The process begins in the "complexes," each of which consists of a feed mill, a hatchery, and a processing plant. Each complex is a more or less autonomous operation in which feed material is literally transformed into finished chicken meat. Here the breeding stock is maintained, the eggs are hatched, and the chicks, along with feed material, are delivered to contract growers. The young chickens are recovered from the growers, killed, defeathered, eviscerated, cleaned, packaged for market, and put in cold storage for shipment. Each of these complexes produces over a million pounds of chicken meat per day.

The feed mill processes corn, soybeans, and fishmeal into chicken feed according to nutritional recipes formulated by feed-research scientists at the Springdale headquarters' R & D facilities. The complex maintains inventories of these raw materials and of finished feed. When substitutes are prescribed in the recipe or authorization is obtained from R & D, the complex manager must occasionally make decisions affecting the type of feed material to be used, based on price and availability. The complex also holds inventories of medicine for treatment and prevention of common fowl ailments. Many of the feed mills are highly automated and computer-controlled for consistency in the quality and composition of the mix.

Once the eggs are hatched, the chicks are delivered by Tyson to a number of contract growers to whom Tyson supplies all feed material, medicine, and procedures on care and feeding. The grower's job is to maintain the flock at a comfortable temperature, give them adequate water and feed, and protect them from predators. The chickens are ready in 7 weeks. (Breeders are grown for 24 weeks, fertilized, and pressed into service as laying hens.) After 7 weeks, Tyson picks up the chickens from the grower and returns them to the complex for processing. Growers are paid on the basis of the mortality rate and the average weight per bird.

The killing and cleaning are largely manual processes performed on a long assembly line of gutters, cutters, deboners, cleaners, and wrappers. However, the firm is rapidly automating and in 1988 opened its first fully automated processing plant in Rogers, Arkansas. The plant encompasses all phases of chicken processing from killing to cooking and deboning.

Tyson Foods Management Information Systems: Purpose, Organization, and Function

The MIS design of this large company must take into account not only its current size and its volume of eight transactions per second, but also the diversity of products, the geographical distribution of production facilities and markets, management's emphasis on efficiency and aggressiveness, and the volatile growth rate of the firm in terms of sales, personnel, operations, and the number of transactions.

The stated purpose of the MIS department at Tyson is the "creation of innovative ideas, coupled with conscientious management and maintenance of the company's vital data via computerized methods." Figure T.1 shows the organizational structure of the MIS department. The organization is by many standards small for a $2 billion company, but the operation of MIS as a distinct function at the corporate vice-presidential level indicates that this function is emphasized and that management recognizes the importance of information. This approach contrasts with that of companies operating their MIS as "DP services" to the accounting or finance departments.

There are approximately 25 programmer/analysts in the department with the application programmers organized along principal functional lines such as sales, payroll, purchasing, etc. This structure allows for the specialization of programmers in particular functions and for increased communication between users and analysts. User support is ultimately improved because the analysts who write the programs communicate directly with the users of these programs. A separate group of analysts is in charge of programming the UNIX machines installed in each production complex. The systems programming group maintains the operating system and system utilities and supports the application programmers.

This MIS structure encourages a bottom-up workflow, with requests for new reports and programs coming directly from users to the appropriate programming group rather than through the programming manager. Since user and analyst work almost on a one-on-one basis, the user is always aware of the analyst's workload and backlog. The direct lines of communication between the users and the analysts ease the backlog, foster realistic schedules, and help lower anxiety levels.

Such an idealized model of workflow in the programming department fails when several individuals from a user area make independent requests. To prevent this situation, the department has implemented the "user group" model, with users organized into application groups. Each group selects a representative through whom all requests and complaints to MIS are funneled. Each user group is assigned a set number of programmers dedicated to servicing only the needs of the user group. The representative user communicates with his or her counterpart in MIS. The objective of this scheme is to set up consistent lines of communication. The suggestion to utilize user groups was enthusiastically received by upper management, and although no policy or procedures were set up to enforce the system, it seems to be yielding positive results.

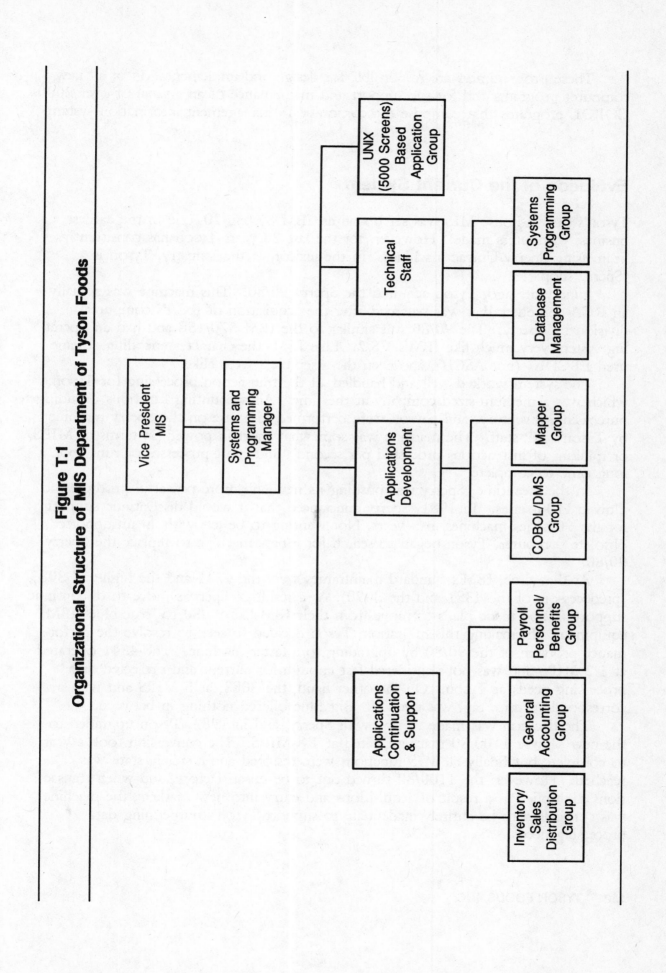

Figure T.1
Organizational Structure of MIS Department of Tyson Foods

These programmers are responsible for design and implementation of all new computer programs and for the support and maintenance of an arsenal of over 2000 COBOL programs that compose the corporation's management information system.

Evolution of the Current System

Tyson's first in-house MIS was set up on an IBM System/20, one of the earliest business computers made. However, for the last 20 years Tyson has consistently been using Sperry/Univac machines. In the lexicon of the industry, Tyson is a "Sperry shop."

Nine years ago, Tyson acquired the Sperry 90/80. This machine was actually an RCA computer that was renamed after the acquisition of RCA's computer division by Sperry. The 90/80 was similar to the IBM 370/158 and had an operating system very much like IBM's VS/2. Like IBM, the character encoding scheme used EBCDIC (not ASCII), and even the assemblers were alike.

The system worked well and handled all the transaction processing for Tyson, which was a medium-sized company at the time. All accounting functions including purchasing, inventory, and payroll were performed in-house on the Sperry machine by Tyson's DP staff. The machine was somewhat short in power (in terms of MIPS, or millions of instructions processed per second), and most processes or runs took a long time to complete.

In the meantime, Sperry was pushing its new and more powerful product, the Univac 1100 series. In 1981, Sperry announced that it would discontinue support for the 90 series machines in 5 years. Not wanting to be left with an unsupported, obsolete computer, Tyson began to search for a new machine to replace the Sperry 90/80.

At that time, IBM's standard mainframes were the 4341 and the high-end 3083 (predecessors of the 4381 and the 3090). As a result of Sperry's move to discontinue support, Tyson made plans to move from their IBM-like 90/80 to "true-blue" IBM equipment. In making this migration, Tyson decided to seek to resolve the performance problem of the 90/80 by upgrading to a faster machine. The 4341 operated at 1.2 MIPS and was not considered fast enough for current and projected data processing needs at Tyson. On the other hand, the 3083, at 5 MIPS and with a corresponding price tag, was overkill. Big Blue offered nothing in between.

The decision was made to stay with Sperry, and in 1982, Tyson upgraded to the new Univac 1100/80 machine, rated at 1.8 MIPS. The conversion took a year to complete but finally all MIS functions were restored and a steady state was reached. However, the 1100/80 turned out to be unsatisfactory, and when transactions multiplied as a result of acquisitions and entry into new markets, the machine was considered to be entirely inadequate to support Tyson's burgeoning data processing needs.

Within one year from the conversion to the 1100/80, Tyson found itself once again needing a hardware upgrade. However, Sperry was ready with a new computer. The 1100/90 was a much better machine overall and, at 7.5 MIPS, offered more "horsepower." The higher input/output (I/O) speed of the 90 was also attractive, since Tyson's data processing was I/O-bound. The 90 was easily much more cost-effective than the 80. Thus, in 1984 Tyson changed over to the 1100/90. Because the 80 and 90 are similar machines, the software changes were minimal and conversion went smoothly. The Univac 1100/90 remained as Tyson's MIS "power plant" for more than a year and a half.

With the acquisition of Valmac (a feed mill and chicken processor formerly in competition with Tyson) and the ballooning of the deboned chicken market, the company's sales, the number of personnel, and the number of transactions proliferated. Simultaneously, the operation became more complex as a result of new business activities. The number and complexity of the reports began to multiply. Addition of more software, disk drives, and main memory to the 1100/90 helped ease the crunch somewhat, but in 1986 it was clear that the 90 would have to be upgraded. Tyson needed more raw computing power to be able to grind through the mountains of data the business was now generating.

By then, Burroughs had acquired Sperry and the merged company, called Unisys, offered a hardware upgrade to a new machine, the Unisys 1100/92. The 92 was similar to the 90 but had two CPUs instead of one. The two processors could operate as a tightly coupled pair, essentially doubling the computing power of 7.5 MIPS. The processors could also be de-coupled in software and operated as two separate computers sharing the same peripherals. The 92 offered an easy but expensive migration path for Tyson, and in 1986 the company changed over to the new machine.

The Current System

The Tyson unit is currently configured with a main memory of 24 megabytes. There are 24 Unisys 600-megabyte disk drives for a total online storage capacity of over 14 gigabytes. Eight tape drives are required to back up this data.

MIS reports are produced on four Unisys Model 7770 high-speed line printers that can each generate output at the rate of 1400 lines per minute. The current level of MIS activity requires about 40,000,000 lines of output per month. Of course, as is typical of MIS, these reports are produced at certain times of the month and year, with associated periods of heavy printer use.

The 1100/92 mainframe serves over 500 online terminals connected to 180 low-speed remote printers via Model 40 series cluster controllers and multiplexers. The terminals are located at the corporate headquarters, and in Tyson plants and offices throughout Arkansas and a wide area from Arizona to North Carolina.

The hardware configuration is summarized in Figure T.2.

Figure T.2
Site Profile for Tyson Foods, Inc.

Hardware:

1100/92
    2 IPs
    2 IOPs
    6 Megawords memory
    1 Cache string with 2 quadrants of cache (1024 tracks total), 8 drives consisting
        of 1 8480, 4 8470s (prepped 1792), Configured as 3 removable, 5 fixed
    2 Non-cache strings
        4 8470s, configured as 2 fixed, 2 removable, 6 8470s, configured as 3
        fixed, 2 removable, 1 hot spare, All prepped 448
    7 U36 tape drives, and 1 U32
    2 SSPs
    4 770 printers
    1 IPCU

    1 DCP 40 with 1.5 meg memory
        16 Local lines, and 15 remote lines
        400 terminals, 150 printers (driven with PDS and FAST4000)
        Terminals consist of PCs, SVT1120, SVT1121, UTS20, UTS20W
        Both PEP and STEP boards in use in the PCs
        Using 4020 and 4040 cluster controllers and Multiplexers

    6 5000/40 Unix machines used for distributed processing

UPS battery backup, with diesel generator for continuous power

Besides the hardware at the headquarters building in Springdale, each of Tyson's production complexes is served by one of twelve Unisys Model 5000/50 Unix-based minicomputers. Each production unit operates a "mini-MIS" on these machines in the departmental computer format using distributed processing architecture. The mainframe database is periodically updated by these machines. The minis and their applications are supported by staff located at the headquarters.

The minicomputer configuration at each complex contains several terminals and printers. A leased line connects each mini to the Unisys mainframe in Springdale at 9600 baud. This connection allows for file transfer between these machines and for direct mainframe access by staff at each remote complex. Mainframe access is made through the mini in a transparent way.

Personal Computers

Over 350 Tyson employees have PCs. The applications used are Lotus 1-2-3 for spreadsheet models, Multimate for word processing, and dBASE III Plus for database management. Most of these PCs are IBM XT/AT compatible clones such as Leading Edge.

The PC users are supported by an information center operated by the MIS department. The center offers training and support, as well as standardization and guidance on software and hardware acquisition.

Approximately 150 of the PCs are connected to the mainframe, using an interface board supplied by Computer Logics, Inc. These PCs can be used as terminals to the Univac or as stand-alone personal computers. File and data transfer utilities have been provided by MIS personnel to allow end users to download mainframe data into PC spreadsheets and upload data and documents for archiving on the mainframe.

An example of mainframe/PC integration at Tyson is the recipe distribution system. The R & D test kitchen, located at the Springdale headquarters, creates all recipes for Tyson's prepared chicken products such as frozen dinners. New recipes and updates to old recipes are produced on the PC, using the Multimate word processor. The ASCII file is then uploaded to the mainframe into a large recipe file and made available to all plants. Individual plant managers can then access the recipe, using MAPPER, and have it printed out on their remote printers. This procedure has significantly improved product consistency and quality control across all plants.

Software: Information Reporting and Transaction Processing Systems

Tyson's MIS operates in a TIP/DMS/DPS/COBOL/MAPPER software environment. The main tool for generating applications is COBOL. The original ISAM file system has been largely replaced with a hierarchical database manager supplied by Sperry called DMS1100. (IBM developed the ISAM file structure to facilitate the process of adding records to or deleting records from the middle of the file while maintaining an access method that appears to be sequential. The letters stand for "Indexed Sequential Access Method," but record retrieval is so slow that many programmers refer to ISAM as "Incredibly Slow Access Method." The method works by allocating disk space using a key index value. The disk allocation method is built into the operating system and the compiler, normally COBOL.)

The change to the hierarchical database manager was dictated by the need to use record-level interlock instead of file locks in the online transaction mode. To increase productivity and throughput, the application programmers are beginning to use MAPPER. Currently, the MAPPER systems process over 30 million lines per day. Some ad hoc query/report programs have been created, and MAPPER is being aggressively promoted to end users. Other system level tools and generators used by the programmers at the MIS department include the following:

ACOB	COBOL Compiler
TIP	Transaction Processing Environment
DMS	Hierarchical database structure
ASM	Assembler
ED	System editor
FTN	Fortran Compiler
MAPPER	Database manager with report and query language
RPG	Report generation language
SORT/MERGE	Facility for combining data from several files
SPERRYCALC	Mainframe spreadsheet program not much used at Tyson

The transaction and reporting functions are programmed mostly in COBOL and include the following:

Accounts payable
Accounts receivable
General ledger
Payroll and benefits
Inventory
Route sales
Trucking
Order entry
Purchasing
Vehicle maintenance
Billing
Sales history

A payables run made in batch mode each night takes a sweep of all payables and "pulls" the invoices that are due to be paid, using predetermined aging and selection criteria. The system then prints the checks, updates the payables files, and generates a summary report of the activity. Payroll with benefits and payroll taxes, another large batch run that is made once a week, is one of the biggest computer runs in the company.

Most of Tyson's sales are made to about a hundred brokers and an equal number of large accounts such as fast-food chains and institutions. The brokers are given access to the system and to programs so that they can enter their orders directly by modem link and make queries on back orders to check the shipping status of orders. Some brokers have the IBM System/36 and use EDINET to leave orders in Tyson's EDI mailbox. These orders are retrieved from the mailbox straight into the transaction processing system (TPS) order files, and an acknowledgment that the order has been received and entered is left in the broker's mailbox. The order information includes a purchase order number and that is all that is needed to ship. No "written" POs are demanded and no significant problems have been encountered with disagreements and inconsistencies. EDINET will support electronic invoices but

Tyson does not use them principally because "nobody wants them." (Most business-people like to wait as long as possible for the invoice. The mail is fast enough!)

The complexes operate their own MISs on their Unix-based mini systems and update the mainframe periodically using batch file transfer through 9600-baud leased lines. The important remote functions include accounts payable, inventory, and payroll information. These files are sent to the mainframe on a weekly or monthly basis (accounts payable files are sent nightly). Time-card data are maintained by the minis and sent to the mainframe weekly but the payroll function is centralized at Springdale.

Tyson's plants operate around the clock every day of the week. So, therefore, must the MIS. The system is online 24 hours a day, 7 days a week. The difficulty of scheduling shutdowns for backups or routine maintenance is recognized as a problem area at Tyson, and the MIS department is currently evaluating options to remedy this situation. System maintenance is scheduled for times when the transaction rate is particularly low. The current average rate is 5 transactions per second but can vary from a high of 10 transactions to a low at night of one transaction per second. Maintenance is performed during these low-volume periods.

Tyson does most of its own hauling all over the country with its fleet of 500 tractor-trailer trucks. Other company vehicles include pickup trucks used by service personnel and company cars for managers. Tyson maintains its own garage and repair shop, fuel depot, inventory of spare parts, and maintenance staff. This auxiliary operation differs considerably from the main line of business but is very data-intensive. The spare parts inventory for the vehicles includes everything from spark plugs to tires and carburetors. MIS tracks the fuel and oil consumption and repair log of each vehicle, and monthly reports show inventories and quantities of all materials used. In addition, monthly reports are produced for each vehicle, showing all activities on a cumulative and period basis. Even though "vehicles" is just a service organization, the data needs are comparable to those of a gas station, trucking company, auto repair shop, and auto parts shop combined.

Transaction Processing and Information Reporting

The Tyson MIS is based on the transaction processing and information reporting system capabilities. A TPS is designed to record and process the normal day-to-day business activities or transactions of a firm. An IRS, or information reporting system, produces periodic (or exception) reports for which the content, form, period, and method are prespecified by management and hard coded by application programmers. In addition, Tyson employs end-user computing in the form of personal computers and ad hoc report capability of the mainframe, thereby avoiding the data currency problems of traditional IRS systems. In a traditional IRS, the end users of the information (management) do not use the computer directly. The MIS programmers and analysts are the only direct users of the system other than the data entry clerks. Managers see only the periodic printed reports they have requested.

Tyson uses online transaction processing, or OLTP. The database becomes updated as soon as the transaction is recorded, and the transaction is recorded as soon as the physical transaction takes place. This is necessary for a system that supports ad hoc inquiries to ensure that all data are current at all times.

When the purchasing department at Tyson sends out a purchase order for plastic wrapping material, a business "transaction" occurs. The details of the transaction, i.e., the amount of plastic, the price, and the supplier, are recorded by the TPS when the purchase order is sent out. Concurrently, all the files are updated. When the plastic arrives, another transaction is recorded and at the same time the inventory file and the accounts payable file are updated to reflect the change. When the bill is paid, another transaction is recorded, and so on.

The OLTP system has inquiry programs that allow line managers to access TPS data directly to produce onscreen reports. If the changes to the files were not made online, managers who rely on MIS for information would not know about these transactions or their effect on the financial position or production capacity of the company until the end of the month, when a monthly summary of purchases is printed out by the IRS.

Custom programs have been written in MAPPER to make the online data available to end users directly. For example, salespeople can use MAPPER to generate customer profiles that summarize a customer's buying history, preferences, and outstanding orders. Frequently, the sales profile analysis is used to provide information to the customer about his or her own purchases when the customer does not have the same sort of data available. An information service of this type engenders customer goodwill and confidence.

Similar data analysis and reporting packages have been written for accounting, personnel, and other functions. The accounting functions include cost variance analysis and other summary cost accounting reports. The personnel inquiry system can be used, for example, to compile a list of employees who are due to retire or who have not been promoted in a given period of time.

Dealing with Backlog

If the information requirements change, the IRS report will be inadequate. Similarly, when the nature of a transaction changes, or the company begins to carry out new transactions, or if new accounting procedures are adopted, the TPS will be unable to record the transactions correctly. In either case, managers will submit a request to MIS to make the necessary changes. MIS will assign a programmer or analyst to make the change by writing or modifying COBOL or MAPPER programs. When more of these requests come in than can be processed, a backlog of requests can occur. Backlogs in MIS can range from several months to years, although they have been eased by the widespread use of "end-user computing" in the form of ad hoc and DSS capabilities, as well as by the proliferation of personal computers.

At Tyson, the principal cause of backlog is that there are not enough programmers to process the number of programming requests being submitted. The growth in staff of the MIS department has not kept pace with the growth of the company. Since 1979, sales have increased sixfold while the number of programmers increased by a factor of only three, from seven to twenty-two. Even with the addition of the phone system as an MIS responsibility, the total MIS staff has only doubled in the same period. Today, the total DP expenses, including voice communication and leased phone lines, are about 0.25 percent of sales, compared with a national average of somewhere above 1 percent.

When MIS is in a state of backlog, software maintenance and development can become limited to "putting out fires," new application development and major rewrite projects becoming shelved. To avoid this situation, Tyson has set up a software SWAT team that is protected from fire fighting and that does not become tied up with day-to-day problems. Thus, it can be assigned to make meaningful long-term improvements in the system that would satisfy a class of requests being made in the long run.

MAPPER and End-User Computing

Ad hoc refers to a capability that allows a manager or end user to sit down at a computer terminal, interact directly with the computer, and order up custom reports on the screen at any time, accessing all data he or she wishes to examine (as long as the access is authorized). The ad hoc method frees the manager from the limitations of the IRS method that restrict the timeliness or the content of the report. The ad hoc query and report method must have a user interface that is designed specifically for a user who is a "non-DP" person. It must have a high tolerance for errors, it must supply online help messages, and it must have language, logic, and relevance that appear to be intuitive to the target user (although not necessarily to the analyst). If the ad hoc system meets these requirements, managers will use these query methods in many cases instead of piling up backlog by requesting program changes.

PCs have a similar impact on backlog by bringing computer and manager together so as to remove the analyst from the loop. Even when the analyst is not completely removed, his or her involvement is reduced. The PC has its greatest impact when the manager's needs require data analysis rather than large volumes of data. In such cases, the manager is able to enter a few numbers into a spreadsheet and develop a model to satisfy his or her requirements rather than submit a programming request. Since these systems were designed from the very start for end users, the adaptation of PCs to end-user computing is superior and exemplary and is frequently used as a model in the design of ad hoc user interfaces.

The Tyson MIS scheme is to take advantage of end-user computing in a significant way.

To accelerate turnaround and implement ad hoc queries by end users, Tyson has been converting much of its programming from COBOL to MAPPER. Most transaction processing systems in business are programmed in COBOL, a procedural language originally developed by the Department of Defense in 1960. The language is well suited to processing large files performing operations such as payroll, benefits, and accounts receivable (invoicing and statements). The data structures used by COBOL are particularly suited to business data processing needs in large-scale TPS and IRS systems. COBOL programs are easy to maintain because, by design, COBOL is easy to read. Unlike most other components of business data processing, COBOL is refreshingly standardized across the industry. Business managers are more likely to invest money in programming when the code is likely to be hardware-independent, and Tyson is a dramatic example of this principle. Even though the company grew across hardware environments, it continued to use its original COBOL code with modifications needed for the changes in the business itself.

The fly in the ointment is that a lot of code is required to perform relatively simple tasks. Development of significant business software in COBOL involves long turnaround when compared to fourth-generation-language (4GLs) such as dBASE III, FOCUS, and MAPPER. The wordy sentence-like syntax becomes a liability, further slowing program development. Fourth-generation database languages have their own problems. Although they offer quick programming turnaround, they generally produce bulky and inefficient code. Execution time can be a tremendous disappointment in large-scale implementations. Currently, more than a day is required to process the payroll for Tyson's 25,000 employees. A 4GL could easily increase this time to a week. Such a disadvantage in execution time would eliminate 4GLs from consideration in huge TPS-type applications.

In the sixties when COBOL was developed, memory, both primary (main) memory and secondary (disk) memory, was very expensive and computers were very slow in comparison with what is currently available. Memory usage and CPU time were critical considerations in compiler design and development of application programs. However, this situation has been turned on its ear. Hardware is now several orders of magnitude more powerful and several orders of magnitude less expensive. In this light, programming time and cost become the critical factors. A recent study by Bechtel showed that the ratio of software to hardware costs has skyrocketed. Although 4GLs are still not suitable for TPS applications, their use in IRS report generation by analysts is likely to slash development time and increase throughput in the MIS programming department.

In view of this situation, Tyson has begun to use MAPPER, a database 4GL supplied by Sperry. Usage is still limited but expected to increase rapidly as more and more end-user report requests are being met with MAPPER. Tyson has set up an internal MAPPER training center for end users so that more users can make ad hoc enquiries and generate their own reports. Many new report generation programs are now being programmed in MAPPER by DP programmers, and it is anticipated that an optimal balance between COBOL and 4GL in the programming department will increase output and efficiency and decrease programming backlog.

Accounts receivable, accounts payable, and inventory data are available to users in an interactive screen report or on an ad hoc query basis. For example, a warehouse supervisor in Rogers can interrogate the system to determine the number of cases of chicken in inventory, the number available for shipment, and the number of in-bound shipments that have left the processing plant and the approximate time of arrival of the trucks. When a truck arrives, the warehouse supervisor interactively and completely electronically acknowledges the shipment and verifies the bill of lading. The system updates the database to show the increase in inventory, the completion of the haul, and the current status of the truck.

Options for the Future

The 1100/92, which at 15 MIPS was impressive even 5 years ago, is now slow in comparison with today's standards set by IBM at around 100 MIPS. In general, computer hardware is undergoing rapid and exciting changes, and Tyson feels that it is being left behind. The 2200 series recently announced by Sperry offers promising advances in computing power that are sorely needed at Tyson. Unfortunately, the 2200 machines are not yet being shipped.

The hierarchical database management structure (HDBMS) is another aspect that Tyson would like to change. Tyson still uses the HDBMS structure while the industry has generally shifted over to relational database management structures (RDBMSs). Many analysts consider HDBMS to be old and antiquated. The scheme goes back to when databases were first designed for mainframe computers, when it seemed natural to view relationships between data as being analogous to parent-child relationships. Some data seemed instinctively to "belong" to other data and had data that belonged to them. (This is the one-to-many type of relationship; that is, a data item can have many children but only one parent. For example, an invoice belongs to a customer, and an invoice line item belongs to an invoice. A customer can have many invoices but an invoice can have only one customer. If you drew a diagram to show these relationships, you would get a tree-like structure with the root at the top — the great-grandfather data — branching downwards in generations to the data at the lowest level.)

In applications in which the data are inherently hierarchical, HDBMSs can be easy to set up since it appears to users to be intuitive. In general, HDBMSs are very efficient in terms of conserving disk storage and accessing data quickly, although lower hardware costs have made these considerations less important than they were in the past. As these costs became less important, the simplicity and flexibility of the relational model (RDBMS) made it more attractive to MIS designers.

The HDBMS is inflexible in two ways. First, the tree-like structure limits the kinds of data relationships that are possible. If other relationships are needed, the programmer must find a way around the limitation, sometimes by using redundant data designations. Second, once data are set up in an HDBMS tree, the structure is very hard to change. To insert data between a parent and a child requires major surgery. For these reasons, a HDBMS may not be suited to installations undergoing heavy maintenance, since by its very nature, the HDBMS discourages changes. Programming changes necessitated by changing organizational information needs at Tyson therefore require longer turnaround and tend to build up backlog.

RDBMS models used in databases such as Informix, Oracle, Ingres, dBASE II, and other well-known databases are popular precisely because they are easy to program and change. The tabular structure is simple and flexible and offers the MIS maintenance programmers a major advantage in turnaround during maintenance.

I/O-Bound Company

Tyson's MIS processes are highly disk-intensive in terms of input/output operations. Most big runs such as payroll and accounts payable require thousands of disk-read and -write operations that tie up the machine for long periods of time. Faster processor speeds have only a marginally greater speed and offer diminishing returns, being limited by disk-access speeds.

The company currently uses twenty-four disk drives (600 megabytes each) and eight more are planned. With this addition, the total data storage will exceed 19 gigabytes. This is an enormous amount of data to sling around and has become a bottleneck in the MIS process.

To leverage the I/O, Tyson has considered adding more cache memory. To be effective, the cache memory would have to be one gigabyte in size, which is not currently available. One vendor sells a half-gigabyte cache memory device that would work with the Unisys machines, but even at today's tumbling memory prices, it would cost over a million dollars and is therefore not feasible.

"The Mainframe Mentality Is Going to Go Away..."

In their search for better response rate, Tyson's MIS staff has several options within the Unisys hardware environment. The Model 1100/94 uses four 90-type processors and has the potential of doubling CPU throughput with a combined CPU speed of 30 MIPS (4 times 7.5). However, this option is not considered cost-effective, since the upgrade costs would be better utilized in the 2200 environment. Another problem is that the idea of more and more processors within the 1100 design is reaching a saturation point and does not provide an open architecture and expansion possibilities for the kind of growth path the company is expected to follow.

Unisys has recently announced a new computer, the 2200. This is a better machine and would be more cost-effective for Tyson. Besides, starting with a bigger frame at a lower level of saturation would be more appropriate, since Tyson needs lots of elbow room for additional capacity that may be required on short notice.

But mainframes may not offer the optimal migration path for a company such as Tyson that faces growth and uncertainty. The reason is that mainframes come in large "chunks." To keep pace with the firm's growth by adding new units would require expansion in chunks that are too large to be logistically or even financially feasible.

Hardware and software costs for mainframes tend to be very high even on the basis of the per unit cost of computing power. An additional problem with large boxes occurs at failure. When a mainframe fails, it takes a large percentage of the computing power with it. MIS managers at Tyson have begun to question the value of "one large box." The general feeling is that the mainframe paradigm may no longer be valid and that "the mainframe mentality is going to go away," to be replaced by distributed and modular systems.

Alternatives to the mainframe are offered by high-powered networks of minis and super-micro workstations. A good example is the DEC VAX series. These computers cost about $150,000 each instead of millions and can be grouped together in "VAX clusters." VAX clusters can be configured so as to exceed the computing power of mainframes and still offer almost limitless growth as more and more VAX units can be added to the Ethernet network. The size and cost of the VAX units offer a more sensible growth path for an MIS department that must keep pace with a volatile business environment. For these reasons, when the MIS managers at Tyson take a hard look at the future, it begins to look more and more like minicomputers and networks.

The minicomputer network option offers additional benefits in terms of redundancy and uptime. If a unit fails it does not bring down the system. Without the full array of machines, the system's performance may be degraded but it will be functional until the unit can be repaired and brought back online. This is possible because the minis work as a group, allocating time slots to the available processors. Disk drives and other peripherals are available to the network as a pool of devices and are accessible by any CPU.

Taking a 5- to 7-year time horizon as a basis, the MIS design today must be such that it can absorb two to three times the current business volume and number of transactions without a major changeover. This kind of growth path in MIS design can be assured either by building in the excess capacity today or by choosing an open-ended system architecture that will allow large growth ratios without a major interruption to service. Budgetary constraints usually dictate the latter approach.

Case Study Questions

1. End-user computing is normally considered to be an MIS headache from a management and control perspective. These perceived disadvantages must be weighed against organizational benefits gained from the improved productivity of knowledge workers. The Tyson case, however, illustrates the direct MIS benefits of end-user computing. Discuss these in relation to the disadvantages of end-user computing and make a recommendation to Tyson MIS managers on future policy with regard to end-user computing.

2. The Tyson MIS managers use MIPS as a yardstick not only for comparing hardware but for assessing MIS needs. What are the pros and cons of this approach?

3. Although IBM seems to own the mainframe market, there are other big players in this field. Unisys, Amdahl, Control Data, and Cray are four large mainframe vendors. As an MIS manager for a company the size of Tyson, under what conditions would you consider using one of these vendors instead of IBM?

4. What special MIS problems are posed by Tyson's furious growth rate? How has the MIS department at Tyson responded to these challenges?

5. The operational structure of Tyson's business is distributed in nature. To what extent does the MIS architecture mirror this structure? How could the architecture be more distributed? What advantages would this offer? What are some potential problems of such an approach?

6. Tyson has been a Sperry shop for 20 years. What problems will it face in changing hardware environments? Make a case for Tyson to stay with Sperry.

7. Tyson's expansion may take their operation geographically beyond the south and southwest so that production complexes could be located as far away as Minnesota and Mexico. What effect, if any, would this have on your MIS strategy for Tyson for the future?

8. Using the information provided in the case material, develop a spreadsheet model to project the growth of the company over the next 5 years. The model should show sales, personnel, number of production complexes, number of transactions, and the rough size and power of MIS facilities needed.

9. The operations of small firms acquired by Tyson are fused with Tyson's, and the MIS of Tyson grows to encompass the added activity. How is this process likely to differ when the target, such as Holly Farms, is the same size as Tyson?

APPLE COMPUTER, INC.

"Window to the World" R & D or MIS?

The best way to predict the future is to invent it.
— Alan Kay, Apple Computer, Inc.

The Commercial Is the Message

Those watching the 1984 Superbowl game between the Raiders and the Redskins saw one of the great running plays of all time by Marcus Allen of the Raiders. From the Oakland 20-yard line, he ran left only to be confronted by a bevy of Redskins. Marcus turned around and ran right – all the way down the field to a stunning touchdown. Immediately following this play, the TV audience was treated to one of the most bizarre commercial messages ever broadcast.

This commercial, which epitomizes the corporate philosophy and religion at Apple Computer Inc., opens in black and white and shows a meeting hall filled with mindless-looking humans being controlled in Orwellian fashion by a computer display. A woman appears like a superhero, in color, running. Swinging a hammer, she shatters the computer display, and the masses are thus set free. This is the dramatic way in which Apple unleashed a completely new kind of computer that its developers promised would "change the way people use computers." Confronted by the IBM PC and "IBM PC clones," Apple too was running right, and, as it turned out, would score a touchdown.

From its very beginnings, Apple has been more than just a business. There is a religious fervor that runs throughout the corporation. One gets the feeling that the company is not just out to make computers but, with ideas distilled from the energy of the sixties, is out to change the world. When former Pepsico executive and veteran "journeyman" manager John Sculley took over in 1982 as president, it was widely predicted that Apple would change their cavalier ways and join the main-stream of American business. Instead, Sculley himself caught the disease and is now its principal spokesman.

The Apple Museum

Exhibited at the corporate headquarters of Apple in Cupertino, California, are artifacts that trace the history of this Cinderella computer maker. The Apple story is now a part of American folklore. In 1976, while working as a hardware engineer at Hewlett-Packard, Stephen Wozniak designed a small 8-bit "personal" computer, which was then a new notion. HP didn't bite, so "the Woz" joined forces with his friend Steve Jobs and began building the Apple II computer in his garage.

At first the Apple II was considered only a computer hobbyist's toy, but sales jumped into the thousands when third-party enhancements increased the screen capacity from 40 columns to 80 columns, and word processing, database, and telecommunications software became available from various software developers.

Then a miracle happened. A software developer produced an entirely new kind of program that changed everything. Developed on the Apple II, VisiCalc allowed nonprogrammers to create sophisticated and useful business programs by writing numbers and formulas onto a grid that used the accountant's spreadsheet as a metaphor. This product was the catalyst needed for businesspeople to take a serious look at the new "toy" computers.

Apple's sales mushroomed into the millions and the garage operation of Jobs and Wozniak took its place among the growing number of high-tech companies in Silicon Valley. By the early eighties Apple had gone public and had risen to prominence as one of the major manufacturers of small computers in the world. But competition toughened in 1982 when IBM entered the personal computer business with its IBM PC and usurped the market almost overnight. Having received IBM's blessings, however, the small computer was finally being taken seriously by big business. It was now up to Apple to respond to the IBM challenge and take advantage of the new opportunities that this competition presented. The stage was thus set for a storybook showdown between the Goliath and the David: between IBM, the establishment, and Apple, the renegade.

The lesson of VisiCalc was not lost on the visionaries at Apple. While other computer companies were looking for new hardware and software, Apple was looking for a new paradigm. While the industry was frantically building faster and cheaper IBM PC clones, Apple was inventing the next generation of personal computers. The company was determined not to become just another clone maker but to develop an entirely new machine that would change the way people perceived and used computers. In 1984, with an advertising campaign as innovative as the product, Apple responded with what turned out to be a promethean development in computing: the Macintosh.

At the time IBM owned the small computer market. Other computer makers that survived did so by making machines that were IBM-compatible. The Macintosh was *not* only not IBM-compatible, but it represented a radical departure from the way computers were being designed and used. The key attributes of the Macintosh are its standardized user interface and the use of graphics and a mouse pointing device as the principal method of user interaction instead of the command-line interpretation of other operating systems. In the Macintosh, Apple had found yet another new paradigm that changed the computer industry in profound ways.

Conventional wisdom would have dictated that Apple abandon its computers and join the fray with an IBM-compatible MS DOS machine. Instead, the company went out on a limb and took a very risky billion dollar gamble. The true extent of the success of this gamble was to be proven four years later when IBM itself dumped its MS DOS machines and announced a new computer that mimicked the Macintosh.

It's a Mac, Mac, Mac, Mac World

By 1987, there were more than 3,000 programs available for the Macintosh, and Apple had sold more than a million of these machines. Fueled principally by Macintosh sales, net revenues jumped from $982 million in 1983 to $1.5 billion in 1984 and rose steadily to $2.66 billion in 1987. Net income almost tripled in the same period, rising from $76 million in 1983 to $217 million in 1987. The 1987 income statement (Figure AC.1) shows that the cost of sales is less than 50 percent; that is, the gross margin in 1987 was more than $1.3 billion. The most significant of the overhead expenses that whittled net income down to $217 million are the marketing and distribution costs of $655 million. These figures point to the emphasis on marketing that has driven Macintosh sales, what Apple calls their "market-driven strategy." Research and development expenses were $192 million, an amount indicative of effort the company is expending in developing new products.

In 1987, the company announced two significant new products, the Macintosh II computer and a piece of software called *Hypercard*. The Macintosh II offers enhanced computing power and capacity that will extend Apple's market to new areas such as CAD/CAM. Hypercard promises to free programmers from the restrictions of traditional database systems and to open up yet another new way to use computers.

Much of Apple's R & D has been directed to networking and communications. From its very inception, the Macintosh has been designed to be a networking computer, with its built-in network connection and a proprietary networking system called AppleTalk.

In 1987, Apple had 7228 employees worldwide. The company is very selective in its hiring policy and prides itself on the productivity of the staff. In 1987, sales per employee were more than $350,000, the highest in the size and industry category.

The company experienced its most explosive growth period during 1988, when the increasing demand for desktop publishing and the introduction of new products such as the Mac II propelled sales to the $4 billion mark. By the end of 1988, the number of Macintosh computers sold had doubled from 1 million to 2 million. To keep pace with soaring sales, the number of employees surged to over 10,000.

Figure AC.1
Consolidated Statements of Income
Three Years Ending September 25, 1987

Consolidated Balance Sheets
September 25, 1987 and September 26, 1986   (Dollars in thousands)

Assets	1987	1986
Current Assets:		
Cash and temporary cash investments	$ 565,094	$ 576,215
Accounts receivable, net of allowance for doubtful accounts of $23,464 ($21,792 in 1986)	405,637	263,126
Inventories	225,753	108,680
Prepaid income taxes	48,798	53,029
Other current assets	62,143	39,884
Total current assets	1,307,425	1,040,934
Property, plant, and equipment:		
Land and buildings	47,599	25,660
Machinery and equipment	132,055	103,963
Office furniture and equipment	49,111	44,237
Leaseheld improvements	60,365	48,179
	289,130	222,039
Accumulated depreciation and amortization	(158,696)	(114,724)
Net property, plant, and equipment	130,434	107,315
Other assets	40,072	11,879
	$ 1,477,931	$ 1,160,128

Liabilities and Shareholders' Equity	1987	1986
Current liabilities:		
Accounts payable	$ 205,929	$ 118,053
Accrued compensation and employee benefits	55,291	37,238
Income taxes payable	20,242	14,652
Accrued marketing and distribution	113,631	83,577
Other current liabilities	83,585	75,015
Total current liabilities	478,678	328,535
Deferred income taxes	162,765	137,506
Commitments and contingencies		
Shareholders' equity:		
Common stock, no par value; 320,000,000 shares authorized; 126, 088,081 issued and outstanding in 1987 (125,255,226 shares in 1986)	263,956	227,075
Retained earnings	573,141	474,287
Accumulated translation adjustment	1,503	(966)
	838,600	700,396
Notes receivable from shareholders	(2,112)	(6,309)
Total shareholders' equity	836,488	694,087
	$ 1,477,931	$ 1,160,128

Consolidated Statements of Income
Three years ended September 25, 1987   (In thousands, except per share amounts)

	1987	1986	1985
Net Sales	$ 2,661,068	$ 1,901,898	$ 1,918,280
Costs and expenses:			
Cost of sales	1,296,220	891,112	1,117,864
Research and development	191,554	127,758	72,526
Marketing and distribution	655,219	476,685	478,079
General and administrative	146,637	132,812	110,077
Consolidation of operations	-	-	36,966
	2,289,630	1,628,367	1,815,512
Operating income	371,438	273,531	102,768
Interest and other income, net	38,930	36,187	17,277
Income before income taxes	410,368	309,718	120,045
Provision for income taxes	192,872	155,755	58,822
Net income	$ 217,496	$ 153,963	$ 61,223
Earnings per common and common equivalent share	$ 1.65	$ 1.20	$ .49
Common and common equivalent shares used in the calculations of earnings per share	131,615	128,630	123,790

President, CEO, and Chairman of the Board John Sculley has set a sales goal of $10 billion to be achieved in the early 1990s. To meet this objective will require Apple to sustain an annual growth rate in excess of 35 percent. The role of MIS in this master plan of growth is twofold. First, the MIS resources and capacity must keep pace with the company's increased transaction processing and information needs. Besides, because growth changes the nature and organization of a company, Apple's structure and character change from year to year as the company grows, matures, brings in veteran managers from other companies, and begins to adopt more conventional business practices. The $10 billion dollar company Apple intends to become by the early 1990s is bound to be a lot different from the $4 billion company that MIS serves today. Allan Loren, vice president in charge of IS&T (Information Systems and Technology), recently organized an internal brainstorming session to define what direction Apple should take in the coming decade and to outline what the company "is going to look like when it hits the $10 billion mark." Whatever it does look like then will be considerably different from now. The MIS strategy for the future will be based on these projections.

Second, MIS has assumed the crucial and unconventional roles of R & D and marketing in constructing and implementing the *Window to the World* project. This project is expected to develop and demonstrate connectivity solutions that Apple needs to open up new markets in the mainframe computing environments of corporate America. Although the company's growth in the last two years has been due primarily to desktop publishing, Apple believes that future growth to the $10-billion mark must be driven by the connectivity issue. It is widely believed that unless Apple finds a way to make the Macintosh a standard tool of the mainstream MIS community, the company's ambitious growth plans will not materialize.

Apple's main office in Cupertino, California, consists of more than three dozen modern office buildings spread out over several blocks in a campus-like setting. The corporate headquarters, Research and Development, Marketing, Developer Programs, and MIS functions are carried out from this location, with the principal manufacturing facility situated just a few miles north on Highway 17, in Fremont. Other important production plants are located in Cork, Ireland, and in Singapore. All these facilities utilize a flexible production line designed to permit production of different products and product specs on the same production line.

Apple maintains distribution facilities in Europe, Canada, and Australia and sales and service operations in 85 countries. The Apple user interface is now available in more than sixteen languages. Foreign sales in 1987 were about $700 million and are expected to increase very rapidly in the 1990s.

In keeping with the perception that the small computer business is a multi-vendor marketplace, Apple uses computer resellers, VAR (Value Added Resellers), and system integrators as the primary distribution channels. (A multi-vendor market is one in which satisfying a single customer's needs involves products from several vendors. In such a market, the customer can be better served by a single source of supply than by a number of different vendors. The computer store serves this function and for this reason has become the primary distribution channel for personal computers.) In addition, Apple pursues direct sales to large single customers and market segments such as the federal government.

Is There Life After Desktop Publishing?

Apple has been very successful in the secondary education market with the Apple II. Increasing numbers of colleges and universities have adopted Macintosh computers. The Macintosh is now in use in over 3000 colleges around the world.

In spite of Apple's success in the educational and consumer markets, as of this writing the company had yet to penetrate corporate America in a significant way. Computer users in what was clearly IBM territory were skeptical about a machine that was so different from their perception of computers. Besides, most corporations by now had hundreds of IBM PCs and, more than ever before, "IBM-compatibility" had become a prerequisite to assure that data and software could be transferred from machine to machine.

The superior graphics capabilities of the Macintosh and its ability to intermingle text and graphics enabled Apple to loosen IBM's stranglehold on the corporate computer market. The graphics capabilities and Apple's laser printer gave rise to an entirely new kind of application called *desktop publishing* or DTP. Using DTP, business managers could produce reports in-house that went beyond word processing and looked as if they had been laid out by a graphic artist. This innovation set a new standard for business reports and created a demand for the Macintosh in the heart of IBM-land.

Having entered the corporate arena, albeit in Trojan-horse style, Apple now sought to reposition the Macintosh as a mainstream business computer by gaining a wider acceptance of the machine than as just a DTP tool. The primary marketing force Apple is using to push the Macintosh in that direction is connectivity. The goal? To make the Macintosh the best-connected personal computer in the market.

Apple has seized upon networking and connectivity as the marketing edge that will finally make the Macintosh *the* corporate computer. Apple's vision is one of seamless connectivity: a networking system that ties together all kinds of hardware and operating systems from mainframes to micros, and that presents all these resources to the user in a transparent and consistent manner through the point-and-click facility of the Macintosh. Apple's objective is to give power to the individual user, starting with the Macintosh and working outward to the full range of MIS and corporate databases.

Figure AC.2 is a graphical model of this new vision. At the center of the system is the individual user, who, through the Macintosh, has all the resources of the network at his or her fingertips. The complexities of the system are hidden. The system appears to the user to be the familiar Macintosh but can serve up almost limitless computing and communications power.

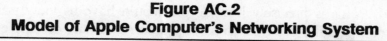

Figure AC.2
Model of Apple Computer's Networking System

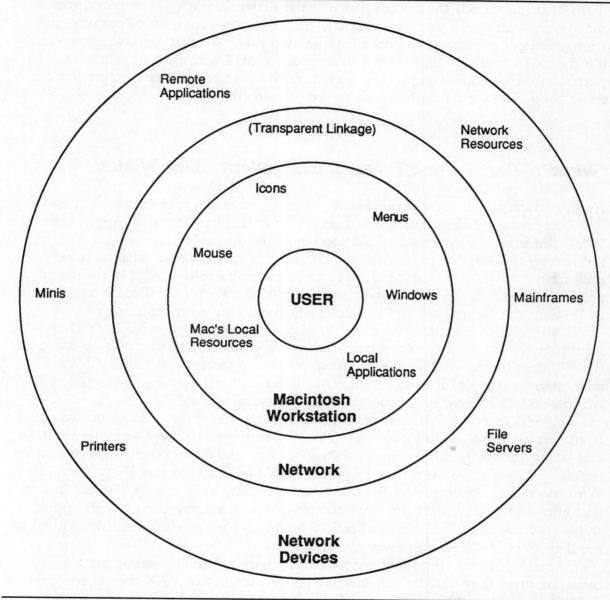

Remote
Applications

(Transparent Linkage)

Network
Resources

Icons

Menus

Mouse

Minis

USER

Windows

Mainframes

Mac's Local
Resources

Local
Applications

**Macintosh
Workstation**

Printers

Network

File
Servers

**Network
Devices**

Apple likes to use the telephone as a symbol of this new paradigm of computing. If you think about it, the telephone is a marvelous device. You can pick up the phone, punch in 12 digits, and make a connection with a single phone out of millions of others anywhere in the world. Although making the connection involves a mind-numbing amount of technology and switching decisions, you do not have to understand or deal with any of this. In fact, you probably never even think about what is involved. This is precisely how Apple would have us view the computer.

A computer is usually referred to as "a system." A part of Apple's new paradigm of computing is the notion that it is the network, not the computer, that is the system with which the user interacts. In this reality, computers, printers, and storage devices are merely devices for facilitating processes that are essential to serving the user's needs. Conventional integration of MIS with personal computers has portrayed the personal computer as an accessory to the mainframe. Apple, on the other hand, views the mainframe as an accessory to the PC.

"Wired": The Life and Times of the Modern Office Worker

Apple's strategic managers decided that this new vision of office connectivity must first be proven and demonstrated at home. The MIS department at Apple, called IS&T (Information Systems and Technology), thus had to assume a dual role. The technology necessary to implement the connectivity office would have to come not only from R & D but from MIS itself. In its indomitable style, Apple christened the project Window to the World and commissioned the R & D and MIS departments to produce the technology and to implement these ideas in the company.

MIS had to take the lead in this project, working closely with R & D and third-party hardware and software developers. Figure AC.3 defines the objective of the Window to the World project. Note that the project scope calls for total connectivity on a global scale. Figure AC.4 shows that 14 major Apple offices worldwide would have to be connected in this grand scheme.

How does one get started on a project of this magnitude? How do we get from here to there? Apple began by taking inventory of the *here,* defining the *there,* and listing the changes, new implementations, and new developments that would be necessary to get there from here. Apple already had Macs on just about every desk. With more than 15,000 Macs in service, the company itself may be Apple's biggest customer and a convenient proving ground for the marketing department. Apple wants to crack open the MIS marketplace for Macintosh products and would like to see their own IS&T lead the way.

Apple's MIS functions and corporate databases are on 35 mainframe and minicomputers from three different vendors. These are five VAX computers from DEC, two IBM 3090 mainframes, 20 IBM System/38s, and four-fault tolerant computers from Tandem. In addition, Apple uses a Cray X-MP and engineering workstations from Sun and other vendors for engineering and R & D functions.

MIS functions at Apple are organized in hardware groups. It is as if each department makes independent hardware decisions guided only by specific MIS needs rather than by arbitrary company-wide standards of hardware homogeneity. All manufacturing functions — including MRP, inventory, and process costing — are on

Window to the World

- From a single Macintosh
  . . . on any desk
    . . . in any Apple office
      . . . anywhere in the world
- A user can access
  . . . any information
    . . . required to do his/her job
      . . . transparently

Figure AC.4
Apple Computer's Window to the World
Connects 14 Major Apple Offices

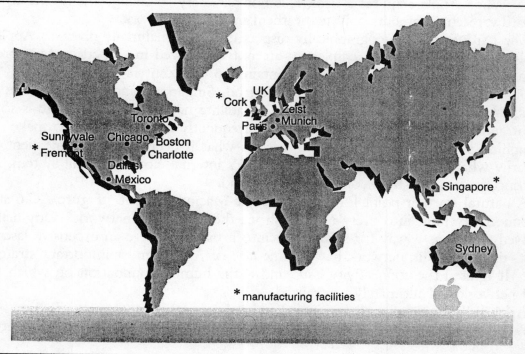

* manufacturing facilities

the Tandems. There is a Tandem at each manufacturing facility (Fremont, Singapore, and Cork) and one at Cupertino used for development work. The Human Resources department (HR) uses a battery of five VAX computers. Apple is also using VAX for office automation. The office automation software, being developed by IS&T, uses the native Macintosh environment as the user interface. It is this activity that has propelled the VAX-Macs connectivity technology. Financial data are maintained on the IBM 3090 mainframes while sales and marketing use the IBM System/38 machines.

Figure AC.5 shows the arrangement of this extremely heterogenous hardware environment that constitutes Apple's current MIS. Most terminals are Macs with terminal emulation for 5291, 3270, 6530, and VT100 protocols. The PBX phone system provides a common access path to the VAX, IBM 3090, Tandem, and the System/38. The connection can be made either through dial-up lines or via a gateway from AppleTalk to Ethernet. Outside data networks and services such as Tymnet and MCI Mail are also routed through the PBX. An important part of the network is the electronic mail system called AppleLink. All Apple employees worldwide as well as many Apple developers, dealers, and user groups use AppleLink to communicate. Apple Sales, Marketing, and Developer Programs use AppleLink as a depository for current information.

Apple's truly multi-vendor MIS environment challenges conventional wisdom, which espouses single-vendor systems. By concentrating on the network rather than on specific hardware environments, Apple's IS&T is leading the way to truly vendor-free MIS designs. Network orientation rather than vendor orientation has many advantages. For example, acquired firms have better access to technological innovation. When Apple acquires a firm, it is not necessary to change them over to a new hardware environment, only to tie them in to the network.

The hardware is as geographically dispersed as it is materially diverse. Apple's computers and its 500 IS&T employees are not centralized in Cupertino but spread out on a global scale. The company maintains 16 data centers in 12 countries, including the United States, France, UK, Ireland, Singapore, and Holland. The data centers, or sites, are connected with an X.25 satellite network. The linkage is so efficient and transparent that hardware usage frequently does not seem to make geographical sense; the hardware being used is what is deemed most convenient, not necessarily what is closest. For instance, Apple's internal electronic mail system, at Cupertino, is operated by a computer in Holland.

A natural starting point for the *here* is the Macintosh itself. Figure AC.6 shows the connectivity built into every Macintosh via the AppleTalk network. Originally conceived merely as a way for several Macintosh users to share an expensive laser printer, the AppleTalk network has become one of Apple's most important strategic assets. It ignited the connectivity issue and is the humble foundation on which the global network will ultimately be realized.

AppleTalk uses inexpensive shielded twisted-pair cable to connect Macs to Apple's LaserWriter printer at a data transfer rate of 230.4 bits/second. The network

Figure AC.5
Hardware Configurations for Apple Computer's MIS

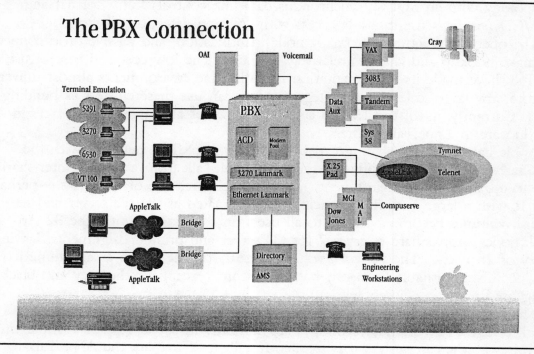

Figure AC.6
Connectivity in the Macintosh Is Provided via AppleTalk

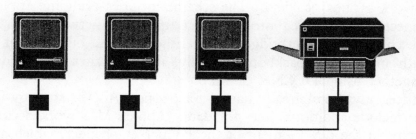

is designed to handle only small clusters of users and has a maximum capacity of 32 nodes within a small perimeter. In most installations a group of six to sixteen users in contiguous offices or desks are tied in to one LaserWriter. AppleTalk uses a serial bus topology with an SDLC (synchronous data link control) frame format and CSMA/CD (carrier sense multiple access with collision detection) protocol.

The open architecture, automatic node identification, and passive drop connections make hookup and changes relatively painless. The low cost and ease of use of AppleTalk have made its implementation in multi-Mac environments almost universal. Therefore, any large scale plan to integrate Macs can use these clusters as building blocks. Currently, all of the 15,000 or so Macintoshes at Apple headquarters in Cupertino are in AppleTalk clusters.

Apple has added file-sharing capability to the AppleTalk network with the AppleShare program, which lifts the status of AppleTalk from a mere printer-sharing device to a data-sharing environment. With AppleShare, one of the Macs — perhaps a Mac II with a large hard-disk capacity — is designated as the file server and its hard-disk volumes become available to all users on the network. Of the 32 AppleTalk nodes, AppleShare reserves 7 for file server and printer assignments, leaving a capacity of 25 users. The network volume appears on the screen as a volume icon that is not distinguishable from other volume icons (except for the grey and black shading used to denote access levels).

The limited node capacity of AppleTalk is easily overcome by the use of network bridges. Two kinds of bridges are currently in use at Apple's complex in Cupertino, or "the campus" as it is frequently called. These are the AppleTalk-to-AppleTalk bridge as shown in Figure AC.7 and the AppleTalk-to-Ethernet gateway as shown in Figure AC.8.

In formulating the master-plan for global connectivity, Apple divided the world of Apple into sites, buildings, and offices. Each geographical location on the globe is a *site*. A site may contain several *buildings,* and each building may contain several segregatable work groups or *offices*. The scheme includes bringing AppleTalk to every desk and connecting each office into a distinct AppleTalk network with the AppleTalk networks in each building interbridged using Ethernet. All buildings at a site will be connected with an Ethernet backbone. Finally, all Apple sites worldwide will be networked together using DECNet or X.25.

Most offices anywhere already have a telephone. Apple's strategy is to expand this wiring to include additional lines for data. Apple's MIS worked closely with Farallon Systems in the development of the PhoneNet product, which allows AppleTalk connections over standard phone cabling. The wiring plan for the "completely wired" office calls for each office to be pre-wired with four sets of telephone lines, at least one of which will be used for AppleTalk (via PhoneNet), with one used for normal voice and asynchronous data multiplexed over a single pair of wires. Each office will be wired into a telephone closet using a star configuration. Use of the "closet" method of connections ensures that AppleTalk networks can be

Figure AC.7
AppleTalk-to-AppleTalk Network Bridge

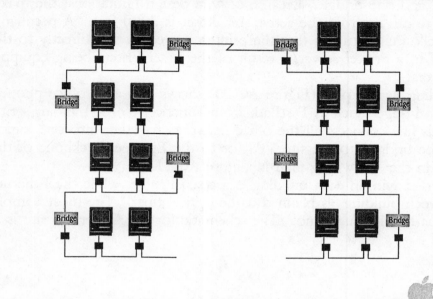

Figure AC.8
AppleTalk-to Ethernet Gateway

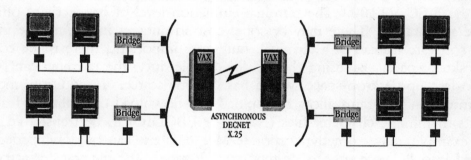

easily reconfigured in much the same way as a switchboard operator used to configure phone lines in the past. The office wiring plan is shown in Figure AC.9.

The typical AppleTalk network consists of 24 workstations, two LaserWriters, one file server, and one bridge. Because of wire design limitations, the maximum distance a device can be from the active star closet is 3000 feet. A peculiar feature of the AppleTalk architecture is that the printers are connected directly to their own port instead of to a printer server, a result of the LaserWriters being equipped with AppleTalk drivers.

The building wiring plan (Figure AC.10) shows that each office phone closet is connected via a bridge (such as FastPath from Kinetics) to the building's Ethernet backbone. This line connects all the office networks together into one logical unit that can then be bridged to the site VAX or to the Ethernet backbone of the site. This is shown in the site wiring plan in Figure AC.11.

The Ethernet wire in each building is a coaxial cable, while the Ethernet backbone between buildings is planned to be optical fiber. The most complex site is Apple's headquarters in Cupertino. The schematic for the Cupertino site is shown in Figure AC.12.

Frontal Lobotomy and Other Levels of Connectivity

Conventional attempts at PC-mainframe integration have focussed on the mainframe as the system and have treated the PC as a peripheral. In particular, the PC has been used strictly as a terminal to the mainframe. Since the PC is programmable, it can be programmed to mimic the communications protocol, keyboard functions, and display parameters of a wide range of mainframe terminal types such as the IBM 327x and the DEC VT100. The terminal emulation level of connectivity offers some worthwhile advantages. There may be some cost advantages in buying the interface board and software instead of a terminal, but more important, there is the consideration of desktop space. By using the PC for double duty, the terminal can be removed to free up desktop space, which has become scarce. In addition, most terminal emulation programs allow file upload and download capability, a feature that permits mainframe character files (ASCII or EBCDIC) to be transferred into PC files. For example, data from the corporate MIS database can be downloaded and incorporated into PC spreadsheets or reports. However, the file transfer across operating systems does not follow the file copy procedures of either operating system but involves a cumbersome sequence of steps specific to the communication software being used.

The user interface of the Macintosh, however, is vastly superior to that of mainframes and their terminals. Thus, the use of the PC to mimic mainframe terminal protocols is a poor use of PC resources. Terminal emulation, therefore, represents the lowest level of connectivity and, according to Apple, is tantamount to a frontal lobotomy if the PC.

Figure AC.9
Office Wiring Plan

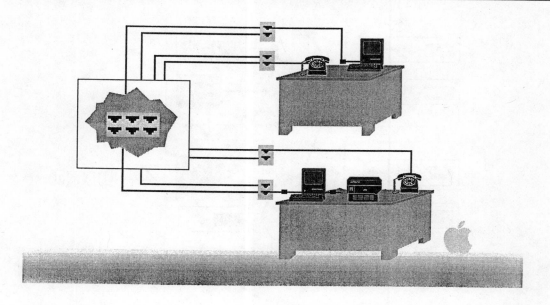

Figure AC.10
Building Wiring Plan

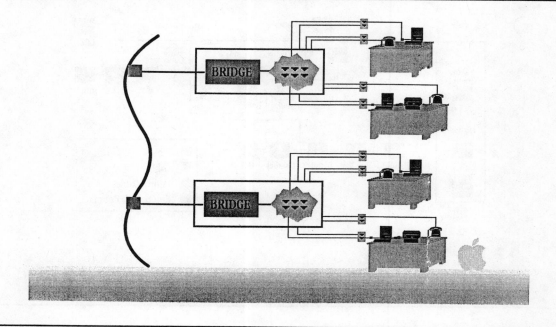

Figure AC.11
Site Wiring Plan

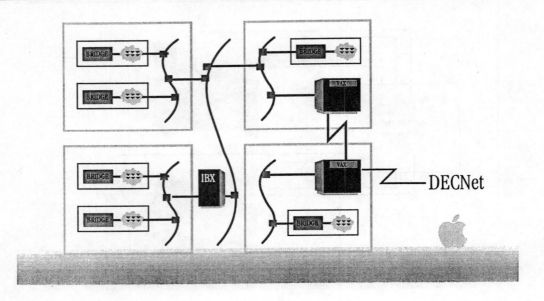

Figure AC.12
Voice/Data Network for Apple Headquarters in Cupertino, California

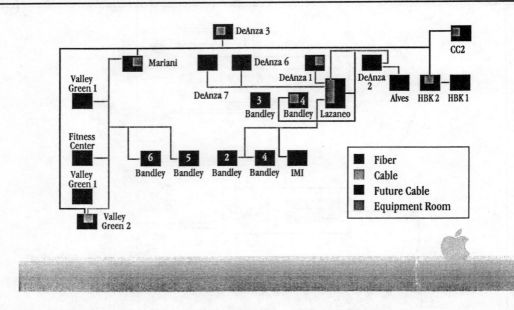

At a higher level of connectivity, the conventional terminal protocols are abandoned and the differences between the two operating systems and the two networks are cemented. In the case of the Macintosh, the screen, mouse, and keyboard functions are retained for both machines. Thus, to the Mac user, the differences between the two operating systems become transparent. What works on the Mac also works on the host machine. For example, file transfer can be performed in the same way as a file copy in the Macintosh, simply by dragging the file icon from one window to another.

The goal of the Window to the World project is to reach an even higher level of connectivity. At the highest level of connectivity a single application can be written that will span both machines. For example, an order-entry program running on the Mac would appear to the user to be entirely a Mac application when in fact it executes and communicates with a companion program in the VAX that accesses the MIS databases and updates them as necessary.

At Apple, many of the MIS machines are VAX computers from DEC, and the machine on all desks is of course the Macintosh. Therefore, Mac-VAX connectivity has been getting a great deal of attention from the IS&T software engineers. The attempts at establishing higher levels of connectivity have been so promising that DEC and Apple have both realized that the mutual benefits of the connectivity would expand and serve both markets. In 1987, the two companies created a stir by announcing a joint development project to attain a high degree of integration between the Mac and the VAX. At a low level, the agreement is aimed at cooperation in the development of common specs for connecting AppleTalk to DECnet. This will provide wide area DECnet support for AppleTalk networks and facilitate access to DEC and Apple PostScript printers from either network. At a higher level, the goals of the alliance are to develop joint specifications so that Macintosh programs can directly access VAX databases and ultimately to set the platform for applications to be written that span both machines.

If You Can't Join 'Em, Buy 'Em

In addition to the strategic alliance with DEC, Apple has augmented its own development efforts by entering into several partnerships with third-party software developers.

Originally developed by Alisa Systems, IS&T's AppleTalk for VMS can be used to run virtual AppleTalk nodes in VAX's VMS environment. The virtual network is bridged to an actual AppleTalk network. Mac users on the real AppleTalk can transparently access files and processes on the virtual AppleTalk nodes in VMS; and voila! the mighty VAX can now be used as a file server on an AppleTalk network.

Apple has cooperated with Alisa Systems in the development of a set of programs, including AlisaShare, that enhance the connectivity between the Mac and the VAX. The objective of this software effort is to integrate the file systems of the

Macintosh and the VAX with a high degree of transparency. The system supports the hierarchical file system (HFS) of both the Mac and the VAX/VMS and maps the directory structure from one to another. To a Mac user, the VMS directories and files appear as Macintosh folder and file icons with access to the normal copy, delete, and move commands of the Mac. To a VAX user, the Macintosh folders and files look just like VMS directories and files, and they can be accessed in the same way as VMS files. An important aspect of AlisaShare is that it supports the AppleTalk File Protocol or AFP so that the VMS directories appear to be on an AppleTalk node and can therefore be accessed through AppleTalk and AppleShare. Although these users can see the files and perform operations on the files (such as "copy") at the operating system level, they cannot "open" a file that is resident in the other system because that involves interpretation of the contents. To do that requires a higher level of integration.

Mac Workstation, another program developed by IS&T to integrate Macs with mainframes, is now an Apple product and is already affecting Macintosh sales. Mac Workstation is host-resident and versions of the software have been produced for VAX, Tandem, System/38, and IBM 30xx series mainframes. Whereas terminal emulation programs run on the micro to make it appear as if it were a mainframe accessory, Mac Workstation runs on the mainframe to make it appear as if it were a Macintosh accessory. The implementation at Apple has been very successful. Manufacturing (Tandems), Sales (System/38), and HR (VAX) all report heavy usage of and reliance on Mac Workstation. The users like it because they don't have to make a mental switch between the Mac user interface and other terminal specific interfaces. Mac Workstation epitomizes IS&T's unique role in the organization and Apple's vision of micro-mainframe integration, which emphasizes the user and the user interface rather than machines.

Of course, IS&T is not primarily engaged in marketing software but in its function as an information service organization to Apple. An example of such a development is an EIS called PRISM that gives managers access to the financial database on the IBM 3090 mainframes. The data are stored under the Nomad database manager on the IBM. IS&T wrote a Hypercard front-end to the data so that executives can access Nomad data on an ad hoc basis, using the user-friendly and familiar point-and-click user interface of Hypercard.

Although Apple's marketing department has been singing the paeans of Hypercard as a business tool and thousands of Hypercard stacks have been developed by afficionados, Hypercard is yet to have a significant application in large MIS shops. However, at Apple, IS&T takes Hypercard very seriously. If Hypercard is to become an MIS tool any time soon, the pace will have to be set by IS&T.

With respect to higher levels of Mac-VAX integration, an important acquisition has been that of Network Innovations, Inc. of Cupertino. The developers of the highly acclaimed CL/1 software are now a wholly owned subsdiary of Apple Computer, Inc. The acquisition is part of Apple's plan to make the Macintosh the connectivity machine of the 1990s. CL/1 is a set of software tools for the Macintosh and the VAX that allows Macintosh application programmers to access VAX

Figure AC.13
CL/1 Architecture: Transparent Integration of Mac-Vax Applications

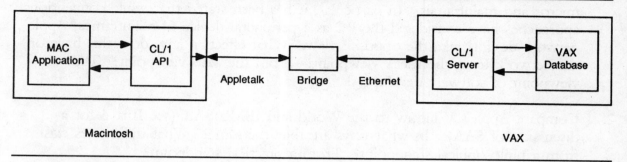

databases such as Oracle and Rdb in a completely transparent way (See Figure AC.13). To the application programmer the process appears to be identical to looking through a database in the Mac. All the translation is handled by the API (Application Program Interface) on the Macintosh and the CL/1 Server on the VAX. CL/1 has been used to link Apple's Hypercard with the Oracle database on the VAX. Through the CL/1 API, the Oracle database looks like a Hypercard stack. This sort application program integration across hardware environments provides the highest level of seamless integration that Apple needs to realize its vision in the Window project.

Various software developers such as Odesta, authors of Double Helix, provide independent support of the VAX-Mac integration at the application level. However, the feeling at Apple is that for the Window to the World project to be successful, Apple has to provide a common software platform such as CL/1 in which application programmers can access both machine resources without having to think about it. Although the emphasis thus far has been on the VAX, similar implementations can be made to other mainframes and minis.

IBM has challenged Apple with the new PS/2 computer and the OS/2 operating system that offers the same window/icon/mouse-based user interface as does the Macintosh. Besides, the IBM machines offer built-in compatibility with the IBM mainframe's DB2 relational database with SQL servers. IBM has not yet delivered these products and most MIS managers in large businesses have adopted a "wait and see" policy with regard to the next generation of personal computers. If the Window project succeeds and Apple is able to achieve the level of connectivity it has envisioned, the $10 billion dream of Apple will be virtually assured.

Case Study Questions

1. Much has been made in the text of this case about the relationship between micros and mainframes. In particular, it has been stated that while conventional approaches have considered the PC as a peripheral device of mainframes, Apple network designs take the opposite view. What effect, if any, does this have on the network from the user's viewpoint? From the MIS viewpoint? The viewpoint of software developers?

2. Compare Apple's Window to the World and IBM's SAA (see Part 4 for a discussion of SAA). In what ways are they the same? What differences exist from a philosophical standpoint? From a practical standpoint?

3. Apple's IS&T uses a heterogenous hardware environment. For example, Manufacturing uses Tandems while Human Resources uses VAXes; Sales uses IBM System/38 machines and Finance uses the IBM 3090. At first glance it does not even appear that the company has an integrated MIS but rather that each department has its own information center independent of the others. Yet IS&T is the only information center and manages information for the whole company. How is this possible? What would Apple have gained by standardizing their hardware? What would it have lost?

4. The function of an MIS department is simply to manage the business data of the firm and make information available for business transactions and managerial decision making as necessary. But at Apple, IS&T fills other roles that might rightly belong to marketing and R & D departments. What are these roles? What activities do they entail? In what way are they helpful to MIS activities? In what way, if any, do they hinder the normal performance of MIS functions?

5. With regard to question 4, compare IS&T's current situation with a hypothetical case where IS&T is restricted to traditional MIS duties while a separate group, say R & D, is responsible for the Window to the World project. What are some of the technical and organizational problems of such a setup?

6. The case makes the statement that Apple's network orientation (rather than mainframe orientation) allows them to become more vendor-independent. What does this mean? What are the advantages of becoming vendor-independent and what are the direct and indirect costs? Select a case from this book that uses a centralized vendor-oriented MIS shop. How would the system you selected be different if the company had used Apple's MIS design philosophy? What are the advantages and disadvantages of these two designs?

7. Apple is a very different kind of corporation compared to the mainstream conservative companies in America. What advantages and disadvantages does this pose to its use as a proving grounds for new MIS technology? Consider both the technological and user-acceptance aspects of the problem.

8. What specific roles are played by the programs CL/1 and Mac Workstation in bringing about the seamless integration of micros and mainframes? Identify three different "levels" of integration and describe where these programs fit into the connectivity scheme of IS&T.

9. List the advantages and disadvantages of PCs. Do the same for mainframes. Compare the two lists. In an integrated MIS that uses both of these types of devices in a seamless network, which functions would you assign to each?

AUTODESK, INC.

AUTODESK, INC.

A PC/LAN-Based Master Plan for MIS

Amazing But True: The Story of Autodesk

In the spring of 1982, 13 systems programmers pooled about $65,000 in personal savings as starting capital for a software company and began holding monthly meetings in their living rooms. Autodesk, the company they founded, is today the world's leading supplier of computer-aided design (CAD) software for personal computers and 32-bit workstations.

Autodesk was named for a desktop organizer program, one of five products the company's founders initially planned for specific markets. In the fall of 1982, the company introduced AutoCAD®, a PC-based (CAD) program that brought the benefits of CAD to users of PCs. Since that time, Autodesk has gained preeminence for its development, marketing, and support of computer-aided design and engineering software — "The Autodesk Family of Products."

The PC CAD marketplace has mushroomed to over half a billion dollars and has attracted many players. But Autodesk continues to eclipse the competition, both in terms of market share and in providing technical leadership, standards, and corporate credibility. AutoCAD has become the de facto industry standard with more than 200,000 installations worldwide.

Autodesk went public in 1985 (NASDAQ symbol: ACAD) and was very enthusiastically received. *Business Week* rated Autodesk the number one hot-growth company two years in a row, in 1986 and 1987.

PC CAD Software

The use of CAD software by engineers, architects, and designers to make and edit engineering drawings is analogous to the way in which a typist might use a word processor to produce written documents. Instead of processing words, however, CAD processes drawings, using the basic pictorial elements such as points, vectors, and polygons in Cartesian space.

The advantages of CAD are similar to those of word processing: compact and convenient storage of drawings on disk, ease of retrieving and editing drawings, fast drawing make-up from a library of parts and components, production of additional copies on the plotter, and ability to produce accurate engineering drawings without drafting skills. As an extra bonus, one can even perform engineering computations, cost estimation, and inventory control functions.

Before the advent of AutoCAD and other low-cost CAD software for the PC, CAD was very expensive and therefore used only by the few very large architectural and engineering firms that could afford it. Most designers still had large rooms filled with huge drafting tables and T-squares, with busy draftsmen pouring over them for endless hours, especially when changes to the drawings were necessary.

Typically, a complete CAD system, including all necessary hardware, software, and manuals, would cost somewhere between $100,000 to $500,000, depending on features and hardware. Now one can turn an inexpensive IBM PC into a comparable CAD workstation with a plotter for about $10,000. Such a system includes AutoCAD software, $3000; digitizing tablet, $500; D-size plotter, $5000; math coprocessor, $250; and enhanced graphics display hardware for the PC, $750. The CAD system that results is at once less expensive by orders of magnitude, much easier to use, and more powerful than many of the older systems. Further, the designer has enormous flexibility in choosing hardware components as well as software add-ons.

One key feature of AutoCAD that led to its early adoption by designers is the use of an open architecture that allowed third-party developers to build customization packages. These made AutoCAD directly applicable to a cross-section of design activities ranging from facilities planning to printed circuit board layout and architectural drafting. Initially, this customization consisted of menus and symbol libraries. Autodesk sensed this advantage early and actively encouraged third-party developers. Software enhancements made it increasingly easier to develop application-specific packages using AutoCAD as a base. This development culminated in the release of the LISP interface (AutoLISP) that, in essence, gave third-party developers a very high-level fourth-generation CAD language in which to write extremely application-specific software.

The PC CAD Market

This low-price range for a CAD system exposed a huge bulge in the demand curve that few had suspected. Hardware vendors were quick to adjust to the new reality by dropping prices to attract the new clientele. Stiff competition helped the precipitous drop in prices and many hardware suppliers went bankrupt in the process.

Despite the temptation to enter the hardware market, Autodesk stayed out of it and followed a strategy of supporting a large number of devices. This strategy increased Autodesk's popularity and helped lower hardware prices, making PC CAD even more affordable.

The PC CAD software market continues to unfold but AutoCAD endures and outshines the other vendors with about 50 percent of the market (see Figure AD.1). In the fiscal year ending 1/31/89, Autodesk alone had sales of $117 million. The market is still undergoing rapid expansion, with no maturation in sight.

Although the market consisted initially of small architectural and engineering firms, even large corporations, government, and the military are beginning to abandon the large mainstream CAD systems in favor of PC CAD. Both of these market sectors are showing strong growth.

Autodesk, Inc. Today

Autodesk Inc. headquarters are located on the waterfront in Sausalito, California, just north of San Francisco. About 300 people work there in research and development, customer support, training, marketing, sales, finance and accounting, production and quality control, management, and management information systems. In fiscal year 1989 (Feb. 1, 1988 - Jan. 31, 1989), Autodesk generated about $117 million in sales revenue and $20 million in net income after taxes (NIAT).

The company occupies three buildings in a campus-like setting. The main offices at 2320 and 2330 Marinship Way are across the parking lot from each other and house approximately 175 employees, including top management, product development, R & D, finance, and MIS personnel. The third building, at 3 Harbor Drive, is about a quarter of a mile down the street and houses 125 employees working in production, shipping, receiving, warehousing, sales and marketing.

Production consists of reproducing diskettes through several disk-copying machines, assembling user manuals, and packaging the disks and manuals together for shipping. The procedure is complicated by the use of a unique magnetic and printed serial number for each product and the simultaneous production of a number of different products, products for different target computers, and a number of different optional enhancements for AutoCAD. Strict quality control and serial number audit are extremely important phases of production.

Autodesk's product line is shown in Table AD.1.

In addition to the IBM PC line of computers, Autodesk has produced versions of its software for high-end workstations such as Sun and Apollo, and for DEC's MicroVAX computers. Versions are also available for IBM's PS/2 line of computers, as well as for Apple Computer's Macintosh II and IIx. In following this aggressive implementation policy, Autodesk has avoided becoming tied to specific pieces of hardware and has been able to address the widest possible marketplace for PC CAD.

Table AD.2 shows the history of the company's growth since its inception.

Figure AD.1
1987 Personal Computer CAD/CAM CAE for Mechanical and Architectural Applications

Market Share by Net Revenues
Source: Daratech, Inc. Cambridge, Mass.

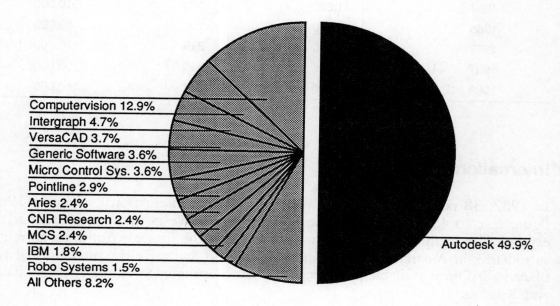

Computervision 12.9%
Intergraph 4.7%
VersaCAD 3.7%
Generic Software 3.6%
Micro Control Sys. 3.6%
Pointline 2.9%
Aries 2.4%
CNR Research 2.4%
MCS 2.4%
IBM 1.8%
Robo Systems 1.5%
All Others 8.2%

Autodesk 49.9%

Autodesk, Inc., 1988 Annual Report, p. 4

Table AD.1
Products Produced by Autodesk

AutoCAD®
General purpose software for PCs and engineering workstations

AutoSketch®
Entry-level, object-oriented CAD program

AutoSolid®
Desktop solid-modeling software for MCAE applications

AutoShade®
3-D rendering software that produces realistic color-shaded images

AutoCAD AEC Architectural®
Add-on package that adapts AutoCAD for architectural applications

AutoFlix T.M.
Animation program that turns AutoCAD, AutoShade, and AutoSketch images into movies or interactive presentations

Table AD.2
Growth in Sales and Employees at Autodesk, 1983 to 1988

Fiscal Year	Sales ($000)	Employees	AutoCAD Installations
1983	15	26	50
1984	1,200	104	10,000
1985	9,800	190	35,000
1986	29,500	313	50,000
1987	52,300	399	100,000
1988	79,200	414	150,000

International Operations

In 1987, 38 percent of revenues were generated by international sales. In 1988, this figure rose to 43 percent. Autodesk is very aggressive in the international arena and expects sales in this sector to grow even faster in the future. Autodesk currently has subsidiaries in Australia, UK, Japan, Sweden, and Switzerland. International versions of AutoCAD are available in French, German, Japanese, Swedish, Spanish, Italian, and Russian.

Dealer Network

Autodesk has more than 1500 dealers worldwide. By providing technical training, financial incentives, and co-op advertising, and by building goodwill, Autodesk has built up a dealer network that has become the envy of the industry. This has been an important factor in AutoCAD's dominance in the market.

According to the *Business Week* article, a key to Autodesk's success stems from this strategy. Using dealers instead of high-priced salespeople to call on accounts differentiates Autodesk from the competition. In effect, Autodesk established a new channel of distribution for CAD software by following the general practice in the PC market. When the large corporate accounts came along, Autodesk set up a plan to let the dealers share in the commissions and did not jeopardize their bread-and-butter channel.

Financial Information

With regard to public offerings, Autodesk went public in 1985 with an IPO at $11/share. A second public offering in 1987 raised an additional $57 million. The shares have been trading around the $30 mark in 1988 after a three-to-one split.

In terms of acquisitions, in addition to diversifying their product base internally, Autodesk has been using their strong cash position to secure related technologies by acquiring small high-technology companies. In 1987, Autodesk acquired Cadetron, Inc. for the company's solid modeling technology and Xanadu Corp. to capture their information management (hypermedia) know-how.

A financial statement for Autodesk is shown in Table AD.3.

Evolution of MIS at Autodesk

Initially, all Autodesk business records were maintained manually on a system of ledger cards. Orders were normally received by phone and recorded manually in a commercial blue book of order forms. The product manufacturing was already complex because of the number of different target devices that were supported, number of different optional features that could be purchased, and the different discount levels at which product was sold. This complexity in manufacturing and order processing was further confounded by frequent releases of product revisions and the need to serialize the software as a means of protection against illegal copy distribution by others. As a result, virtually every order had to be treated as a custom order.

Orders were normally taken by phone and recorded manually in an order book. They were then delivered to production, where the staff cut the appropriate disks, serialized the program, packaged the disks with the relevant manuals (in three-ring binders), and shrink-wrapped the entire package. The product was then packed for shipment via United Parcel Service (UPS). At this point the invoice and packing slip were prepared by typewriter. One copy of each was enclosed with the shipment and two were filed. Credit shipments were recorded on customer ledger cards.

This order entry system took a long time to process and was prone to errors and delays. Customer queries about the orders were not easily answered.

As Autodesk began to grow in 1984, orders from dealers and end users began to pour in by phone and mail. It soon became apparent that a computerized order-entry system was needed. Being a high-tech company with lots of programmers and computers in-house, Autodesk felt that MIS functions, such as order-entry system design and implementation, could be handled by the staff in an unstructured way.

Table AD.3
Financial Statement (in thousands of dollars except per share amounts)

Description	1988	1987
Income Statement		
Revenue:		
Sales	$79,257	$52,382
Cost of sales	10,552	7,864
Gross margin	68,705	44,518
Expenses:		
Marketing and sales	19,641	12,465
Research and development	7,206	3,366
General and administrative	10,649	7,049
Total	37,496	22,880
NOI (Net Operating Income)	31,209	21,638
Income from other than operations	3,838	1,287
EBIT (Earnings before income and taxes)	35,047	22,925
Interest Expense	0	0
Taxes	14,506	11,305
NIAT (Net income after taxes)	20,541	11,620
Shares number outstanding (000)	23,180	21,030
Income per share	0.89	0.55
Balance Sheet		
Current Assets:		
Cash and marketable securities	$ 96,631	$ 24,301
Accounts receivable	11,353	8,130
Inventory	1,712	1,123
Prepaid taxes and expenses	3,880	1,918
Total current assets	113,576	35,472
Fixed Assets:		
Furniture and equipment	11,432	4,927
Less accum. depreciation	(3,886)	(1,429)
Capitalized software	1,668	395
Other assets	2,661	982
Total fixed assets	11,875	4,875
Total Assets	**$125,451**	**$ 40,347**
Current Liabilities:		
Accounts payable	$ 2,327	$ 1,438
Accrued compensation	1,016	594
Income tax payable	3,181	2,390
Other current liabilities	2,334	1,133
Total current liabilities	8,858	5,555
Long-term Debt:		
Deferred income taxes	1,548	500
Other	280	310
Total LTD	1,828	810
Shareholders' Equity:		
Retained earnings	40,082	19,870
Common stock	72,897	13,355
Foreign currency translation adj.	1,786	757
Total shareholders equity	114,765	33,982
Total Liabilities and Equity	**$125,451**	**$40,347**

Computers at Autodesk

By the time the MIS department was established in 1986, Autodesk had several hundred computers of a dozen different makes. Most were IBM PC XT or AT machines and clones. Other makes included S-100 machines, Sun Microsystems workstations, MicroVAX supermicros from DEC, and computers from Apple Computer and Atari. The majority of the systems were used for product development; some were used for office and MIS functions, and still others were used for both.

Development of a Formal MIS

A fresh start at an MIS presents a challenge and an opportunity. Autodesk had to pull together a cohesive MIS out of seeming disarray. On the other hand, in the absence of extant policy and procedures, Autodesk could design a system that matched current technology to the company's information needs.

There was one potential problem. Being an MIS manager for a high-tech company meant that many of the system's users were likely to be computer professionals. This meant they would be very technically oriented and they would have opinions and prejudices about MIS architecture, database systems, and information technology that could interfere with the plans of the MIS designer. The job was not for someone whose technical competency could be tested or questioned. This problem was solved by hiring an MIS manager who reported to the president as the head of a separate department.

Segregating MIS from Development Systems

Autodesk decided that the initial task would be to (a) set up a network to connect all their computers into one system, (b) set up a corporate MIS database, and (c) draw clear and unambiguous boundaries between the development system and the information system.

The seminal and perhaps controversial decision Autodesk made at the very outset was to design an information system framework for Autodesk that would use only PCs. There would be no minis or mainframes in the MIS, only PCs and networking. It was a bold and innovative move.

Autodesk believes that PCs offer more computing power per dollar than any other hardware environment available. Besides, they are easy to use and have a large base of sophisticated and inexpensive software. Multiplicity of units provides redundancy in case of breakdown, resulting in a very high uptime for the system as a whole.

It is interesting to note here that the old school of thought considers software that is difficult to use to be more sophisticated. The new generation of MIS executives holds a different view. Software that offers equal functionality but that has been programmed to be easier to use (by end users) has to be more sophisticated than software that is easier to program but that requires sophisticated users who can follow its complex syntax.

Users today are accustomed to powerful, useful software that anyone can learn to use in a matter of hours. The new word for sophistication in software is *slick* and refers to a well thought out and intuitive user interface in combination with useful functions and bug-free operation. The mainframe environment has been slow to respond to this shift in the winds.

The Network

Autodesk implemented a company-wide PC network consisting of two parts connected by a bridge: a 3Com system for MIS and a UNIX system for technical users and software development. These networks were linked using a microwave bridge, a configuration that effectively segregates the two hardware environments but retains connectivity for occasional data and file transfer operations.

The development network consists of about 50 devices in a UNIX network running at 10 megabits/second data transfer rate. It is served by a Sun file server and serves a variety of dissimilar devices, including Apollo and MicroVAX mini computers and Sun Microsystems workstations in addition to Macintosh II and IBM PC AT and IBM-compatible 386 machines. The IBM PC-type machines at Autodesk are mostly compatibles or so-called clones. Their 386 machine of choice is the Compaq.

Buildings 2320 and 2330 were connected into one MIS network also operating at 10 megabits. The two buildings are connected via underground conduit, since they are only about 50 meters apart, separated only by a portion of the parking lot. The two networks are connected via a microwave bridge carrying 40 phone channels and operating at the reduced speed of 3 megabits/second.

The MIS network consists of roughly 400 devices including about 330 workstations, 40 printers, and 35 file servers. On the whole the system runs efficiently, with very little downtime and excellent network response. Many of these workstations are Compaq 286 and 386 machines, utilizing the Intel 80286 CPU chip and the Intel 80386 CPU chip, respectively. The servers are a mix of Compaq and proprietary 3Com devices supplied by the network vendor. Each has a 386 processor, 2 megabytes of RAM, 450-megabyte hard-disk storage partitioned into three logical 150-megabyte devices, and a 150-megabyte streaming tape backup unit. The 3Com servers are preferred over DOS machines because of their larger disk storage and RAM addressing capacity.

The IBM PC DOS versions 3.X and earlier limit the directly addressed RAM to 640 kilobytes and disk storage to 32 megabytes. As you will see in other case studies, this turns out to be a very serious limitation in large-scale networking and corporate MIS environments. Other companies, for instance, have had to resort to a MicroVAX network server at considerable expense to skirt this problem. A cost-performance comparison between the MicroVAX server and the 3Com server options would be an interesting exercise. With their proprietary servers, 3Com can break this barrier, allowing up to 250 megabytes in a disk partition.

Software

In addition to the 3Com network software, the principal software packages used at Autodesk are as follows:

Autodesk chose the Foxbase fourth-generation language database program as the foundation on which to build their MIS. Not only is it compatible with their accounting package, it provides a powerful dBASE-like relational database that compiles to yield fast run-time modules. But its most important attribute is that its data structure uses both record- and file-level interlock and supports the use of a common database across a network by multiple users. This was a critical criterion necessary to fulfill the needs of an MIS or corporate database. Almost all the software development by the MIS department is done in Foxbase. The final applications implemented are a mixture of purchased Foxbase packages and in-house development. The in-house Foxbase programmers provide complete application packages in addition to customization and patches to purchased canned software.

The MIS database with manufacturing and accounting functions is programmed on Foxbase and runs across the network in a noncritical implementation. The package is tailored for a distributed environment and maintains records for and provides reports of accounts receivable, accounts payable, order processing, and general ledger.

Lotus 1-2-3 is the software most used by Autodesk management. Top- and middle-level managers use Lotus to prepare everything from expense accounts to summaries of financial analyses and sales forecasting.

Word from Microsoft is the word processing software used at Autodesk. In addition to providing common databases, network services include electronic mail, automatic file backup, file transfer, and network help.

Management Support Strategy

The MIS department consists of nineteen people, including six programmer/analysts. These six analysts serve a key function in the MIS implementation. Each is assigned to an individual department and maintains a one-to-one relationship with the department (see Figure AD.2). Their responsibilities consist primarily of providing user support, hardware and software debugs, and software development. Their job is to understand the function and information needs of their assigned department and, in essence, to be "their person" in MIS. As such, an important role of these analysts is to analyze information needs and design and implement systems to meet these needs. Additional programmers and technical personnel are used for routine tasks including systems programming, operation, backups, routine coding, documentation, and support.

The departments directly supported by MIS are management, customer support, sales, accounting, marketing, purchasing, product support and product management (see Table AD.4). Management includes top executives and strategic decision makers of the firm whose primary needs are oriented toward decision support systems (DSSs) and executive information systems (EISs).

From a management perspective, department activities are distinguished from functions and goals. Activities are those things people do on a day-to-day basis that are designed, in the long run, to accomplish the functions and achieve the goals of the department. Although DSS designers pay particular attention to functions and goals, MIS designers must also study the activities, because it is these activities that must be directly supported by the information system on a day-to-day basis.

As in most successful software companies today, the product support department is a large and important operation in Autodesk. The staff answer technical questions from users and dealers over the telephone. In addition, they provide training courses and interact with user groups and the CompuServe bulletin board on AutoCAD to make sure that all user queries are answered. A crucial function of this department is to process, distill, and synthesize user feedback and feed this information to marketing, production, and R & D.

The information needs of product support relate to producing bug reports and making a large amount of technical information available to the people on the phones. They also maintain training-schedule and enrollment data and dispense publications about the training program.

The sales department is the critical line of communication with Autodesk's lifeline — its more than 1500 dealers. Most of the activity consists of taking phone and mail orders and routing them to production promptly and with the correct product, shipping, and billing information. Business and dealer goodwill may be lost by unnecessary delays caused when orders are mixed up or lost. The functions of the customer service group include expediting orders, tracing lost orders, reshipping damaged or incomplete orders, and generally taking care of the dealers and making them feel comfortable.

Of course, the sales staff are the users of one of the standard MIS products, the order-entry system. They need a dealer and order database and need to know production backlogs and turnaround. They also need call-logging, since many small

Figure AD.2
Autodesk MIS Relationship to Other Departments

nonrevenue items promised to dealers (such as a user manual or a fix-disk) can be easily missed.

The marketing department activities have to do predominately with advertising, promotion, trade shows, and AutoCAD expositions. Their information needs consist largely of effective lead tracking systems, mail list databases, and database searches.

Finance and accounting are in many respects principal clients of MIS in the traditional sense. The Accounting Information System, including A/P (accounts payable), A/R (accounts receivable), G/L (general ledger), and the order processing form the bulk of MIS systems and activities. The A/R package is written in Foxbase. G/L and A/P are on purchased commercial packages. Inventory and shipping information from the production department is fed into the accounting system. In addition to standard financial reports, DSS-type interfaces to the accounting data are needed for managers to be able to make financial decisions involving investments and acquisitions.

In addition to manufacturing product, the production department performs the crucial functions of product serialization, serial number audit, product quality control, and product shipping/expediting. They also produce the source documents that validate the A/R entries. With an increasing product line, the production department is saddled with the increasing complexity and sensitivity of the production operation.

Table AD.4
Autodesk: MIS Requirements

Department	Functions/Activities	MIS Needs
Management	Managing/decision making/ strategy planning	Decision support and executive information systems
Customer support	Technical support for users and dealers	Report generation
		Data retrieval for user support
	Training/interaction with user groups	Generation/maintenance of training schedules, enrollment data, training program information
	Integrating/routing user feedback	
	Monitoring illegitimate acquisition of software	Call-logging/cross-referencing serial numbers
Sales	Order taking	Order/dealer database
	Routing orders to production	Tracking system for turnaround
	Expediting/tracking orders	Call-logging
	Dealer support	
Accounting	Accounts payable	Financial reporting system
	Accounts receivable	Decision and information support for investment managers
	General ledger	
Marketing	Advertising/promotion	Online data: promotional publications, advertising rates, campaign calendar
	Trade shows, expositions	
		Calendar/budget data
Production	Serialization/auditing	Production of invoices
	Production operations	Generation/updating of production schedules and reports
	Quality control	
	Shipping/Expediting	Tracking system for shipping

An MIS Plan for Rapid Growth

Sales Forecast

The current sales forecast calls for continued growth for the next several years (see Figure AD.3). History dictates a rapidly growing environment, but plans for the

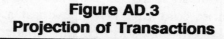

Figure AD.3
Projection of Transactions

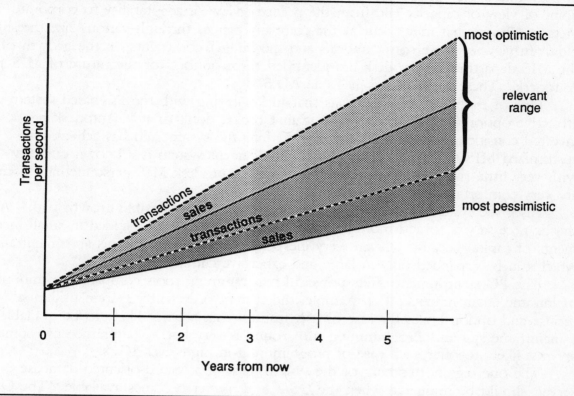

future must also look at the "worst case" scenario. Long-range strategic and operational planning must take both the optimistic and pessimistic scenarios into account.

In the case of the MIS department, planning for the future must be such that the proposed system will not be overloaded in the most optimistic scenario. On the other hand, managers cannot commit the firm to such enormous fixed expenses that the firm will suffer financial adversity, should the most pessimistic forecast come to pass.

An added complexity to the sales forecast has to do with an MIS sizing criterion called *number of transactions*. We must estimate the number of discrete tasks the system will perform per day and per accounting cycle. Normally, the number of transactions is assumed to be linear with sales. However, in this case, we expect the transactions, or activity, curve to be steeper than the strictly linear curve for several reasons. Autodesk is expanding its product line, and adding more products introduces additional complexity to the inventory and the order processing systems, as well as to the manufacturing and serial number auditing system. In addition,

Autodesk management has put an increased emphasis on product traceability, which will require progressively more computer power even at a constant level of sales.

Autodesk's PC-based system may soon become inadequate, both from a strict point of view of capacity and from the point of view of adaptability to corporate metamorphoses that may occur as the company pierces through various size thresholds. In view of these considerations and the budget constraints on the growth of the MIS department, Autodesk has identified three options for the future of MIS at Autodesk. These are outlined in Table AD.5.

One of the main considerations that make staying with the PC-based system an attractive option is that "it works; if it ain't broke, don't fix it." Autodesk has invested considerable capital and manpower into the system and has achieved a customized MIS that meets their needs. The current system is a known quantity with very little risk and virtually no unknowns. Autodesk MIS personnel and users are very comfortable with this system.

Also, the system is inexpensive and provides a highly flexible growth path. All that is necessary is to add more equipment. Equipment can be added in small increments of capital because PCs are very inexpensive compared to minis and mainframes, which can be expanded only in large and expensive chunks.

The PC environment offers powerful programming tools compared to mini and mainframe environments. For example, the current order-entry system utilizes a mouse and option boxes for ease of use, features that are not likely to be available in a mainframe system. Programming turnaround is very fast. Mainframe environments are not likely to offer such ease of programming in high-level 4GLs.

The one big shortcoming of the system, lack of a record-oriented database server, should be mitigated when the OS/2 SQL server becomes available. The OS/2 SQL server will offer true multi-user relational database functionality. OS/2 is likely to become available in the third quarter of 1989. In general, the increase in power of PCs both in hardware and software has been impressive. As the PCs become more powerful, they will meet future needs better.

When end users are the heaviest system users, it is very important to maintain a commonality in the look and feel of the user interface. This has been achieved in large measure at Autodesk.

Autodesk has purchased hundreds of personal computers and associated peripherals to set up the current MIS. The investment is significant and the system cannot be simply abandoned. Staying with the current system would preserve the investment already made in PCs.

In addition, software for PCs is very inexpensive compared to mini and main frame software. This assessment is not based on functionality or power but on simple accounting. The installed base of PCs is so much bigger than that of large computers that the cost of development and support activities of software companies can be distributed among a larger number of customers, each of whom has to pay less.

Table AD.5
MIS Options at Autodesk

Option A:
Stay with current PC-based system
and wait for OS/2 technology

Advantages:
1. Meets the needs of the company
2. Inexpensive and flexible
3. Ease of programming as compared with mainframes
4. Increased capabilities of PC hardware and software
5. Consistency of user interface among various applications
6. Preserves value of previous investments in PCs
7. Lower software costs
8. Preserves value of previous investments in software
9. User familiarity with the current system

Disadvantages:
1. Limitations of PC DOS
2. Strained PC file capacities
3. Limited capabilities as compared with mini computers
4. Difficulty of future hardware upgrades
5. Weak vendor support
6. Need for higher level of computer literacy among users
7. Continued reliance on custom-developed software

Option B:
UNIX-based solution with Sun Microsystems

Advantages:
1. Availability of advanced database software
2. Inherent multi-user capability
3. Larger disk storage capability
4. Benefits of UNIX open architecture
5. Benefits of being a UNIX shop
6. Ease of integrating PCs with UNIX-based minicomputers
7. Potential for integrated systems solution
8. Availability of public domain UNIX software

Disadvantages:
1. Inadequacies of UNIX environment
2. Difficulty of use of UNIX interface as compared with PC interface
3. Necessity to recompile code
4. Risks associated with using an unfamiliar system

Option C:
The VAX/VMX Solution

Advantages:
1. Well known and well regarded; poses little risk
2. Preserves existing investment in PCs
3. Growth capability offered by VAX clusters
4. Guaranteed vendor support for hardware and software
5. Capability to support large-scale businesses
6. Higher performance, higher reliability, and increased up time
7. Benefits of using a centralized machine with remote capabilities

Disadvantages:
1. Expense
2. Restrictions posed by dependence on DEC system
3. Prevents utilization of relational database structure
4. Loss of user-friendly interfaces available of Foxbase system
5. Necessity to train MIS staff in use of VMX system

AutoCAD and AutoLISP are registered in the U. S. Patent and Trademark Office by Autodesk, Inc.

Autodesk has invested heavily in software development in Foxbase for the current system. These programs would have to be rewritten and debugged for a new system or else functions would have to be replaced by the packaged software to be installed.

Lastly, autodesk MIS users are familiar with this system and would require retraining for the new system.

Some arguments against staying with the PC system include the fact that the 32-megabyte file size limitation by PC DOS is a problem for large databases, and the high growth in transaction files and history files are straining PC server capacities. Record locking, data integrity, and multi-user capabilities on network database are still fairly primitive compared to minicomputer capabilities. There is no easy hardware upgrade path in the event of unexpected growth or "maxing out" of a server. Autodesk is already using the most powerful PC servers available.

Also, vendor support is weak compared to minis. This is related to lower costs of hardware and software. Higher user computer literacy is required for PC-based solutions. Continued reliance on custom-developed software would be necessary to a larger degree than with alternate systems.

Considerations that favor the UNIX approach to MIS include the fact that Sybase and Informix, advanced database software with full multi-user capabilities, are now available for UNIX-based systems. Multi-user capability is inherent in this operating system and not a patch created by the network vendor. In addition, large disk storage capability is available. Disk storage capacity is not limited by the operating system.

The open architecture of the UNIX operating system promises continued development in the future both within Autodesk and in the user/developer community as a whole. Also, AutoCAD is written in C and the company developers use UNIX heavily. In this respect, Autodesk is a UNIX shop. If MIS also goes with UNIX, there will be a synergistic relationship with the development programmers. The existing network of PCs can be easily integrated with a UNIX-based minicomputer.

Application packages are available that would give Autodesk an integrated systems solution. Finally, UNIX offers a huge selection of quality public domain software that will be useful to the MIS programmers.

On the other hand, there are some good reasons why UNIX-based MIS would not work at Autodesk: First of all, available application packages for normal MIS functions such as manufacturing, order processing, and accounting are not mature. UNIX is still a programmer's environment. The UNIX user interface is not as friendly as the PC interface. Users accustomed to the PCs will find UNIX systems hard to use, with a long learning curve.

Even though UNIX offers machine independence so that code can migrate from machine to machine on a chosen growth path, frequently the code must be recompiled. For instance, the Sun/3 and the Sun/4, though from the same vendor, are not binary-compatible.

Autodesk MIS personnel are not familiar with UNIX systems and therefore the UNIX approach presents additional risks. The UNIX system is not the known quantity that the PC system is.

The VAX/VMS solution appears to be an ideal answer to Autodesk's problems. It is an extremely well-tested and stable MIS platform with an array of mature application packages. As an MIS machine, the VAX is a known quantity with very little associated risk. DEC offers a 99 percent uptime guarantee with these machines. The VAX has a good reputation and is highly regarded in the MIS community.

The VAX/VMS operating system supports both DECnet and Ethernet networks with IBM PCs and Macintosh personal computers as workstations. This would allow Autodesk to utilize the existing investment in PCs as well as preserve the familiar interface and work environment of the MIS users.

The VAX/VMS solution offers an almost limitless growth path with the availability of larger machines and the use of VAX Clusters (see Part 4).

The vendor offers guaranteed support for both hardware and software and has a very good reputation in the industry. This contrasts sharply with the PC option, which offers inferior support.

Other large and successful software companies use the VAX as their MIS machine. The list includes Microsoft, Lotus, and Digital Research. There is comfort in the notion that this machine is applicable to operating a large-scale software business. The VAX also has a reputation for high performance and high reliability and uptime, factors that are crucial to an MIS designer. (In many ways MIS is like the weather. Nobody notices it when it's good, but everybody complains when it's bad.)

A centralized machine offers many advantages in implementation, development, maintenance, and control to the MIS manager. Additionally, it allows for remote dial-in capabilities for other Autodesk offices and dealers.

However, the VAX installation would present certain difficulties. VAX is the most expensive option. The flexible growth path mentioned above must be added in large chunks. Each of these growth steps is also expensive.

Autodesk would be tied in to DEC's proprietary operating system. This limitation, in contrast to a hardware-independent operating system line UNIX, is restrictive in terms of enhancements and software availability. Growth outside of DEC is limited.

The applications available do not use the relational database structure. This is viewed as a disadvantage for the long run, since the relational database structure is most suitable for the MIS design at Autodesk and a data structure they are familiar with. VAX applications use older file systems and network database schemes as the underlying structure.

Autodesk would lose the user-friendly interfaces they have built up on the current Foxbase system. Although the VAX will allow them to use PCs as workstations, it is unclear to what extent the same user interfaces could be used and how much reprogramming would be required.

The Autodesk MIS department is not familiar with the VMS operating system and would have to go on a learning curve itself as part of the implementation.

Case Study Questions

1. "As the company has grown, MIS has failed to keep pace and continues to cling to the PC-based system." As MIS manager of Autodesk, how would you respond to this criticism?

2. Develop a model to forecast sales and transactions for the next 3 years, using optimistic and pessimistic growth rates. Assume that the number of transactions per dollar of sales will grow at a rate of 10 percent per year. Plot these lines and shade the region between these lines. The shaded region represents the range of information needs for which MIS must budget. What design problems does this uncertainty present?

3. Summarize the arguments for using PCs instead of larger machines in the MIS. As a senior Autodesk manager, what concerns might you have in this regard?

4. Assume that you are the MIS manager at Autodesk. Compare the three alternatives given and write a report to top managers with your recommendation.

5. Many medium-sized manufacturing firms are operated quite successfully with System/38- and HP 3000-based MIS systems. In particular, HP 3000 systems with ASK software are very popular. Develop a fourth alternative using one of these systems and compare it to the three options presented.

6. The case refers to special problems faced by MIS staff in high-tech firms in which the users are sophisticated computer users. What sort of problems might one encounter? What are the advantages of such a user environment?

7. The alternatives presented for future MIS capacity planning at Autodesk imply that they are mutually exclusive. Develop an alternative that combines the best attributes of the VAX and PC options.

WAL-MART

WAL-MART STORES, INC.

Electronic Data Interchange:
Toward a Paperless Economy

"I have a feeling we're not in Kansas anymore."
— Dorothy in *The Wizard of Oz*

Information Technology Holds It Together

Drive down a country road to Bentonville, Arkansas, pull into an ordinary-looking parking lot, enter what appears to be an ordinary office building, and you will find yourself standing in the eye of the world's largest private, fully integrated satellite network. This is the electronic nerve center of Wal-Mart Stores, Inc. From here, one can almost feel the pulse of this $20-billion retailing powerhouse that came literally out of nowhere to join in the discount merchandising market in head-to-head competition with such established industry stalwarts as K-Mart, Sears, and JCPenney.

The satellite network connects the Wal-Mart MIS to every Wal-Mart store and distribution center in 26 states, using video, audio, and data signals via more than 1400 earth stations. It maintains instant communication between the firm's information center and all its operations and suppliers. With this network, every store is, in effect, "plugged in" to the corporate nerve center at Bentonville so that each transaction can be made "online." For example, when a customer at a store in Topeka, Kansas uses a charge card, the credit card number is flashed electronically to Bentonville through the network, the bank is electronically contacted, an electronic approval is obtained, and the authorization is then sent back down to the store. The entire process takes less than 6 seconds.

The network is targeted toward providing better customer service not only in speeding credit card transactions but in improving business efficiency and monitoring inventory and movement, tracking trends item by item, and ensuring product flow from supplier to distribution center to stores to guarantee that products in demand are flowing in at the desired rate. The result? An enviable in-stock rate, a high asset utilization ratio, and industry leadership in keeping waste and costs down and keeping productivity and profits high. The high asset utilization contributes to a healthy (return on equity) ROE value of more than 37 percent.

Bentonville, Arkansas, is sometimes said to closely approximate the proverbial *nowhere*. Yet, with an arsenal of satellite dishes and computers and an army of information specialists, Wal-Mart operates a far-flung empire of over a thousand stores located throughout 26 states. The firm has achieved spectacular success by running a tight ship with a high degree of managerial control. In doing so, Wal-Mart has ushered in a new paradigm of the American corporation. Information technology has obviated the need to locate headquarters in large urban commercial centers.

In this case study, we will peek into the MIS department of Wal-Mart to appreciate the role it plays in this unique organization. By studying their use of EDI (Electronic Data Interchange) for business transactions, we will see how new technology in computing and data communications has been used to bridge geographical barriers and enhance managerial control and overall integration of a dispersed business enterprise to achieve lower cost of operations. Information is a vital ingredient in the retail business, especially in discount merchandising, where competition is based on price and cost is everything.

Wal-Mart has achieved low-cost leadership in the industry by combining common sense and information technology. The company's sale circulars list the same "everyday low prices" (no "sale" prices), cutting the cost of advertising. Because of the sheer volume of data, the satellite network is much less expensive per byte than alternate means such as leased telephone lines. The result is that even when Wal-Mart cuts prices, sales and profits continue to increase.

The Rise of Wal-Mart: "The Customer Is the Boss"

The success of Wal-Mart and its unique corporate character has been ascribed to the energy and philosophy of its enigmatic founder and chairman. His unique management style and approach to retailing has propelled Wal-Mart into national prominece.

Wal-Mart is a no-frills discount merchandiser offering everything from apparel and household items to drugs, electronic goods, sporting goods, cosmetics, jewelry, toys, and hardware at bargain prices. The store's motto, Low Prices Every Day, underscores its primary marketing strategy and target.

Chairman of the Board Sam Walton identifies as reasons for the success of the company "our people" ("The answer is so simple, yet very few people really understand it: our people make the difference") and "our customers" ("The customer can fire everybody in the company from the chairman on down and he can do it simply by spending his money somewhere else").

With this simple business philosophy and a yen for the retail industry Walton turned a "5-and-10" store in Bentonville into a multibillion-dollar retailing giant.

Company History

Sam Walton's retailing career began with a position as a manager trainee with the JCPenney Company in 1940. After the war, he operated Ben Franklin franchise stores in several Arkansas locations, joining forces with his brother, "Bud" Walton. In 1961, unable to convince Ben Franklin management to try an innovative discount merchandising format, Sam opened his own discount store in Rogers, Arkansas. The venture was immediately successful and in 1962 he formed Wal-Mart Stores, Inc. and began to spawn new discount stores throughout a four-state area (Arkansas, Oklahoma, Missouri, Kansas). In 1970, with 18 stores and $44 million in sales, the company went public and constructed its present-day headquarters and distribution center at Bentonville.

By the end of the decade, the company had grown to 276 stores in eleven states, with annual sales well over the billion dollar mark. The expansion included two major acquisitions and penetration into other markets such as shoes and auto service.

The 1980s saw a very aggressive growth curve for the company, which multiplied its size by opening new stores and by acquisition. The growth pattern is chronicled year by year in Table W.1.

The annual report for the fiscal year ending on January 31, 1988 shows 1114 stores in Alabama, Arkansas, Colorado, Florida, Georgia, Illinois, Indiana, Iowa, Kansas, Kentucky, Louisiana, Minnesota, Mississippi, Missouri, Nebraska, New Mexico, North Carolina, Oklahoma, South Carolina, Tennessee, Texas, Virginia, and Wisconsin. Net annual sales had grown to $15.96 billion. Reported sales for fiscal 1989 are $20.65 billion from a total of 1382 retail outlets which include 1259 Wal-Mart stores.

The distribution system plays a pivotal role in Wal-Mart's strategy. By the close of 1988, the company was operating 16 distribution centers throughout its marketing region. These included six in Arkansas, three in Texas, and additional centers in Iowa, Louisiana, Mississippi, Alabama, Georgia, and South Carolina. When a purchase is made from a vendor, the goods are delivered to one or more of these distribution centers, which are strategically located to serve the expanding network of retail stores. More than 80 percent of all store merchandise are replenished from the distribution centers, saving middleman costs.

The firm prefers to deal directly with the manufacturer of the goods and eliminate as many distribution channel markups as possible. There are important reasons other than cost considerations for this policy. Wal-Mart works very closely with its vendors to control product quality and to automate and streamline the supply lines. For example, they require that vendors connect to their EDI system. Manufacturer's representatives simply do not have the knowledge or the authority to negotiate terms at such levels. Such prudent business practices, augmented by a high level of automation, have helped Wal-Mart achieve the lowest distribution costs in the industry.

Table W.1
Wal-Mart Stores, Inc. New Stores, 1980-1987

Year	New Stores Opened	
1980	54	
1981	161	(92 by acquisiiton)
1982	60	
1983	91	
1984	103	
1985	114	
1986	121	
1987	120	

Although distribution is decentralized, management, data, and control are highly centralized at the corporate headquarters in Bentonville. The policy to centralize has significant consequences for MIS, as we shall see. The centralized control structure means that every transaction, every individual inventory item, every individual sale in Wal-Mart's 1300-plus stores is tracked, stored, analyzed, summarized, and printed into reports at the data center in Bentonville. The sheer volume of the bits that are necessary to carry out such an operation over a large geographical region presented unique challenges to the MIS designers at Wal-Mart. They have answered these challenges by building the world's largest satellite network to tie more than a thousand stores into one, huge, logical "store" managed from one control point.

The company's growth has been phenomenal. Rapid growth continues with the addition of new Wal-Mart stores at the dizzying rate of one every two days. In the time that it took to generate this case study, more than 50 new Wal-Mart stores were opened. The growth in sales since 1968 is shown in Table W.2.

Next to each column of figures are the annualized growth rates (percentage of growth per year). The table shows that Wal-Mart has sustained its growth not only by opening more stores but also by steadily increasing sales per store. In the last decade, almost a thousand new stores have opened and during the same period the sales per store have more than quadrupled.

This growth points to the increasing complexity of Wal-Mart's business. The stores are becoming bigger and more multi-faceted, as shown by the size of the stores in square feet, the total inventory being carried, the number of different items in the inventory, and the number of different kinds of business activities and market segments being addressed. In the period covered in the table, store sizes have gone from less than 30,000 square feet to more than 80,000 square feet.

Sam's Wholesale Club and Hypermart*USA represent ventures into new market segments, new retailing strategies, and innovative store formats. These operations present new MIS challenges in information integration and centralization as a large, dispersed, and diverse business becomes even more diverse.

Table W.2
Wal-Mart Stores, Inc. Sales, 1968-1989

Year	No. of Stores	% of Growth	Sales ($ milliions/yr)	% of Growth	Sales/Store ($ millions/yr)	% of Growth/yr
1968	24		$13		$0.542	
1973	64	22%	$125	57%	$1.953	29%
1978	195	25%	$678	40%	$3.477	12%
1983	551	23%	$3,400	38%	$6.171	12%
1987	980	12%	$11,910	37%	$12.153	18%
1988	1114	3%	$15,950	34%	$14.318	18%
1989*	1231	2%	$20,500	29%	$16.653	16%

* projected figures

Hypermart*USA is a variant of the so-called Hypermarket format of retailing, which uses large store sizes and combines supermarket (groceries) and general merchandising under one roof to achieve certain economies of scale. This approach has been tried in the past in the U.S. without much success (Fed-Mart and Carrefour) but has flourished elsewhere, most notably in Canada (Hudson Bay Company) and in France (Carrefour). The new formula being tried by both Wal-Mart and K-Mart features monstrous store size and emphasizes deep-cut discounting in collaboration with an existing discount grocer.

Wal-Mart's arrangement employs a collaboration with Cullum Supermarket in a store exceeding 200,000 square feet. The prices are kept low not only by cost cutting in packaging and shelving design but also by using very low margins. The format combines all the features and retailing savvy of Wal-Mart stores, Sam's Wholesale Clubs, and Cullum Supermarkets. The stores shelve about 60,000 stock units, divided about 40/20 between merchandise and food items, and generate revenues of about $100 million annually. Advertising has emphasized the convenience of "one-stop-shopping" and low prices. The store format and way of doing business is new and is expected to test the firm's MIS and control mechanisms. For example, the grocery segment adds new inventory items, new suppliers, new ways of doing business, and new measures of performance and control.

"Sam's," the wholesale club business, makes use of yet another emerging retail format in America. The club format uses large warehouse-style outlets that bring near-wholesale prices to consumers who wish to buy in bulk from forklift pallets and forego the display and packaging of normal retail stores. This approach has been a very fruitful venture for Wal-Mart. The wholesale club format has matured beyond the experimental stage and currently contributes significantly to the overall revenue. In 1988, the firm operated 105 of these stores, with sales of almost $4 billion or over 20% of total revenues. Further diversification within the retail format has included addition of jewelry stores, shoes stores, and even craft shops.

Wal-Mart has identified the average working-class American as the target consumer. As such, the chain stresses low cost and low prices to its consumers and downplays fancy shopping frills that would add costs without providing equal value to these consumers. The firm's long-term strategy is to keep pace with changes in the retail buying habits of its targeted consumer group.

Success in retailing requires staying abreast of changing political, economic, and social conditions that affect consumer attitudes, expectations, and objectives. Retail businesses that attach themselves to the format rather than to the market will atrophy when their customers' shopping habits change. Wal-Mart has chosen a broader self-definition. The firm will not, therefore, rise and fall with evolutionary changes in retail formats but only with the fortunes of its customers — working Americans.

Keeping Working-Americans Working

In the long run, the success of the business will depend on the size and buying power of this consumer group. As part of its long-term corporate strategy, Wal-Mart has decided to actively participate in helping to sustain this power with its "Buy American" program. Founder Sam Walton's passion for selling more goods made in the U.S. and for creating more jobs at home has resulted in a corporate strategy that is tilted towards domestic suppliers. Wal-Mart works closely with its suppliers to help them achieve cost-effectiveness and even to replicate products currently made overseas.

A company that buys tens of billions dollars of merchandise per year can indeed foster significant economic changes in the region it serves. The objective of the "Buy American" program is to induce American manufacturers to produce products that they had given up to foreign competitors. Wal-Mart buyers are instructed to buy from manufacturers that employ Americans whenever possible except in cases where the quality and price are significantly different. The suppliers are forced by the purchase contracts to improve their products and their productivity and to become more competitive with foreign manufacturers.

This policy extends to domestic suppliers the special advantages normally enjoyed only by foreign suppliers. For instance, foreign manufacturers are usually given long-term contracts and prompt payment. The Wal-Mart "Buy American" plan makes the same terms available to American suppliers. Wal-Mart estimates that since 1985, more than a billion dollars of foreign goods have been replaced by U.S.-made goods as a direct result of this policy. Using the Department of Commerce ratio of 23 jobs per $1 million in sales revenue, Wal-Mart estimates that 42,000 new jobs have been created for Americans.

In a stroke of marketing genius, Wal-Mart heavily promotes their "Made in USA" program at each store and displays on U.S.-made products large red and blue banners showing the number of new jobs created in America as a result of Wal-

Mart's purchase of that particular product at home. This display is viewed with patriotic fervor by customers who feel that their jobs are threatened by unfair competition from overseas. The "Buy American" program therefore strengthens the economic base and buying power of its customers and at the same time creates goodwill among them.

Although this technique is effective as a business strategy, there is considerable evidence that the firm is genuinely concerned about the trade deficit and the plight of the American worker. The program is ultimately conceived in patriotism and a desire to create new jobs here at home.

Wal-Mart's MIS: Hardware/Software/Humanware

Wal-Mart's MIS is an IBM-based system that utilizes two 3090 mainframes in tandem to achieve a total computing power of 120 MIPS. The operating system is IBM's MVS/XA (Multiple Virtual Storage Extended Architecture) with CICS (Customer Information Control System) to facilitate real-time terminal access and transaction processing. More than 300 gigabytes of data are available online. Two hundred data lines support more than 35,000 online terminals, including all POS terminals at the stores. The system processes over two million transactions per day. It is located at the central office in Bentonville, where it is operated, maintained, and supported by an IS team of roughly 400.

A notable feature of the Wal-Mart MIS is the amount of direct electronic control and monitoring that can be exercised from the corporate headquarters. The enormous computing and data communication power concentrated at Bentonville makes this possible. Each store is fitted with a communication controller and a satellite dish. The POS terminals are connected to an in-store mini computer (micro in some cases). The store computer is connected with the satellite network via a communications controller and can be accessed directly by the corporate mainframes at Bentonville. The mainframes will pull sales information, item movement data, performance information, and payroll data and push POS/UPC data, price changes, and programming changes. The CICS communication lines are open from 5 a.m. to 2 a.m.; other communication lines are open around the clock. Although the information from the stores follows a store-and-forward operation, in many critical services such as credit card verification, the data moves in real time.

This architecture is not quite the same as the conventional distributed systems used by many retail chains. In the conventional scheme, as at Wal-Mart, each store is operated by a small mini or super-micro computer that monitors the POS ter-minals and maintains the UPC (Universal Product Code) database and price list. Periodically (usually nightly), the store mini contacts the mainframe at the central office and communicates sales and inventory information using standard phone lines or leased lines. At that time, the mainframe may "push" (download) UPC codes and prices. The mechanism maintains communication with the main office and ensures that the store can continue to operate on its own even if the communications channels or the central mainframes go down.

The difference is in the connectivity between the stores and the mainframe. Using the dedicated satellite network, the mainframes at Bentonville can monitor and update the in-store minis as frequently as necessary 24 hours a day. As a result, Wal-Mart is able to maintain a higher level of control and chain-wide uniformity in prices and store policy from transaction to transaction. A price change made at Bentonville can immediately affect all POS terminals in all stores. Some links, such as that used for credit verification, use real-time direct links between stores and Bentonville. Varying degrees of interactive to batch communications occur between Bentonville, and stores and distribution centers around the clock. All of this traffic is controlled from Bentonville using asynchronous communication on a regular pull/push schedule although stores may initiate synchronous traffic.

Because the chain is vulnerable to failure of either the satellite communications network or the home office mainframes, Wal-Mart has taken steps to minimize this possibility. First, it operates two 3090s in tandem. If one goes down, the other will pick up the load. Although response time will be high for a period of time, the network will be functional. Wal-Mart has a standby diesel power generator at Bentonville so that the satellite network and the mainframes would continue to operate after a power failure. Line voltage is conditioned through a phalanx of batteries before being brought into the computer room. If line voltage fails, the batteries will keep the machines running for the critical minutes needed to bring the diesel generator online. An underground tank of diesel fuel waits at the ready.

In spite of its centralized high-connectivity command center at Bentonville, Wal-Mart's total computing power is actually geographically and functionally dispersed in a highly distributed architecture. In terms of pure CPU capacity, there are only 120 MIPS at the headquarters compared with 140 MIPS in the distribution centers and over 1500 MIPS at the stores. Each store contains an IBM Series/1 computer that manages the POS terminals as well as communications with the satellite network. About 200 stores have microcomputers for special functions such as management of layaway plans. The sixteen distribution centers operate their own information centers. Each maintains its own IBM 4381 midrange mainframe with the MVS/XA/-CICS operating system. These operate fully automated warehouses and maintain accurate real-time inventory and shipping records; and of course they are plugged into Wal-Mart's satellite network.

All communication between stores and distribution centers is via Bentonville. A store manager can use a hand-held terminal to enter his orders. Orders from all stores are received over the network at Bentonville, where they are recorded, approved, and forwarded electronically to the 4381s at the appropriate distribution centers. (The location of a distribution center is selected automatically by taking various factors into consideration such as geography.) At the distribution center, orders are processed by producing picking lists. The goods are loaded onto the designated truck, and picking and shipping information is sent to Bentonville. Thus, even though computing power is distributed, control is not compromised, as Bentonville serves as the hub of the network, monitoring and controlling all traffic.

Electronic Data Interchange

Information is a key commodity in effective discount merchandising in today's intense competitive environment. In head-to-head competition between discount retailers the key ingredient is price. Other important factors include cleanliness, friendliness, trust, and service. Customer service provided by Wal-Mart is unconventional by the standards of the discount industry. (For example, Wal-Mart offers completely "hassle-free" returns of merchandise, a service that one would normally expect to receive only at more pricey department stores.)

Nevertheless, in competitive discount merchandising the retailer that can keep costs lower than the competition's will win out. One way to keep costs down is to reach higher efficiencies of operation through automation. Automation in retailing implies the use of UPC with scanners at POS terminals and effective communication between operations and MIS and between the retailer and its suppliers. A practical retail MIS can spot trends and alert managers through online control of all sales, purchases, inventory, scheduling, and movement of stock. To keep stocks flowing smoothly from suppliers to distribution centers Wal-Mart has automated its purchasing and has achieved a high level of communication with its suppliers by the use of a standardized form transmission protocol called EDI.

EDI (Electronic Data Interchange) as formalized by the ANSI (American National Standards Institute) X.12 committee and the VICS (Voluntary Inter-industry Communications Standards) offers a way to reduce the amount of paperwork necessary to carry out business transactions with other businesses through the use of standardized communication protocols and product identification techniques. UPC is a technique of representing numbers by the use of dark bars on a light background, which can be read by laser scanners to identify all merchandise at every point in its journey from manufacturer to retailer to customer. EDI is a standard way of sending business forms such as purchase orders, shipping slips, remittance advice, order acknowledgments, and invoices from one computer to another by using electronic mail technology.

Wal-Mart's purpose in using EDI is to improve service to the customer by increasing the overall "in-stock" rate at minimum inventory levels, as well as by reducing the prices he or she will pay by reducing costs and improving productivity. In general, the use of EDI improves communications with vendors, reduces paperwork and associated costs, and shortens the product pipeline. Accurate inventory data, reduced stock counts, and faster POS transactions result in reduced markups and increased sales.

Though EDI initially was slow to catch on because of a dismal lack of standards, the ANSI X.12 and the VICS standards have accelerated the use of electronic forms in the retail trade as a means of cutting costs of transactions and gaining greater control of the supply pipeline. The reduced transaction costs make it more feasible to use JIT (Just In Time) and QR (Quick Response) techniques in purchasing and to simultaneously reduce costs and increase product availability.

Printed Forms: The Paper Chase, Business-Style

Under the very nose of the great electronic information revolution, American companies are sending each other literally tons of forms every day printed on paper to record business transactions. Our initial attempt to improve this process using computer technology has been mired in conceptual limitations. Instead of getting rid of the paperwork, we used computers to generate more paperwork and to make the paper-form process itself more efficient. We continue to use paper forms as the only acceptable record of a business transaction, a method that is replete with waste, duplication, errors, and inefficiency.

Suppose that Buyer, Inc. wishes to purchase a widget from Vendor Corp. The "computerized" form process would involve the following activities: A purchasing clerk at Buyer enters the data into a computer to generate a purchase order. The computer now contains the details of the purchase, such as items ordered, the quantity of each, the price of the items, method and cost of shipping, ship-to and bill-to addresses, terms of payment, total amount of the purchase order, and so on. Buyer's computer then prints out the order on paper in multiple copies. At least one copy is filed by the purchasing department, and at least one copy is mailed to Vendor.

In one to four days, the U.S. mail delivers the purchase order to Vendor. An order-entry clerk then sits down at a computer terminal at Vendor and enters the data from the printed purchase order into Vendor's computer. Recall that the data already exist in digital form in Buyer's computer. Vendor's computer then prints out an order acknowledgment form, which specifies that the order has been received and will be filled according to the stated delivery schedule and payment terms. A copy of this form is filed and another copy is mailed to Buyer, where it is also filed.

When the order is shipped, a Vendor order clerk pulls up information from the order-entry system into an invoice, enters any changes and additional information that is required, and prints out two more forms: the invoice and the shipping advice (slip). A copy of the shipping advice is attached to the widgets being shipped and another is filed. A copy of the invoice is mailed to Buyer and another copy is filed at Vendor.

Vendor's invoice is entered once again into Buyer's accounts payable system. When the goods are received and payment is authorized, Buyer generates yet another form, the remittance advice form, to inform Vendor that the goods have been received and will be paid according to a specified schedule.

How Information Technology Can Do Away with the Paper Chase

The business forms that businesses send each other include purchase orders, invoices, packing slips, and scores of other related documents. The Department of Defense alone sends out more than 1.4 million bills of lading annually, enough to make a pile more than three times as high as the Empire State Building. These serve as written business contracts that are legally valid. They contain the exact description of the transaction "in writing" and are signed by the appropriate officer of the firm. This legal aspect of business forms has perpetrated their use and will continue to extend their lifespan into the information age.

However, from a business standpoint, these forms are inefficient when compared with electronic data transfer. EDI form transfer does away with paperwork. Generating, filing, and archiving of paperwork consumes a major portion of the activities of the firm's workers but does not necessarily contribute to their functionality. The advantages of paperless EDI business transactions are many and widely recognized. They include the following important considerations:

1. *Does away with paperwork*
   Since EDI does not use printed paper forms, there is no paper and therefore no paperwork. Thus, no physical paper business forms need be printed out, mailed, and filed.

2. *Reduces duplication of data entry*
   When firms do business with each other, most of the output generated by the computers of one firm is manually re-entered into the computer of the other firm. According to Wal-Mart, "statistics show that 75% of one company's output is another company's input." By transferring the information directly from one computer to another using EDI, duplication of data entry is reduced or can be eliminated.

3. *Speeds up business transactions*
   The paperwork method of business transactions requires that a piece of paper be physically moved from one place to another through the mail or otherwise. This movement is subject to mailroom lag time as well as to delays in transport and delivery of the document. Purchase orders can take up to 3 weeks to turn around. EDI transfers are instantaneous in comparison.

4. *Allows "Quick Response" and lowers inventory*
   Because of the reduced lag time, purchasing decisions can be made on a very short time horizon. Quick Response, or QR, is a restocking method that requires close cooperation between retailer and vendor. EDI allows the vendor to react quickly to changes in

inventory counts. Merchandise supply can be matched to consumer demand by placing frequent and rapid tactical reorders. The paper method does not allow the retailer to follow the sales trends very closely and fewer and larger reorders are made to follow trends on a longer time cycle. When using QR, the retailer can lower inventory levels and the associated carrying costs. The accurate history of the inventory and reorder data can be used as a basis for forecasting demand in future periods. The benefits of QR are most notable in stocking of time-sensitive items that need constant replenishment. Using EDI, the demand can be tracked and the supply replenished on a daily basis. This reduces the chances of oversupply or lost business due to undersupply. (Inventory is nothing but a hedge against uncertainty. As uncertainty is reduced, inventory can also be reduced.)

5. *Lowers the cost per transaction*
Elimination of the costs involved in producing, processing, and mailing the paperwork results in a dramatically lower cost per order and lowers the EOQ (economic order quantity) amount. Wal-Mart has identified five areas of cost reduction: reduced inventory carrying costs, savings in data re-entry costs, reduced paperwork expenses, reduced mail expenses, and lower labor costs. The purchasing pattern begins to approach the JIT pattern. Large inventories are replaced by many frequent reorders and items arrive as they are needed for sale.

6. *Better in-stock percentage*
Using EDI, Wal-Mart has achieved in-stock positions approaching 100 percent on some items. (Wal-Mart tracks the in-stock rate on selected items only, so this figure applies only to those items and not to the overall in-stock rate.) By reducing order lead times, stock can be replenished very quickly. The end result is that the store is less likely to be out of any item that is being depleted by heavy demand.

7. *Efficient retailer-vendor communications*
There are many intangible benefits achieved when the communication lines between retailer and vendor are improved. Wal-Mart in particular works very closely with vendors. The company policy is to view vendors as "trading partners" and to establish a symbiotic relationship. This effort is aided by the efficiency of communication afforded by the EDI link.

8. *Better inventory management*

Accurate and timely data on inventory counts and reorder flows lead to better decisions on inventory levels on an item-by-item basis. EDI enhances inventory control and simultaneously reduces inventory costs and increases item availability.

The Need for Standards

Although most businesses are enthusiastic about the advantages of paperless electronic transactions, the movement to EDI has been slow, not only because of the standards issue but also because EDI changes the way business transactions are conducted. It is not just a DP issue but one that involves the whole company from top management to purchasing, sales, finance, accounting, and the legal department. Therefore, the move to EDI is not simply an MIS decision but one that requires total involvement and commitment from the firm.

EDI was originally put into use by McDonnell Douglas in the 70s but was slow to catch on with other firms because of the reasons mentioned previously, as well as a debilitating lack of standards. Although most business transaction documents were similar, they varied sufficiently so that no common basis existed for electronic data interchange between firms on a consistent basis. To build such a common basis, all firms that do business with each other must use exactly the same format in their business forms and must use the same data communication protocols. However, the EDI that were in use historically used proprietary methods that were designed in isolation. The EDI formats and protocols differed not only from industry to industry but also among firms in the same industry. Without a common basis for data communication and form interpretation, the EDI revolution stalled.

This situation was relieved somewhat when ANSI formed a committee for EDI standards and issued the initial set of ANSI X.12 standards. These established communication protocols and document formats for purchase orders, invoices, and most other business forms that were generic in nature and could be used, theoretically, by any industry. Some of the issues that must be addressed in standardizing EDI are as follows:

1. *Hardware*

How the physical connection is to be made. Most systems use dial-up phone lines. Other systems may specify leased lines. The type of hardware must be specified. If the system is to be hardware-independent, it must be so specified and the methods of ensuring hardware independence must be prescribed.

2. *Data encoding method*

How characters are to be coded (usually some commonly used method such as ASCII or EBCDIC); whether the data transmission will be synchronous or asynchronous, full or half-duplex; word framing to be used with the number of bits used to encode each character and the number of start and stop bits; parity checking method, if used; transmission speed in bits per second; the type of handshaking and acknowledgment; the methods of error detection and re-send methods to be used; etc.

3. *Availability*

Times during which the EDI system should be available for data communications and the grade of service that should be maintained during that time. The "grade" of service refers to the percentage of time that the system is in use. Wal-Mart likes to maintain a grade of 0.05, which means that the line will not be busy 95% of the time.

4. *Security*

How access is to be controlled and how the parties are to be identified. Normally, this means sign-on identification numbers and passwords. Business data and forms are very sensitive and unauthorized access or alteration by vandals can cause large headaches and losses for many businesses. In critical service, call-back provisions may be used. In simple call-back, the sending computer calls the receiving computer requesting call-back and hangs up. The receiver then calls the sender back for data transmission. In a variation of this, the receiver receives the data on the first transmission, then calls the sender back after a prespecified interval and verifies selected data sent.

5. *Format of each business form*

The types of business forms that are supported and the exact format and content of each; how each form is to be encoded for transmission and how transmitted forms are to be decoded. This is the most difficult and most voluminous part of the standard specifications and accounts for most of the disagreements and negotiations during standards formulation. The reason is that the forms encapsulate how each firm conducts its business, and changing forms has implications beyond that of simply changing an MIS procedure. These specifications are necessarily so detailed and inflexible that normal procedure is to encode these rules in a computer program. The program can be written in COBOL, a 4GL, or in assembly language and performs the data encoding and decoding operations between the corporate database and the electronic mail system. Most firms prefer to purchase a commercial EDI formatter. The only in-house programming consists of customization and installation for compatibility with database and file systems with which the program is to interact.

6. *Legal and contractual*

Another difficult area during standards negotiation may be the legal terms of the electronic transfer and the remedies in case of disagreement, since no signed contract can be produced by either party. A blanket paper contract between two firms may be used to govern the validity of all electronic transfers for the period of the contract and a system of "reference numbers" and "authorization codes" may be used to validate each transmission. The danger of electronic transmission is that an error in transmission or reception can result in business losses. The possibility of these errors must be minimized and the liabilities and remedies in case of losses must be predetermined to the extent possible. Historically, this limitation has been an impediment to the widespread use of EDI. The legal system must eventually address the issue of paperless electronic business contracts to put the legal concerns completely to rest.

EDI Standards

With the impetus provided by the ANSI X.12 standards, many large firms and government agencies, burdened with paperwork, began to join the EDI bandwagon, although each implementation was customized to some degree. It became evident early on that the business transactions were so different from one industry to another that a single set of specs such as X.12 could serve as guidelines but were too general to be useful in a direct implementation. The X.12 standards required interpretation to address the format, security, translation, and legal issues of various types of users from government agencies to trucking companies.

Each industry began, therefore, to formalize its own interpretation and implementation of the X.12 standards, and a plethora of standards evolved that were at once useful and confusing. By 1986, under the auspices of the Uniform Code Council (UCC), several industry-specific standards had been pushed into service. These were UCS (Uniform Communication Standard) used by the grocery trade, CIDX (Chemical Industry Data Exchange) of the chemical industry, the EDX (Electrical Data Exchange) in the electrical industry, TAMCS (Textile Apparel Manufacturer's Communication Standards) and TALC (Textile Apparel Linkage Committee) of the textile industry, WINS (Warehouse Information Network Standards) for the warehousing industry, TDCC (Transportation Data Coordinating

Committee), and VICS (Voluntary Inter-industry Communication Standards) for the general merchandisers such as Wal-Mart. Other proprietary and standard interpretations of X.12 standards were being used by the railways, aerospace, Department of Defense, and ocean liners.

EDI-VICS was spearheaded initially by Wal-Mart's Jack Shewmaker and Bob Martin to develop a common interpretation of the X.12 Purchase Order Specification. Martin later served as chairman of the VICS technical committee. What the merchandisers wanted was a way to use the same EDI purchase orders with a variety of vendors. The effort was so successful that the VICS standard grew to encompass a complete set of EDI specifications for the general merchandiser. The set of X.12 standards with VICS specifications addresses most of the transactions between a merchandiser and its suppliers. The partial list below shows the standard number and description of the major business forms supported.

850	Purchase Order
810	Invoice
856	Advance Ship Notice (Packing Slip)
846	Inventory Advice
997	Functional Acknowledgement

Figure W.1 shows the complete specifications for the 850 purchase order.

Figure W.1
Complete Set of Specifications
for the ANSI X.12 850 Purchase Order

850 - Purchase Order - Version 2000

This is the layout for the 850 purchase order, version 2000. All segments that Wal-Mart uses are given in the sample below. Not all segments are used for each purchase order.

Note: All insignificant digits are dropped.

Example: $5.10 is transmitted as 5.1.

Example of a Formatted Purchase Order - Version 2000

```
ISA*00*     *00*        *13*9254850000*01*RECV'R ID*YYMMDD*HHMM*U*00201*100000011*0*T>
GS*PO*5012734672*RECVR ID*YYMMDD*HHMM*10050*X*002000
ST*850*100850001
BEG*00*NE*0420159891***YYMMDD
LS*0100
N1*VN**92*145029050
N1*ST*WAL-MART WHSE #4*09*0519577696041
N3*809 'P' ST. -REGULAR
N4*BENTONVILLE*AR*727160000
LE*0100
REF*PD**HOLIDAY BUILDUP
PER*BD*BUYER'S NAME*TE*5012734000
ITA*A*AX*UM*03**4.32**Z*2*144*CA
ITD*03*04*2.5*YYMMDD*10*881130*5*****002.5%10  N5 MMDDYY
DTM*010*YYMMDD
DTM*001*YYMMDD
FOB*PP*OR*ANYWHERE, US*02*FOB
TD2*0***CALL5012736556
NTE*GEN*COMMENTS CONCERNING PURCHASE ORDER IF NECESSARY
PO1**5*CA*117.6*PE*UI*07872970111*PI*001506591*VN*072
PO4*24**CA***G*17.*CA
PO1**45*CA*107.88*PE*UI*07872900203*PI*001506592*VN*060
J2X*DS*F*COMMENTS CONCERNING ITEM IF NECESSARY
PO4*12**CA**G*18*CA
ITA*A*AX*QD*02*SA*4.32**Z*1*83*CA
CTT*2*50.
SE*20*100850001
GE*1*10050
IEA*1*100000011
```

Figure 3-2. X.12 Formatted Purchase Order - 2000

Figure W.1 Continued

ISA Segment - Interchange Control Header

Marks the beginning of the transmission and provides the sender/receiver identification.

ISA*00*   *00*   *13*9254850000*01*RECV'R ID*YYMMDD*HHMM*U*00201*100000011*0*T >

Element Reference Number	Description	Qualifiers/Definition	Length Min/Max
ISA01 744	Authorization information qualifier.	00 No authorization sent 01 UCS authorization	2/2
ISA02 745	Authorization information.		10/10
ISA03 746	The qualifier indicating security information.	00 No security information 01 Password	2/2
ISA04 747	The actual security information.		10/10
ISA05 704	Code used to identify the sender.	01 Duns number 12 Phone number 13 **UCS Code**	2/2
ISA06 705	The sender identification.	Wal-Mart's ID - 9254850000	15/15
ISA07 704	Interchange ID qualifier code used to identify the receiver of the transmission.	01 Duns number 12 Phone number 13 UCS code	2/2
ISA08 706	The receiver identification number.	Senders identification	15/15
ISA09 373	The date the information was created in the sender's system.	YYMMDD format	6/6
ISA10 337	The time the transmission was created.	HHMM	4/4
ISA11 726	The interchange standard identifier.	U = X.12	1/1
ISA12 703	The transaction set version.	00200 = version 2, release 0	5/5
ISA13 709	The control number assigned by the sender.	Control number sequential by trading partner.	9/9
ISA14 749	Acknowledgement request.	0 Acknowledgement not requested 1 Acknowledgement requested	1/1
ISA15 748	Test indicator.	P Production T Test	1/1
ISA16 701	Sub-element separator.	>	1/1

GS Segment - Functional Group Header

GS*PO*9254850000*RECVR ID*YYMMDD*HHMM*10050*X*002000

Element Reference Number	Description	Qualifiers/Definition	Length Min/Max
GS01 479	Code identifying the type of information sent.	PO	2/2
GS02 142	Code identifying the party sending the transmission.	Your company code.	2/12
GS03 124	Code identifying the party receiving the transmission.	Phone Number 501-273-4672	2/12
GS04 29	The date the transmission was generated.	YYMMDD	6/6
GS05 30	The time of the transmission.	HHMM	4/4
GS06 28	The control number assigned and maintained by the sender.	Control number sequential by trading partner.	1/9
GS07 455	Code identifying the transaction type.	X = X.12	1/2
GS08 480	The version and release of the EDI standards.	002000	1/12

ST Segment - Transaction Set Header

ST*850*100850001

Element Reference Number	Description	Qualifiers/Definition	Length Min/Max
ST01 143	The transaction set code that identifies the type of document.	850 = Purchase Order	3/3
ST02 329	The identifying control number assigned by the sender for a transaction set.	Control number sequential by trading partner.	4/9

BEG Segment

The beginning segment for a purchase order application.

BEG*00*NE*0420159891***YYMMDD

Element	Description	Qualifiers/Definition	Length Min/Max
Reference Number			
BEG01	The code identifying the purpose of the transmitted set.	00 Original	2/2
353			
BEG02	The code specifying the type of purchase order.	NE New Order	2/2
92			
BEG03	Purchase Order Number.		1/22
324			
BEG06	The purchase order date.	YYMMDD	6/6
323			

LS Segment - Loop Header

LS*0100

Element	Description	Qualifiers/Definition	Length Min/Max
Reference Number			
LS01	Indicates that the next segments begins a loop.		1/4
447			

N1 Segment - Name

N1*ST*WAL-MART WHSE #4*09*0519577696041 *or* N1*VN**92*145029050

Element	Description	Qualifiers/Definition		Length Min/Max
Reference Number				
N101	The code identifying the type of party being defined.	**BD**	Buyer/Department	2/2
98		**BT**	Party to be billed other than freight company	
		BY	Buyer	
		SN	Store Number	
		ST	Ship to	
		VN	Vendor	
N102	The name.			1/35
93				
N103	The code identifying the system used for the identification code.	**09**	Duns with 4 digit suffix	1/2
66				
N104	Code identifying one of the party in the transaction.	The last four digits denotes the specific location.		2/17
67				

N3 Segment - Address Information

N3*809 'P' ST. - REGULAR

Element	Description	Qualifiers/Definition	Length Min/Max
Reference Number			
N301	Free form description area for address information.		1/35
166			

N4 Segment - Geographic Location

N4*BENTONVILLE*AR*727160000

Element Reference Number	Description	Qualifiers/Definition	Length Min/Max
N401	Free form area for the city name.		2/19
19			
N402	Standard state abbreviation code.		2/2
156			
N403	The zip code.		5/9
116			

LE Segment - Loop Trailer

LE*0100

Element Reference Number	Description	Qualifiers/Definition	Length Min/Max
LE01	Indicates that the loop preceding this segment is complete.		1/4
447			

REF Segment - Reference Number

REF*PD**HOLIDAY BUILDUP

Element Reference Number	Description	Qualifiers/Definition	Length Min/Max
REF01	Code identifying the reference number.	**PD** Promotion/Deal Number	2/2
128			
REF03	Free form description.		1/80
352			

PER Segment - Administrative Communications Contact

PER*BD*Buyer's Name*TE*5012734000

Element Reference Number	Description	Qualifiers/Definition	Length Min/Max
PER01 366	The code identifying the responsibility of the person named.	**BD** Buyer/Department	2/2
PER02 93	Free form area.	The buyer's name.	1/35
PER03 365	The code identifying the type of communication.	**TE** Wal-Mart Telephone Number	2/2
PER04 364	The complete communication number.	5012734000	7/21

ITA Segment - Allowances

ITA*A*AX*UM*03**4.32**Z*2*144*CA

Loop Id's equal to zero indicate purchase order level discounts. Loop Id's equal to 200 indicate line level discounts.

Element Reference Number	Description	Qualifiers/Definition	Length Min/Max
ITA01 248	Code indicating an allowance.	**A** Allowance	1/1
ITA02 559	A code identifying the agency assigning the code.	**AX** ASC X.12	2/2

Element Reference Number	Description	Qualifiers/Definition		Length Min/Max
ITA03 560	Special services code. **Note:** These allowances may appear at line level or purchase order level.	**CM** Advertising Allowance **FA** Freight Allowance **FG** Free Goods **HD** Handling **LA** Labeling **QD** Quantity Discount **TD** Trade Discount **UM** Unsaleable Merchandise Allowance **WH** Warehousing **ZZ** Mutually Defined There are 6 discount types that Wal-Mart uses that are not defined in the **X.12 850 Purchase Order.** When these are used the following procedures applies: 1. You will receive a ZZ (other allowance) in **ITA04.** 2. You will receive the Wal-Mart discount code in **ITA05.** These codes are: **EB** Early Buy Allowance **ND** New Discount **NW** New Warehouse **SA** New Store Discount **SB** Special Buy **TL** Truckload Allowance		2/10
ITA04 331	The code identifying the method of handling payment for the allowance.	**02** Off Invoice **03** Vendor Check **04** Credit Customer Account **ZZ** Mutually Defined		2/2
ITA05 341	The number assigned by a vendor referencing an allowance or promotion.			1/16
ITA06 359	The allowance rate per unit.			1/9
ITA08 378	The code indicating what basis the allowance percent is calculated.	**Z** Mutually defined		1/1
ITA09 332	Allowance percent.			1/6
ITA10 339	The allowance quantity.			1/10
ITA11 355	Code identifying the basic unit of measurement.	**CA** Case		2/2
ITA12 379	The free good quantity.			1/10

ITD Segment - Terms of Sale

ITD*03*04*2.5*YYMMDD*5*****2.5%10 N5 MMDDYY

Element Reference Number	Description	Qualifiers/Definition		Length Min/Max
ITD01 336	Code identifying the type of payment terms.	**02** **03** **ZZ**	EOM Fixed Date Mutually Defined	2/2
ITD02 333	The beginning date of the terms period.	**02** **03** **04** **ZZ**	Delivery Date Invoice Date Specified date Mutually Defined	1/2
ITD03 338	The terms discount percent (%).			1/6
ITD04 370	The terms discount due date.			6/6
ITD05 351	Terms discount days due.			1/3
ITD06 446	The terms net due date.			6/6
ITD07 386	The terms net days.			1/3
ITD12 352	A free form description.			1/80

DTM Segment - Date and Time References

DTM*010*YYMMDD

Element	Description	Qualifiers/Definition	Length Min/Max
Reference Number			
DTM01	The code specifying the type of date.	**001** Requested Cancel Date **010** Requested Ship Date	3/3
374			
DTM02	The date.	YYMMDD	6/6
373			

FOB Segment - F.O.B. Related Instructions

FOB*PP*OR*ANYWHERE, US*02*FOB

Element	Description	Qualifiers/Definition	Length Min/Max
Reference Number			
FOB01	The code identifying the payment terms for transportation charges.	**CC** Collect **PP** Prepaid	2/2
146			
FOB02	The code identifying the transportation location.	**OR** Original shipping point	2/2
376			
FOB03	Free form description of the shipping point.		1/80
352			
FOB04	The code used to describe the transportation responsibility.	**02** Trade Term Code	2/2
334			
FOB05	The code indicating the trade terms which apply to the shipment.	**FOB** Free on board	3/6
335			

TD2 Segment - Routing Information

TD2*0***CALL5012736556

Element Reference Number	Description	Qualifiers/Definition		Length Min/Max
TD201 133	Routing sequences code.	**0**	Original Carrier	1/2
TD204 387	Routing or origin carrier.			1/35

NTE Segment - Notes

NTE*DEL*COMMENTS CONCERNING PURCHASE ORDER IF NECESSARY

Element Reference Number	Description	Qualifiers/Definition		Length Min/Max
NTE01 363	Code identifying the purpose of the note.	**GEN** **ZZZ**	Entire transaction set Mutually defined	3/3
NTE02 3	Free form description.			1/60

PO1 Segment - Purchase Order Item Information

PO1*1*5*CA*117.6*PE*UI*07872970111*PI*001506591*VN*072

Element Reference Number	Description	Qualifiers/Definition		Length Min/Max
PO101 350	The purchase order line number.			1/6
PO102 330	Quantity ordered.	*Example:* Number of cases		1/9
PO103 355	The code identifying the basic unit of measurement.	**CA**	Case	2/2
PO104 212	The unit price.			1/14
PO105 639	The code defining the basic unit prices.	**PE**	Price per each	2/2
PO106 235	The code identifying the type of the descriptive number used.	**UI**	UPC 11 digit item code	2/2
PO107 234	The identifying number for the item.			1/30
PO108 235	The code identifying the type of the descriptive number used.	**PI**	Wal-Mart's item number	2/2
PO109 234	The identifying number for the item.			1/30
PO110 235	The code identifying the type of the descriptive number used.	**VN**	Vendor's stock number	2/2
PO111 234	The identifying number for the item.			1/30

PO4 Segment - Item Detail

PO4*24**CA***G*17*CA

Element Reference Number	Description	Qualifiers/Definition		Length Min/Max
PO401 356	The number of items in a pack.			1/6
PO402 357	The size of the vendor/supplier units in a pack.			1/8
PO403 355	Code identifying the basic unit of measurement.	CA	Case	2/2
PO404 352	Free form description.			1/80
PO406 187	Code identifying the type of weight.	G	Gross Weight	1/2
PO407 384	Gross weight per pack.			1/9
PO408 355	Code identifying the basic unit of measurement.	CA	Case	2/2

J2X Segment - Item Description

J2X*DS*F*COMMENTS CONCERNING ITEM IF NECESSARY

Element Reference Number	Description	Qualifiers/Definition		Length Min/Max
J2X01 348	Code indicating the group or industry.	DS	Department/General Merchandise	2/2
J2X02 349	The code indicating the format of a description.	F	Free form	1/1
J2X03 372	The item description.			1/80

CTT Segment - Transaction Totals

CTT*2*50

Element	Description	Qualifiers/Definition	Length Min/Max
Reference Number			
CTT01	The total number of line items in a transaction set.		1/6
354			
CTT02	The dollar amount of the data elements.	Cumulative figure	1/10
347			

SE Segment - Transaction Set Trailer

SE*20*100850001

Element	Description	Qualifiers/Definition	Length Min/Max
Reference Number			
SE01	The number of segments in the transaction set.		1/6
96			
SE02	The transaction set control number.	Control number sequential by trading partner.	4/9
329			

GE Segment - Functional Group Trailer

GE*20*100850001

Element Reference Number	Description	Qualifiers/Definition	Length Min/Max
GE01 97	The number of transaction sets in the functional group.	*Example:* The number of purchase orders in the set.	1/6
GE02 28	The functional group control number.	Control number sequential by trading partner.	1/9

IEA Segment - Interchange Control Trailer

IEA*1*100000011

Element Reference Number	Description	Qualifiers/Definition	Length Min/Max
IEA01 405	The number of segments in the transmission.		1/5
IEA02 709	The transmission control number.	Control number sequential by trading partner.	9/9

EDI at Wal-Mart

Wal-Mart has been a pioneer in EDI technology and a driving force behind the standardization and adoption of EDI specifications in the general merchandise retailing industry.

The company began using EDI as early as the seventies to transmit purchase orders to selected vendors who had the requisite technical capability and managerial willingness. The system used a proprietary "standard." Wal-Mart designed its own custom format and developed its own custom software to support the EDI transfers. Connection was by dial-up phone lines and vendors were required only to support a simple modem link. By 1986, 500 vendors had been brought online with this proprietary EDI system.

By 1985, however, Wal-Mart senior executives began to realize the real benefits of the elimination of paperwork. Then Vice-Chairman Jack Shewmaker and Senior VP Bob Martin took an active interest in EDI. They realized that the real benefits of EDI would not be available until a wholesale conversion away from paperwork was made. It was apparent, however, that wholesale conversion would be achieved only with industry-wide standards. They therefore took the initiative and began to move the industry toward a standard.

The ANSI X.12 standard needed interpretation. UCS, the "retail" standard, was grocery-oriented and not a good fit. Besides, it was an independent set of specifications that did not conform to the ANSI X.12 standard. Transportation (TDCC), warehousing (WINS), and manufacturing (TALC, EDX, etc.) had their own standards. What was needed was a way for merchandisers such as Wal-Mart to set up EDI links with all these parties, using one set of formats and protocols.

Wal-Mart decided to stay strongly X.12-committed and participated in the VICS committee to put together a common interpretation of EDI standards, starting with the purchase order. This standard was released by the VICS committee in 1987.

The success of the VICS effort provided the impetus for a new vision — that it would be feasible to go completely paperless with vendors. Thus, in 1987 Wal-Mart made a commitment to EDI and to the X.12 standard. The proprietary (custom) system in use at Wal-Mart prior to VICS was phased out and the company began to convert to the X.12 formats. The 700 vendors Wal-Mart had on the proprietary system at the time were encouraged to switch to the X.12 system. By 1988, 450 new vendors were added to EDI, all of them on the new VICS X.12 system.

The original ANSI system was PC-based and used commercial data communications software with some custom patches to support an in-house EDI mailbox. This was essentially a low-investment prototype to test the waters and prove the system. The PC system grew to 150 vendors. By then the system began to outgrow the capacity of the PC, but it had shown that EDI could work and Wal-Mart's MIS department could justify further investment on that basis.

Wal-Mart then moved the EDI system to the large computer by purchasing commercial mailbox software and an EDI formatter. In-house programming was necessary to set up the interface between the MIS database and the EDI system and to make some enhancements to the system. This in-house mail box then became Wal-Mart's EDI system.

Currently, all EDI vendors have been converted to electronic purchase orders and the most important trucking companies are on EDI freight bills. Less than a dozen trucking companies account for most of Wal-Mart's freight bills. EDI remittance advice is under development and will be added in the near future.

Wal-Mart has made it a corporate mission to deliver the lowest possible price to the consumer and has recognized EDI as a means towards this end. To achieve total conversion of all vendors, Wal-Mart is using a combination of its marketing skills and muscle power. The company's size gives it a negotiating advantage with most vendors. This leverage is used to make it "a Wal-Mart requirement" for new vendors to be EDI-VICS compatible. In conjunction with this requirement, Wal-Mart has also launched a marketing crusade to educate and persuade vendors of the advantages of EDI. In keeping with the "trading partner" attitude, Wal-Mart engenders a mutually beneficial and cooperative relationship with vendors in the EDI implementation.

To come online, the vendor must typically acquire software for EDI document formatting and modem communication. Wal-Mart offers specs and guidelines to vendors for selecting the software. If the vendor wishes to use a third-party network such as Ordernet, Wal-Mart provides assistance in attaining the electronic linkage. Using EDI promotion and vendor education, Wal-Mart hopes to achieve its goal of having every vendor online by 1990. In 1988 Wal-Mart had approximately 4000 vendors, of which 1100 were on EDI.

Documents Currently on EDI at Wal-Mart

Purchase Orders

Wal-Mart supports the ANSI X.12 version 2000 and 2001 (used by most general merchandise retailers) and the UCS formats (used mostly by the grocery industry). Wal-Mart suppliers are required to use the EDI purchase order.

Invoices

Wal-Mart is currently testing EDI invoices and will be going online with selected vendors within several days of this writing. The firm will be actively encouraging vendors to use electronic invoicing. The invoices will be automatically matched with the purchase orders and processed for payment. Acceptance of EDI invoices may seem to be a disadvantage from a financial standpoint, since it reduces the float time. As it turns out, there is no float loss at all, since the payment terms are not contingent upon the date the invoice is received.

Remittance Advice

As invoices are paid, the vendor is sent a remittance advice via EDI. This electronic message or "document" shows the amount being paid and the corresponding invoice numbers against which the amount applies.

Direct Link Versus Third-Party Network

EDI data are usually transmitted directly from one computer to another. This is the preferred method and Wal-Mart encourages all vendors to support direct link to the company's EDI system. This method allows Wal-Mart to have more control over the data transmissions, poses lower security risks, and lowers costs by avoiding third-party network charges. The connection is made over dial-up phone lines at 2400, 4800 or 9600 baud, using a synchronous modem and the IBM 3780 BISYNC protocol.

However, vendors who wish to use third-party networks can do so by leaving the EDI message in Wal-Mart's EDI mailbox in one of the networks the company subscribes to (see Figure W.2). Currently, Wal-Mart uses GEIS (General Electric Information Services) and Ordernet. Wal-Mart checks these mailboxes for messages on a regular basis and leaves the response in the vendor's mailbox. Third-party network charges can be substantial, especially when EDI message transmission is frequent. Wal-Mart's goal is to convert completely to direct connection. To ease the conversion for a wide range of vendors, Wal-Mart has installed the electronic mailbox system as a common method of conducting EDI transfers with a large number of different retailers who may differ with respect to communication protocols (see Figure W.3).

Going Online with Wal-Mart

The conversion of a vendor from paper forms to paperless is a careful and formalized process, with testing and verification at each stage to reduce chances of erroneous transmissions or misinterpretation of EDI documents.

Initially, the physical communications line is tested with sample text exchange to ensure that there are no transmission errors. Once satisfactory data communication is established, a "format verification" is performed. A sample purchase order is transmitted to the vendor for verification against the paper PO that was sent in the mail. The vendor is asked to compare the two POs and for a consistent interpretation. Inconsistencies are resolved and additional sample POs are sent until the electronic PO compares with the paper invoice. In a normal conversion, this process may involve up to six different transmissions.

Figure W.2
EDI Transfer Using Third-Party Electronic Mailbox

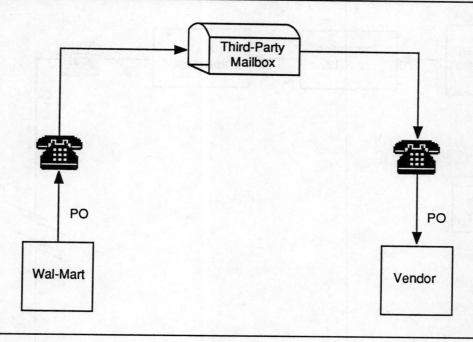

During this test-and-verification phase, Wal-Mart sends the vendor a list of all of the vendor's items carried by Wal-Mart. The vendor is asked to verify this list, which shows the UPC code and description. This is a critical step, since once the vendor comes online electronically, the UPC code interpretation must be consistent with Wal-Mart's. After a successful test period, the vendor goes "live"; that is, the vendor begins to receive purchase orders via EDI. However, Wal-Mart continues to send the vendor confirming paper purchase orders. In time, the vendor begins to rely more on the electronic PO and less and less on the paper PO.

After three months of parallel operation of the paper and electronic purchase orders, the vendor is weaned completely from paperwork and goes paperless. Wal-Mart MIS staff works very closely with the vendor in making this important transition to the total elimination of paperwork in the purchase order process.

Figure W.3
Computer-to-Computer EDI Transfer

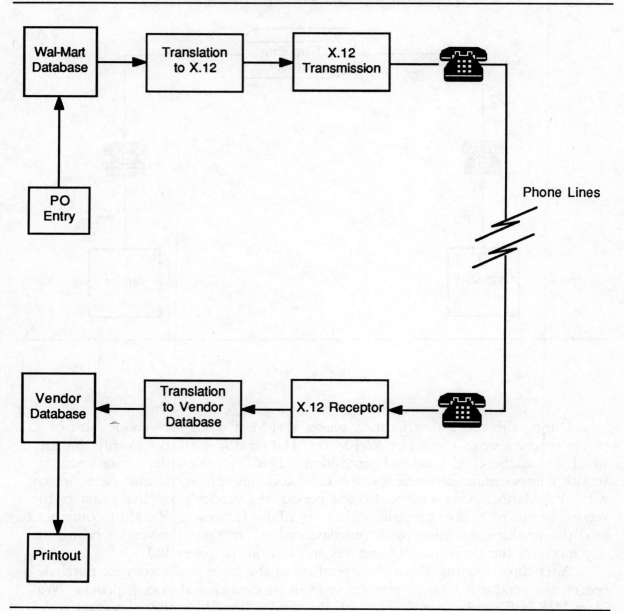

EDI Activity and Future Plans

Of the 4000 Wal-Mart vendors in 1988, 1100 were online and receiving EDI purchase orders. It is not known how many vendors are actually processing the EDI POs electronically, since some vendors are known to use the EDI mechanism as a glorified Fax machine by printing out the incoming EDI PO and then processing the printout as a paper PO. The best guess is that fewer than 75 percent of the vendors are fully electronic in the EDI PO process.

Wal-Mart Electronic Services Group is responsible for EDI implementation. As part of the implementation, they have engineered an educational and promotional push for EDI. It is hoped that an additional 1500 vendors will be on EDI purchase orders by the close of 1989, and all vendors will be receiving EDI purchase orders by 1990. However, because certain small, infrequent, or seasonal suppliers cannot and will not convert, the paper PO process must remain extant to serve these needs.

To date, Wal-Mart has implemented EDI purchase orders and freight bills. The firm issues about 50,000 purchase orders and 3,000 freight bills every week. Approximately 50 percent of the purchase orders and 90 percent of the freight bills are now on EDI. Plans call for getting 50 percent of the vendors and 80 percent of the purchase orders on EDI PO by the end of 1989.

The conversion to invoices is less spectacular. Because these source documents originate with the vendor, Wal-Mart can exert less control on the process. The development of the EDI invoice acceptance system by Wal-Mart Electronic Services has been completed and is expected to be implemented by the first quarter of 1989. However, the conversion process is expected to be slow. Wal-Mart uses a computerized "invoice-matching" algorithm to determine the validity of invoices and to make payment. In this process, invoices are compared with the corresponding PO and payment is automatically authorized by the computer. In a majority of the cases, there is no human intervention at all in the payment process. Invoices are aged and paid automatically. However, since the incoming invoices are paper, these must be manually entered into the computer for this matching process to begin. The process is expensive, slow, and subject to error. A further cost of the paper invoice process is that all the invoices must be microfilmed and archived for a number of years as required by law. What Wal-Mart needs is EDI invoices. The fully electronic invoice would make the invoice-matching process automatic and the data could be archived more conveniently in magnetic tape cartridges. To automate the invoice-matching process the company has placed a high priority on conversion to EDI invoices.

Security Concerns of EDI Implementations

Recently there has been a proliferation of data vandalism by "hackers." Computer systems and networks accessible via dial-up lines have proven to be particularly vulnerable to such mischievous or criminal access to sensitive data. Thus, EDI must address the issue of vandalism. As implied earlier, much of the resistance to EDI has been psychological. A single security breach could stiffen this resistance and arrest the growth of EDI adoption or even torpedo the process altogether.

If unguarded, the EDI network could be vandalized in several ways, with the severity of the security breach ranging from the benign to those causing significant financial losses. For example, a vandal could leave false purchase orders in a vendor's EDI mailbox, causing the inconvenience and expense of a bogus shipment, which would, of course, be returned by Wal-Mart. In more severe cases, a break-in could involve the generation of false purchase orders and corresponding invoices, prompting the highly automated invoice payment system to issue checks. There are other possible avenues of electronic embezzlement from an EDI system.

Although no system is ever completely break-in proof, prudent measures must be taken to guard against known methods of the data vandals. Wal-Mart recognizes the importance of these security needs of EDI. The company has assigned the best technical people to the security aspects of the project and has been very cautious in the implementation so that security issues could be properly addressed. Some aspects of the Wal-Mart security system that can be made public include the following:

1. *Vendor ID and password*
   Vendors are given unique identification codes and passwords by Wal-Mart to control access to the in-house mailbox. Third-party networks also utilize user-ID's and passwords. This strategy offers a first line of defense but has not proven to be vandal-proof. Unscrupulous or discontented employees or ex-employees may release the passwords to others or use them to cause mischief themselves. In many publicized cases of data vandalism the hackers have been credited with ingenious ways of bypassing this method of access control.

2. *RACF*
   Wal-Mart uses IBM's Resource Access Control Facility (RACF) as a second line of defense. This piece of software, resident in the IBM 3090, monitors all activity performed by remote-access users and limits their functions to a permissible subset of the operating system and to a limited subset of the EDI system. This limits the amount of damage a vandal can cause but doesn't eliminate the possibility of vandalism.

3. *Limitation to data only*
   Remote access to the system is limited to supplying or receiving data only. This data-only limitation prevents the user from executing programs or changing the way programs work. This feature, if unpenetrated, would make it impossible for the remote user to

generate a bogus purchase order in Wal-Mart's system, although he or she could leave one for the vendor. However, since Wal-Mart's database would not contain the bogus PO, neither the shipment nor any invoice against the PO would be accepted. Thus, the amount of the damage resulting from the break-in would be limited.

4. *Authorization and security codes*
   In addition to the previously mentioned measures, the EDI access and activation method contains a system of security codes and data validation techniques that are checked at each stage of the process. These security codes make it very difficult, although not impossible, to make an unauthorized entry.

Wal-Mart is monitoring their EDI implementation very closely from the security standpoint and expects to beef up these measures in the future. As the company's VICS brochure points out, no method is absolutely safe; however, the electronic method as installed is at least as secure and reliable as the paper method and future enhancements will make it even more so.

Case Study Questions

1. Critics of JIT purchasing claim that it simply shifts the inventory burden to the supplier and does not eliminate inventory from the system as a whole. Yet in this case, we have seen that QR can reduce inventories at both ends. Explain how this is possible and, using this explanation as your ammunition, respond to the critics' charge.

2. Some advocates point to EDI as a means by which American industry can again become competitive in the international arena. Is there sufficient evidence in the Wal-Mart case to support such an optimistic view?

3. Assume that you are the MIS manager at Wal-Mart. The president of the company expresses some concern to you about the vulnerability of centralized control to a failure in the mainframes or the satellite network and wants you to draw up a design and a budget for a more distributed architecture. Prepare a memo to the president describing what would be involved, what would be gained, what would be lost, and defending your decision to maintain the centralized system. Is it possible to have both a centralized and distributed architecture? Remember that Wal-Mart is a very lean machine and the firm's very definition and survival is based on keeping costs down and bringing the lowest possible prices to the consumer.

4. When Wal-Mart implemented their EDI system, they considered a stand-alone system versus the one on the 3090 mainframe. What are the pros and cons of each option? As MIS manager, defend your decision to go with the 3090 option.

5. What role did the PC-based system play at the inception of EDI at Wal-Mart? Describe the type of system development life cycle used in the EDI implementation at Wal-Mart.

6. In spite of the high priority placed on EDI by Wal-Mart's top management and in spite of its enormous influence with most suppliers, conversion to EDI has been slow. After 2 years of effort, only purchase orders have been implemented and only about a fourth of the vendors are on EDI. What are some reasons for this slow progress?

7. Plans are to bring the rest of the vendors (2900) online in the next 2 years with full EDI implementation of purchase orders, invoices, freight bills, invoice matching, and remittance advice. The president of the company sends you a memo questioning your projections based on the rate of progress thus far. As MIS manager at Wal-Mart, write a memo supporting your implementation schedule.

8. The extreme degree of automation at Wal-Mart is exemplified by invoice-matching and QR purchasing. In both instances, the computer takes action without human intervention, automatically issuing payment to vendors (in invoice matching) or automatically ordering goods to maintain inventory levels. What are the risks of such a system? What safeguards would you take as MIS manager?

9. The basic technology of EDI is surprisingly simple. It involves little more than the expertise needed to operate an electronic bulletin board system (BBS), hundreds of which have been operated out of hobbyists' spare rooms since the seventies. What then are the issues and concerns that have retarded complete conversion to EDI at Wal-Mart?

10. As VP of MIS, you are asked to make a presentation on EDI at a company strategic planning meeting. You feel that there are too many dangers and security risks to abandon paper documents. Prepare a presentation, urging caution in the rush to go "electronics everything" at Wal-Mart.

11. As MIS manager at Wal-Mart, prepare a report to the your boss, who is skeptical about the benefits of EDI. Draft a presentation in which you urge top priority for conversion to EDI. Use the title "EDI: The Coming Revolution."

12. Prepare an MIS and EDI capacity planning report for Wal-Mart for 1994 if current rates of growth in sales, number of stores, and EDI conversion are sustained.

13. Can you identify aspects of organizational, managerial, and business climate at Wal-Mart that have encouraged or required a high reliance on information technology? What are some innovations that Wal-Mart might use in the future to stay ahead of the competition?

PART 4

Topics in Information Technology

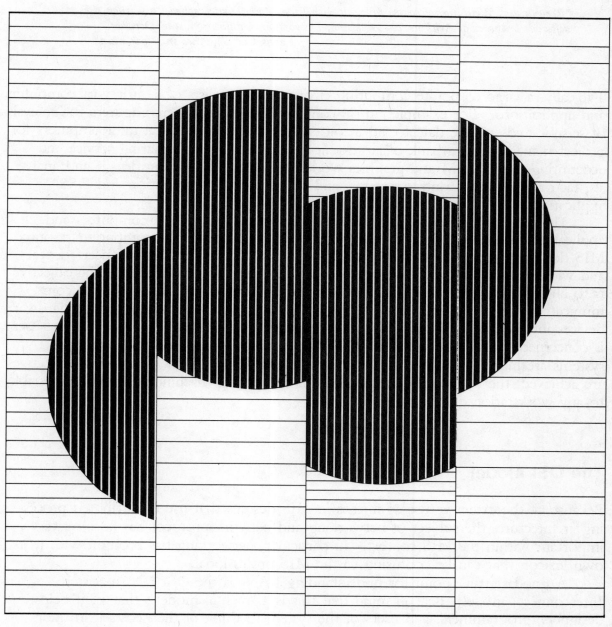

Data Communications/
Local Area Networks

"Reeling and Writing, of course to begin with," the Mock Turtle replied, "and then the different branches of Arithmetic – Ambition, Distraction, Uglification, and Derision."
— Lewis Carroll, *Alice in Wonderland*

Typically, a large corporate computing environment consists of a variety of computers and applications. For example, an oil company may have supercomputers for analysis of seismic and satellite data to aid in oil exploration, departmental minicomputers for project management, a bank of large-scale mainframes for timesharing service and accounting, CAD/CAM and graphics workstations for engineering design and analysis, factory (refinery) control systems, and PCs for office automation and DSS applications.

The challenge for MIS professionals today is to tie all these computers and applications together into a cohesive and logically homogeneous computing resource. MIS designers seek to make the physical heterogeneity invisible to the user. Local and wide area networks (LANS and WANS) are used for this reason. The objective is to allow all users to share data and hardware resources and to be able to communicate with each other. A high degree of integration welds the disparate hardware devices into a unified "system" that is consistent across the network as far as the user is concerned. This means that all differences between computers and operating systems are hidden from the user. In an ideal MIS installation, when these objectives are achieved, the huge corporate resource in computing machinery becomes accessible to any workstation on the network.

The OSI Model

Because of the extensive use of micros in MIS designs that use a distributed processing architecture, the subject of networking and network protocol has become very important within the MIS context. In particular, networking has brought with it its own lexicon that can be confusing to the MIS professional.

A good starting point for understanding LANs is the OSI (Open System Interconnect) model. Bear in mind that this is a "mental model"; that is, it helps designers, programmers, and users of the system to think of the network in these terms so that they can communicate with each other on a consistent basis. This model was first proposed in order to bring about some standardization in the industry at a time when vendors were engaging in open warfare with each other over hardware and software protocol. Each vendor claimed that their system was best in terms of data transfer rate (megabits per second or MPS), data integrity, and network response time. The MIS designer became the victim, caught in the middle with technical "gotchas" and massive system integration headaches.

The OSI network model provides a common integration basis and, at least theoretically, renders the network design "vendor-free" to some degree as long as the vendors conform to standards that can be described within the OSI framework. It then becomes possible for the MIS designer to establish compatibility at each OSI level and, as a result, begin to integrate a multi-vendor network.

According to the OSI model, the network is considered to consist of seven "levels." These are, from top to bottom

7. *Application:* the user's application program

6. *Presentation:* user interface/screen display

5. *Session:* conversation between two nodes

4. *Tranport:* message-encoding protocol

3. *Network:* system for keeping two messages separated

2. *Link:* data encoding scheme

1. *Physical:* hardware — wires, connectors, voltage

Level 1 defines the type of cabling and connectors to be used in the network. Cable designs attempt to reduce the effects of magnetic interference to increase the maximum length of cabling that can be used before the signal begins to deteriorate. As Sir James C. Maxwell demonstrated so eloquently a century ago, electricity and magnetism are actually two manifestations of the same reality. A moving charge creates magnetism and a moving magnetic field creates electricity. Data signals put on a wire consist of a series of fluctuating electrical charges beating out a rhythm according to a code (and producing magnetic fields, according to Maxwell's equations). As the signal travels down the line, the magnetic environment of the office and the earth's magnetic field may oppose and weaken the signal. Eventually the signal will dissipate and be indistinguishable from noise.

In the twisted-pair design, the signal and ground lines are woven or twisted around each other so that the magnetic field is not uniform. This renders the signal less susceptible to its magnetic environment. The twisted-pair, currently the least expensive cable available, severely limits the distance between nodes. The situation can be improved somewhat by encasing the wires in a conductive sheath to provide protection from ambient magnetism. The shielded twisted-pair wires are heavier and more expensive, however.

An innovative approach has been the coaxial cable or *coax,* as it is normally called. In this design, the signal, ground, and sheath are arranged in concentric cylinders. The geometry causes the magnetic fields to become self-cancelling. Since the resultant (net) magnetic field produced by the wire is weak, ambient forces are not able to interfere with the signal. It was this bit of geometric wizardry more than computer technology that ignited the networking issue, since the development of coaxial cable allowed engineers to lay thousands of feet of wire and still transmit a clean, 12-volt, low-energy signal with very little distortion. The catch is that these wires are very expensive, very heavy, and hard to work with. But they continue to be the mainstay of most LAN designs.

Products such as PhoneNet from Farallon Computing make it possible to use existing phone lines. The hardware interface sits between the network cable and the phone lines, translating signals between the network and the phone lines. The idea is attractive economically because most offices are already wired with phone lines. The single biggest headache when installing a LAN is the laying of cable. "Power line modems" are available that utilize the existing AC wiring as data lines but these are limited in speed to 19.2 kilobits per second (or 0.0192 megabits per second) and are therefore not suitable for the massive data fluxes of local area networks. Data transfer rates in LANs are typically in the range of 230 kilobits per second (Apple-Talk) to 10 megabits per second (Ethernet).

Another important aspect of cable design is the frequency of the carrier wave that can be imposed on the medium being used. Higher frequencies offer a larger bandwidth and faster data transfer but increase inductive losses and heat generation in conventional metallic media. Bandwidth is a variable that affects the number of different data paths or channels that can be defined within the frequency range of the carrier wave.

Optical fiber technology defuses the magnetic issue by using high-frequency electromagnetic waves (light) as the carrier and by avoiding metallic conductors. A very narrow beam of light shining through a specially constructed tube is used as the signal carrier. The signals can be run for miles without any perceptible degradation of signal quality. But even more important, the high frequency greatly increases the bandwidth and the possible data transfer rates. The bandwidth makes it possible to carry hundreds of channels integrating video, voice, and data in a single strand of light. Current research aimed at cutting the cost of these tubes, if successful, will have a staggering impact not only in data communications, but in the cable TV and telephone industries. Many technology analysts feel that the eventual impact of fiber optic technology may transcend that of the telephone and television combined.

Cabling design can affect the maximum data transfer rate and the maximum distance between nodes and of course must be taken into consideration in terms of cost and compatibility with existing cabling in the building. Data transfer rate is a very important network design parameter. Cabling costs can account for more than half of the network cost in large installations. Coaxial cable, shielded twisted pair, telephone cable, fiber optics, and microwave are some methods of connection that are normally used.

Now that networks have matured beyond the stage when we used to quarrel about wires, today it is not uncommon to find MIS designs that use different wire schemes in the same network. This is possible because of compatibility at higher OSI levels. The same vendor may offer cabling schemes that differ only in the lowest two levels of the OSI model. Nowadays, in network standards that follow the OSI structure, higher-level specifications are insulated from the lower levels, so that the kind of wires used is no longer an issue.

The next two levels up, Levels 2 and 3, contain the specifications that determine how each LAN "standard" encodes and decodes data and also the identification of each node on the network as a distinct address. Since the data transfer is synchronous, the timing, the number of bits per packet, the interpretation of these bits, and the method by which transmission errors are to be detected must be specified.

Levels 4 and 5 specify how communication of entire messages between two nodes will be set up. Long messages must be cut into pieces and fed to the lower levels in a format they can handle. A "session" or conversation must be established between the two nodes with a beginning and an end so that the entire message is properly transmitted.

The presentation level (Level 6) contains specifications that determine how the network operating system will present information on the user's screen display. The top level (Level 7) contains details by which a user's application program can utilize network resources through the network operating system.

Various industry "standards" (the word is used to denote vendor specifications) are available in the LAN market that address one to four of these levels. No standards are yet available or necessary that specify all levels.

Ethernet

Ethernet is a network standard designed by three computer companies working together: Digital (DEC), Intel, and Xerox. (These three companies are sometimes collectively referred to as *DIX*.) Rugged and flexible in design, Ethernet is by far the most popular network in use today. It is utilized mostly in large networks of micros, mainframes, and minis. The design uses the CSMA/CD protocol in a bus topology.

A typical architecture in large organizations utilizes an Ethernet backbone to connect mainframes to micro networks through gateways or through departmental minis such as an IBM 9370 or a MicroVAX. Ethernet is used today largely to provide specifications for the wiring and the datalink levels (Level 1 and Level 2) of the OSI model.

Because the standard is backed by three different companies and because many network vendors use the Ethernet specs for the low OSI levels, Ethernet is generally deemed to be vendor-free. This perception has encouraged third-party support and widespread adoption in disparate hardware and software environments ranging from AppleTalk to DECNet.

The Ethernet design has been ratified as standard 802.3 by the Institute of Electrical Electronics Engineers (IEEE), 802 committee, which has been active in establishing network standards. The design offers data transfer rates of 10 megabits per second through a baseband coaxial cable. The cable length can be more than 3000 feet between nodes. More important, end to end, the network can be over a mile long. Ethernet networks are commonly considered to be very reliable. They are simple and robust in construction and offer ease of expansion and a great deal of flexibility to the network designer.

Ethernet has been criticized for its use of heavy and expensive cable, but many vendors of Ethernet systems have started recently to offer other cable types. For example, 3Com offers lighter, inexpensive cable with their "Ether Series" systems. The IEEE has issued a twisted-pair Ethernet standard referred to as the 802.3 10BaseT that uses telephone wiring. Hopefully, the heavy, bulky, expensive, and difficult coax will go the way of the 25-conductor RS-232 cables, and the tonnage of copper under the floor of our office buildings will be greatly reduced.

Fiber optic technology has been incorporated into the Ethernet design. The principal benefit of this technology thus far has been that the maximum distance between nodes can be increased from 3000 feet to 10,000 feet and data transfer rates have been bumped all the way up to 100 megabits per second.

Other LAN Standards

LAN "standards" normally specify the lower levels of the OSI model. Most specifications cover Levels 1 to 3 while many, including SNA and Ethernet, also specify level 4. DOS-specific interfaces, such as IBM's NETBIOS and Apple's AppleTalk address the higher levels of compatibility.

IBM's System Network Architecture (SNA) was one of the early datacom standards set up. It was not designed for local area networks but rather for high-speed data transfer between large-scale mainframe computers. Because of IBM's dominance in the mainframe market, SNA has a large installed base. In most corporate MIS settings, it is important for LANs to be connected to the SNA line. Evaluation of PC LANs, therefore, includes SNA connectability as a criterion.

Datapoint's *ARCnet*, the grandfather of LAN specifications, owes its longevity to a solid design and trouble-free operation. This token-passing network was originally designed to link Datapoint's minicomputers. It is gaining a new life as a LAN for personal computers. Because of the relatively large installed base of ARCnets, new network vendors typically offer ARCnet-compatible bridges to interconnect the two networks.

The Department of Defense (DOD), frustrated by the network wars between vendors and a lack of standards, designed and enforced its own standard, called the

Transmission Control Protocol and *Internet Protocol TCP/IP.* Because the DOD is such a large buyer and because the network method has been adopted by the educational and research community, the TCP/IP has become an important standard. It is normally associated with UNIX only because of the popularity of this operating system among researchers. The standard addresses the Network and Transport levels of the OSI model (levels 3 and 4) and installations typically use Ethernet specifications for the lower levels.

Xerox Network System (XNS) from Xerox Corporation is a similar low-level standard that can ride on top of Ethernet. It is widely supported by PC networks.

Some Vendors of PC LANs

AT&T *StarLAN* is a personal computer network based on AT&T's own StarLAN network standard. Its primary feature is that it supports MS/DOS and Unix-based workstations seamlessly on the same network. AT&T, the developers of Unix, believes that this will offer the proper platform for the migration of personal computing from MS DOS to Unix. Zealots like to argue that Unix is the operating system of the future. They claim that personal computers will become too large and powerful for simplistic operating systems (such as MS DOS) that were conceived for smaller computers, and when that happens Unix will be widely adopted.

The wiring uses a fiber optic backbone and twisted-pair telephone wire distribution to individual nodes. Coaxial cable is not used. The network architecture makes use of AT&T's Network Extension Unit (NEU), which is used as a central connector board or "hub," making network hookups very simple. NETBIOS is supported at the Session and Presentation levels of OSI.

TOPS is a personal computer network designed and marketed by a Sun Microsystems subsidiary. It is designed to integrate Unix-based Sun Workstations, Macintosh computers, and IBM personal computers into a single network. Ethernet is used at the low OSI levels for the network, including all cabling and connections. Linkage to TCP/IP is provided at the Network and Transport levels of OSI. Normally, the Sun Workstation would be used as the network server, providing network resources to Macintosh and IBM PC PS/2 workstations. TOPS is viewed as a natural link between AppleTalk and the Unix world.

DECnet from Digital Equipment rides on top of Ethernet levels 1 and 2 and provides specifications for OSI levels 3,4, and 5 (Network, Transport, and Session). DECNet has been used to set up large-scale MIS networks of Digital's VAX machines and PC clusters. The link between Apple's AppleTalk and DECnet has been particularly successful and could be the promethean development in connectivity. DEC has expressed enthusiasm for the OSI standards and is introducing a new and more extensive network standard called Digital Network Architecture (DNA).

AppleTalk from Apple Computer is an extensive network standard that specifies OSI levels from Physical up to Presentation, leaving only Application to node-specific

DOS or application programs. It is designed to link Apple's Macintosh computers together into small "work groups." The Macintosh computers were designed to be networked and are shipped packaged with AppleTalk hardware and software support. AppleTalk has a high degree of integration with the operating system and user interface.

Although initially designed only as a means of sharing the expensive LaserWriter printer, AppleTalk has been greatly expanded and linked to more powerful networks such as Ethernet, DECnet, and SNA, principally because of third-party products. The speed limitation of 0.23 megabits per second has been overcome with cable changes. Hardware add-ons are available to run AppleTalk on top of Ethernet at 10 megabits. The limitation of 32 nodes has been increased to 230.

Other improvements that have enhanced AppleTalk are the AppleShare file server and the Laserserve print spooler from Apple Computer. A particularly impressive enhancement at the Presentation level has been Apple's AFP or AppleTalk Filing Protocol. AFP supports the Mac's visual filing system and user interface. If a network folder is "open" and a file is added or deleted, then all open windows are automatically updated. Contrast this with systems such as FTAM (in the IBM world) in which the user must ask for a new directory listing to get the updated file list.

The VAX-Mac Connection

In 1987, DEC, the second largest computer manufacturer in the world (after IBM), and Apple Computer, the second largest PC manufacturer in the world (after IBM), entered into a strategic partnership. The objective is to integrate Macintosh and VAX systems into a single system. The partners take a systemic view of the LAN concept and recognize the complementary nature of micros and mainframes within this system. Acknowledging that the Macintosh with its mouse-driven, icon-based interface was the ideal user access to the network, it was decided that this should be the medium (workstation) through which users would access all network resources, including VAXs, mainframes, printers, high-capacity disk storage, optical disk, and other devices. The VAX and other large computers should simply concentrate on larger capacities and higher speed to provide this resource to the network.

The synergy has resulted in a high degree of seamless connectivity between the Macintosh and the VAX. This makes it possible to use Macs as workstations to the VAX while retaining the familiar windows and icons and the point/click/drag user interface of the Macintosh Finder. There are several possible configurations of Mac-VAX connectivity.

In the simplest configuration, individual Macs are connected by asynchronous link to a DEC terminal controller that is itself a node on the Ethernet network on which the VAX resides. The Macs can work as terminals to the VAX but have limited functionality beyond that on the network.

A better configuration is achieved when the Macintosh computers are nodes on the Ethernet backbone. The Mac user has much better access to the network and works at the full speed of the Ethernet cable (10 megabits per second). However, each Mac requires an expensive Ethernet interface card and occupies an Ethernet node address. In large networks this would tend to degrade the response rates.

An even better configuration is to organize each department or small functional or geographic group into an AppleTalk network. Macs on the network can utilize local file servers and laser printers without accessing the Ethernet backbone. The AppleTalk network, in turn, is connected via a network bridge to the Ethernet backbone. This makes it possible for each Mac on the AppleTalk network to access the VAX (and other Ethernet resources) via the bridge. This connection is seamless in that it is hidden from the user. The user accesses files and resources as if they were on the Mac, without much thought about where they are and how exactly the network physically brings them to the user.

Terminal Emulation Modes

The Mac (or the IBM PC) can be programmed to behave like a VT100 or similar DEC terminal. The user physically uses the Mac to access VAX applications but logically uses only the facilities of the VT100 (or VT220, VT241) terminal. The advantage is that the user does not need to purchase another terminal, thus saving "footprint" space on the desk. The term *footprint* has gained popularity in MIS circles. With the increased emphasis on "desktop" equipment, desktop space is becoming squeezed and the area occupied by telephones, computers, fax machines, and the mouse is at a such a premium that MIS designers must take it into account. Other than savings in terminal cost and footprint, the user gains little in terms of connectivity and functionality by using terminal emulation instead of the physical terminals.

TPS on PC Networks

With the increasing sophistication and popularity of PC networks and the adoption of PC networks in MIS design, the personal computer is becoming less personal and more public. In a strictly personal computing environment, the software designer could assume that the files would be accessed by only one user at a time, but information systems that use PC networks may require more than one user to be able to access the same database. In particular, online transaction processing systems (OLTPS) make some specific demands of databases that are not normally available in PC-based database software.

Changes made to a record and new records added should be made available to all users as soon as the record is entered. While a record is being changed by one user, other users must not be allowed to access the record or to change it. However, the other users must have access to the file at all times. These requirements generally mean that record level, rather than file level interlock, should be used. Also, to make the same data available to all users, the database must be kept on a network file server. The server must pass only the specific records requested and not the whole file. This requires the server to be more discriminating than a file server, and it is variously referred to as a database server or, when compatible with IBM's SQL, a structured query language (SQL) server.

Although MIS database managers of traditional multiuser mainframe environments solved these problems years ago, PC software, which had been designed for single users, is generally immature in this regard. The push to build more PC networks has finally provided the needed impetus for PC software vendors and computer makers to address the issue. Most popular PC database programs including dBASE III, Paradox, R:Base, Foxbase, and Revelation now have multiuser or network versions that offer many of the features necessary to carry out OLTP in a PC network. Team-up, a new database software product from Unlimited Processing, was designed from the ground up to serve a PC network-based OLTP with heavy data traffic. Speed is a very important feature in OLTP, since updates must be posted immediately, and record-passing to several users can cause response degradation. Efficient OLTPs are designed for high throughput and high availability of shared resources. Because the program was designed differently to be suitable for fast response on a network, Team-up is much faster than the database programs that are modified versions of single user programs.

IBM 3270 Communications

The IBM 3270 is a data communication protocol and terminal display definition used for accessing IBM's System/370 mainframes as hosts from terminals and other systems that serve as the workstation. The display and keyboard definitions normally used are those of IBM 3278 and 3279 terminals. The 3270 supports bisync (binary synchronous) communication as well as SDLC (synchronous data link control) at speeds up to 256 kilobits per second. In addition to the 3278 and 3279 terminals, 3270 communication support is available that provides gateways to most local area networks and for IBM personal computers, including the PC and the PS/2. Direct linkage to fast mainframe-to-mainframe communication protocols such as SNA and X.25 is also available. For full System/370 communication support, a PS/2 or PC requires a 3270 adapter card as well as 3278/9 terminal emulation software.

IBM's Token-Ring Network

The IBM Token-Ring local area network is a popular and versatile LAN. The networking protocol is designed primarily for the networking of personal computers within a building to facilitate the sharing of printers, other peripherals, and files on hard-disk servers. The network supports a data transfer rate of 4 megabits per second over coaxial cable connections. The personal computer LANs can be bridged to each other or to IBM mainframes. Bridges and gateways are available to interconnect the Token-Ring LANs to System/370 host machines, System/3x computers, and to the new IBM 9370 midrange computer. IBM uses specially fitted and programmed PCs to perform gateway and bridge functions.

In the Token-Ring scheme, the network devices are connected to each other in a circular path. An electronic header flag, or token, goes round and round the ring. The token can either be free or carry an encoded message. If it is free, any one of the network computers can capture the token, change the flag to busy, and attach a message to it. If it is busy, it is carrying a message for a specific node address, which is encoded into the token. The node addressed copies the message and sends the token and message frame back to the sender as acknowledgment. The sender then removes the message frame and returns the token as free back to the ring.

This scheme has proven extremely reliable. Both data integrity and response time can be predictable as opposed to CSMA/CD systems, in which the response time varies widely with network load.

IBM Mainframe and Mini Computers

The IBM System/3x

The IBM System/38 has been one of the most successful MIS machines ever built. It has been an MIS workhorse in small- and medium-sized companies and is popular as a departmental computer in large organizations. The System/3x computers were designed from the ground up to drive an MIS database environment and introduced many innovations in computer design.

The low cost of the machines made computerization possible for many businesses that were too small to afford or use large mainframes. These computers broke down many installation barriers. Whereas mainframes were housed in large, inaccessible, air-conditioned "computer rooms," the System/3x consisted entirely of one or two file-cabinet-sized machines that were wheeled right into the office and made completely accessible. The System/3x computers are simple to operate, rugged and robust in design, and extremely reliable. Reliability of operation has been a major factor in their success since programmers, users, and MIS managers began to trust these machines. It was one of the first machines built for the user as well as for the data processing professional.

But what has made this computer such an MIS success story is undoubtedly its database orientation. Other computers provide a simple data platform with access to disk sectors and files. Then software engineers develop database environments on top of the operating system. But the System/3x is, in every respect, a "database engine." The unique system architecture integrates database functions right into the operating system, the microcode, and the hardware. This architecture makes it easy for MIS programmer's to integrate all the company's data into one database with as many functional user views as necessary. Many database functions such as creating user views of data can be performed by making system calls instead of writing code. Software developers responded enthusiastically to this new opportunity and today the System/3x environment enjoys a rich array of MIS software ranging from accounting to MRP.

Built in to the System/3x is an ad hoc query facility (Query) designed for end users. The menu-driven query system can access any data in the database without any programming assistance.

System/38 configurations include choices of several peripherals and system units. The model 700 is normally configured with 16 to 32 megabytes of main memory, using IBM's new one-megabit chips. Up to sixteen IBM 3370 and 9332 disk drives (direct access storage devices, or DASDs) can be configured for a total direct access external storage of 13.6 gigabytes. Although the usual display device (terminal) used in System/3x installations is the IBM 3179 terminal, IBM also offers IBM PC terminals as an option. The terminals are connected to the system unit via SNA/-SDLC, using the IBM 5294 communications controller. Each System/38 unit can support up to 256 users and 12 communication lines.

"Silverlake," the IBM AS/400

IBM introduced this minicomputer in 1988 for the same market as that served by the System/38 — small- and medium-sized companies. IBM perceives this market segment as the fastest-growing market in the world for computing machinery. Although this upgrade was expected to replace the System/3x product line, demand for 3x systems continues to be strong and the AS/400 has been slow to catch on.

Code-named "Silverlake," the AS/400 machines can be considered to be an upgrade to the System/3x. Rather than use the cutting edge of technology in terms of speed and hardware components, the system designers have emphasized good engineering and changing technological priorities. Incorporation of new technology and new system design priorities are the major differences. The units are more compact, generate less heat, run on standard 110-volt power, and offer plug-and-go-type installation similar to that for PCs. Compared to the 3x machines, the AS/400 has faster processing speeds, more storage capacity, enhanced network connectivity, and better PC compatibility.

An important attribute of this machine is that it has been designed to be completely compatible with IBM's Systems Application Architecture (SAA). As long as IBM retains the SAA architecture, this feature of the AS/400 will ensure full compatibility with future IBM hardware and software products, from super mainframes to PCs encompassing System/370, RPG, and PS/2 machines. SAA gives the AS/400 a higher degree of connectivity than System 3/x machines offer. This advantage includes enhanced integration with PCs and facilitates distributed processing designs using System/370-based networks.

But the most useful features for System/3x users who might wish to migrate are increased storage and faster execution cycles. The reported transaction processing speed of 45,000 transactions per minute is twice that of the System/38 and five times that of the older System/36. The main memory capacity of 96 megabytes is three times that of the System/38's 32 megabytes and the DASD capacity of 27.2 gigabytes is twice that of the 38 and 19 times that of the 36.

The number of local workstations supported has been increased from the System 38's 256 to a whopping 480. The AS/400 can run 32 communication lines using IBM's Token Ring LAN. Connectivity has been an important issue in the AS/400 design. MIS designs can employ a number of these machines linked together with a high-speed network into a distributed processing system with a System/370-based network operating system. A program called *PC Support* provides a high degree of integration between IBM PC and PS/2 computers with the AS/400.

Like the 3x systems before it, the AS/400 is designed for MIS applications with a built-in relational database. To ease conversion to the AS/400, IBM has even made it System/36-compatible, so that existing System/36 users can convert without software rewrites. They can simply transfer their files over. To date, however, the MIS marketplace is still waiting to see how the industry will evolve in the short term. Utilizing what it has learned about user-friendliness in the PC market, IBM has given the AS/400 a menu-driven front end, complete with an online help facility.

The IBM Model 4381 Mainframe

IBM's Model 4381 is a mid-sized machine between the high-end 3090 and the low-end System/38s but has not been used as extensively in MIS environments. Its low cost and fast floating point math capabilities have made it a popular mainframe for universities and for engineering and scientific applications.

The 4381 is an upgrade to the older Model 4341 and offers almost 2.5 times the computing power of its predecessor. The processor cycle time of 56 nanoseconds represents a significant improvement over past models. (A 56 nanosecond cycle time corresponds to $1000/56 = 18$ MIPS.) It supports IBM's VM or MVS operating systems, with interactive support provided by the CMS and MUSIC systems in educational environments and the TSO or Customer Information Control System (CICS) in commercial MIS installations. The main memory capacity is 32 megabytes, using 256 kilobit chips. A multiplication chip is used to speed math computations and special microcode is provided to enhance the speed and accuracy of mathematical computations. A software package called Mathematical Function Facility is used to improve performance in engineering and scientific applications. Floating point numbers can be computed to 128-bit precision. Fifty-one floating point instructions are available with the machine. In extended precision floating point, numbers can be computed to 34 decimal digits of precision. The 4381 is able to use any of IBM's standard DASDs such as the 3370, 3380, and 3390.

The IBM Model 3090 Mainframe

IBM's 3083 and its most recent incarnation, the 3090, are the mammoths of the MIS world. With the MVS operating system and the CICS software for OLTP support, these fast, high-capacity, high-end mainframes have become the standard MIS machines in large corporations.

IBM sees the 3090 as the basic MIS frame for business computing through the nineties. The advanced processor operates at a cycle time as low as 17.2 nanoseconds (Model 180E), which corresponds to about 58 MIPS. The raw computing power of the 3090 machines is setting new standards for MIS hardware designers.

The 3090 has a primary memory capacity of 256 megabytes and supports the MVS and the VM operating systems and the System/370 Extended Architecture. The advanced models use two to six tightly coupled processors, each of which has access to the primary memory address lines and to all the communication channels and the DASD devices. The processors are able to work together in a parallel processing configuration by allocating CPU cycles to each other. Special programming techniques can be used to exploit the multiple processors more fully. If one CPU fails, the other(s) takes over. The overall system response and throughput goes down but the system does not.

In our case studies we have seen that Apple, Bechtel, WalMart, and FFIC all use the 3090 as an MIS tool. One reason for its popularity in transaction processing applications is the CICS software. CICS/MVS Version 2 is the CICS product recommended by IBM. The ideal hardware environment is the multiprocessor 3090 machine running the MVS operating system. CICS/MVS is a set of productivity tools for programmers of terminal-oriented transaction processing systems that can be used directly by customers and suppliers as well as employees of the firm. It greatly reduces the amount of programming needed to access data and offers advanced system features such as multi-region programming and recovery when developing online transaction processing systems.

SAA by IBM

"If, any one of them can, explain it," said Alice, "I'll give him sixpence. I don't believe there is an atom of meaning in it."

— Lewis Carroll, *Alice in Wonderland*

SAA is a promising solution to a messy problem. Here is the problem.

By the late eighties, IBM had put out a number of different kinds of systems that were incompatible with each other. The midsize 4381 and the mainframe 3090, under the VS, MVS, and VM operating systems, functioned according to the System/370 architecture. However, the System/3x machines did not follow this architecture at all. A software specialist or end user familiar with the System/370 was lost in a foreign world with the System/3x machines. Whereas the System/370 used a file system geared primarily for programming in COBOL, the System/38 used a database core with an RGP (report program generator) interface. Each system had its own communications and terminal protocols; the System/370 environment used the 3270 while the System/3x world used the 5250. Software developed in one environment would not work in the other, and it was hard to get these machines to talk to each other.

The internal heterogeneity took a turn for the worse with the introduction of the AS/400 relational database machine and that of the desktop PS/2 systems with the OS/2 operating system. IBM had created four different computing environments that were incompatible and that had very little connectivity. Software development was fragmented as software engineers had to concentrate on one system or the other. So different are these systems that even the keyboard layout was different from machine to machine. MIS managers, software developers, end users, and manufacturers of peripheral devices alike were openly critical of Big Blue for continuing to spawn incompatible system architectures. Compared to DEC VAX systems, for instance, these systems have poor connectivity and do not offer an easy migration path with compatible software environments.

To remedy this situation IBM has developed SAA, or System Application Architecture. SAA is a grand unification plan. It will, we are told, make all IBM systems from the personal computers to mammoth mainframes look the same to programmers, users, networks, and devices. Programmers have to know only one architecture and end users must familiarize themselves with only one user interface. For example, programs can be developed on one machine and executed on another. Moreover, since SAA is network-oriented and allows multiple processors and devices, applications can be developed that run on more than one machine. For example, an order entry system could be developed that resides in a 3090 mainframe and that uses the PS/2 for some functions and a System/38 for others.

This architecture works by standardizing and controlling the methods by which the computer interacts with its environment, consisting of programmers, users, devices, networks, and other computers. The standardized methods are called common interfaces. For example, the CPI, or Common Programming Interface (Can you expect anything less from a company whose name itself is an acronym?), provides a single programming environment for programming any of IBM's machines from the mighty 3090 to the pesky PS/2. Development tools supported by SAA/-CPI include COBOL, FORTRAN, RPG III, C, and a 4GL application generator.

The Common User Access (CUA) standardizes the user interface. It specifies the hardware (including the keyboard!), the dialog and command lexicon, and the screen presentation method and style. The SAA/CUA is a radical departure from conventional IBM software and represents a bold new development for the giant computer maker. For example, the CUA's window and icon-based, Macintosh-like presentation style brings the best aspects of personal computers into the integrated large-scale computing arena. The CCS, or Common Communication Support, standardizes the way data can enter and leave the SAA environment and includes terminal as well as network support.

To what extent the industry or even IBM will support SAA remains to be seen. Like all standards, SAA is without support, just so many specifications. Even while IBM is proclaiming SAA as the framework on which it will build the future, another part of the same firm is pushing the 9370, a brand-new IBM "departmental computer" that does not incorporate SAA. Then there is CICS, a user interface and development platform for transaction processing that seems to have been developed from the ground up without any SAA elements. Regardless of what the future holds, it is clear that SAA will play a major role in design of IBM-based MIS.

IBM PC and PS/2 Personal Computers

Personal computers from IBM are significant components of MIS designs and are used primarily for end-user computing, networking, as front ends to mainframe applications, and even for software development in MIS environments.

The Veritable IBM PC and XT

The humble IBM PC, now outdone by the AT and the PS/2, is still widely used. It was IBM's initial offering in the PC arena. The machine employs the Intel 8088 CPU at 4.77 MHz and can be (and usually is) configured with 640 kilobytes of primary memory. The PC version has dual 5¼-inch 360 kilobyte floppy disk drives (FDDs) while the XT version has one floppy drive (also 360 kilobytes) and a 20 megabyte hard disk. The systems have limited communications capability and do not have a built-in networking port such as the AppleTalk port of the Macintosh. There are two RS232-compatible serial ports capable of asynchronous communication at up to 19.2 K baud. A Centronics-compatible parallel printer port is also provided. Two types of screen display controllers are offered, one for text display and a "color graphics" controller that has bit-mapped color graphics display capability. The graphics resolution of 320 x 256 pixels is poor by today's standards.

The operating system was a variant of "86-DOS," a DOS from Seattle Computer for their 8086 board for the S-100 bus. Microsoft adapted it to the IBM PC and marketed it as MS DOS, while IBM called their implementation PC DOS. It is a simple single-user, single-machine, single-task operating system for the 8088 CPU that supports floppy and hard disks, a good memory-mapped video display system, extended keyboard functions including function keys, and a well-conceived set of interrupt-driven function calls.

IBM brought this machine to market with almost no software besides the operating system and a BASIC interpreter (both from Microsoft). They wanted to get the product out quickly. By using third-party components, they were able to bring the PC to market in about nine months. IBM then waited for third-party software and hardware developers to fill in the blanks. They didn't have to wait very long.

Within a year of introduction, the IBM PC was supported by a large array of hardware add-ons that remedied almost all of its shortcomings except for the RAM addressing limit (640 kilobytes) and the maximum addressable disk and file size (32 megabytes). Support from software developers was overwhelming. A microcomputer software industry had been built up by the CP/M (central program microcomputer) operating system. These programmers jumped onto the IBM bandwagon and filled the PC software void with good word processing, spreadsheet, database, CAD, and other programs. The most notable program was 1-2-3 from Lotus Corporation. This spreadsheet program with graphics capabilities helped give the IBM PC a firm grip on the large-scale business market that it has yet to loosen.

The IBM PC AT

The AT, or Advanced Technology, version of the IBM PC was the first actual hardware revision of this product. It incorporated what was then Intel's state-of-the-art CPU, the 80286, as its main processor. The new processor boosted the speed of the machine and opened it up for more sophisticated software and applications. The video display was enhanced to 480 lines in color and the floppy disk capacity was increased to 1.2 megabytes (from 360 kilobytes). The hard disk capacity was increased to 40 megabytes.

MS DOS (currently Version 3.3 and soon to be updated to Version 4), continued as the operating system. In essence, the AT was a 286 machine with an 8088 operating system. Since the 286 would execute all 8088 instructions, not only the MS DOS operating system but all software written for the MS DOS 8088 PC would work on the new machine. This was excellent from a compatibility standpoint but it also meant that no one wrote any 286 code and the AT simply used the 286 as a fast 8088.

However, because of the memory map used by the PC design and Intel's segmented memory addressing, the machine was still saddled with the 640-kilobyte limit on main memory. As programs and applications grew in sophistication, this RAM limitation became a bottleneck in the development of the AT.

The Intel 80386, PS/2, and OS/2

The PS/2, or Personal System 2, is IBM's current line of personal computers. Besides using more advanced hardware and software technology, the design of these machines has incorporated features such as IBM's proprietary Micro Channel Architecture that make it difficult to copy or "clone" these machines as easily as the PC line.

The PS/2 computers represent a complete departure from the PC architecture and the MS DOS operating system, and no attempt has been made to retain compatibility between these systems. The primary design features are mainframe connectivity (in the SAA architecture), enhanced user-friendliness, better graphics, faster processing, and increased primary memory and disk storage. A number of popular features of the PC line have been integrated into the system board. These include serial and parallel ports, graphics output, mouse interface, clock/calendar, and disk controller. IBM has used the lessons it learned from the PC experience to design the PS/2, allowing the PC marketplace and the third-party hardware vendors to determine the configuration and options that a personal computer should contain.

Using the Micro Channel Architecture, the PS/2 has overcome the 640-kilobyte memory limitation and can offer an addressable RAM space of up to 16 megabytes.

Whereas in the PCs, the graphics display generator was an add-on card with strong competition from third-party vendors, PS/2's VGA (Video Graphics Array) or MCGA (Multi Color Graphics Array) is built into the system board. These graphic controllers can display 640 x 480 pixels per screen in sixteen colors.

In developing the PS/2, IBM has finally discarded the aging 8088 for good and has gone to Intel's 80386 and the 80286 as the primary processors for personal computers. MS DOS, which was an operating system for the 8088, has been replaced by OS/2, written for the 80286 in 286 code. OS/2 and a bigger version, OS/2 Extended, along with the user interface, Presentation Manager, include many features that address new priorities for PC users and for IBM, including multi-tasking, built-in database support, integration with mainframes, and a mouse-driven window and icon-based user interface that make the computers easier to use and give IBM a chance to catch up with gains made by Apple's Macintosh along these lines.

OS/2 has been slow to stake its claim as the successor to MS DOS as the dominant PC operating system. It will probably continue to be slow going for OS/2 until the faster 386 machines with large memory and disk space become more popular. Compared with MS DOS, OS/2 is large and slow. Ironically, although OS/2 is an operating system for the 286 processor, the 286, even at 12 MHz, does not have the power to run OS/2 at a usable speed. OS/2 actually requires a 386 at 20 or 25 MHz to incorporate all its features with a sufficiently fast response for interactive usage without long waits. Many industry observers have criticized OS/2 for this reason and for its large memory and disk space requirements.

In any case, because of the enormous computer power required to run OS/2 and especially OS/2 Extended, these operating systems are not likely to become household words until 386 systems (such as IBM PS/2 models 70 and 80, the Compaq Deskpro 386, and similar computers) proliferate to the same extent as have 8088 systems. As in the AT model, in which the 286 was used to drive an 8088 operating system, a 386 is needed to operate a 286 operating system. What some analysts are wondering out loud is whether there will ever be an operating system or any code written for the 386 or whether it will be used as a fast 286 until the next generation of processors breaks onto the scene.

Along with the 8088 processor, IBM has also dumped the 5¼-inch floppy disk drive in going to the PS/2 line. The floppy drives used in the new machines are the 3½-inch drives originally designed by Sony and made popular by Apple's Macintosh computers. These new drives have a capacity of 1.44 megabytes compared to the 1.2 capacity of the AT floppy drive. The diskettes themselves are much better designed for easy and safe handling, shipment, and storage. IBM's stamp of approval means that the older floppy designs are obsolete and that floppy drives will be 3½ inches for the foreseeable future. Most models also feature very high capacity and fast hard-disk systems.

The PS/2 Model 70 and 80

If the "something-for-everyone" style of PS/2 models and options is bewildering, perhaps it is only IBM's way of test marketing to see which ones survive the consumers' scrutiny. For MIS applications using OS/2- and SAA-compatibility as a basis, only the two 386/MCA models are usually considered. These are the model 70 and the model 80 in their various optional configurations. The price-performance leader seems to be the model 70, with its advanced 25-MHz 386 processor and all the high-powered features of the PS/2 line. It is, in many respects, superior to the higher-priced model 80. The most notable difference between the two, other than price, is that the model 80 is a floor unit and has more expansion slots than the 70, a desktop unit. Both units use the Intel 80386 CPU and IBM's Micro Channel Architecture and can use either the OS/2 Standard or the OS/2 Extended Edition as the operating system.

The standard processor in both models is the 16-MHz 386. Both units offer the 20-MHz CPU as an option while the model 70 can also be purchased in a 25-MHz version. Both systems require 0 to 2 wait states although the 25-MHz version of the model 70 can operate without wait states with a 64-kilobyte memory cache. Both systems come with either 1 or 2 megabytes of main memory (RAM) on the system board. The memory capacity of the system board ranges from 4 to 8 megabytes. Plug-in "adapter boards" can be used to increase the memory size to the maximum addressable range of 16 megabytes. A minimum of 4 megabytes is recommended for proper operation with OS/2 and the anticipated increasing size and complexity of PS/2 software. The model 70 is configured with either a 60- or 120-megabyte 3½-inch disk while the model 80 uses 5-inch hard disks with capacities of 44 (standard), 70, 115, and 314 megabytes (optional). All seven expansion slots in the model 80 can be used for 16-bit devices, and three can also be used for 32-bit boards. The model 70 offers only two 32-bit slots and one 16-bit slot.

The PS/2 Model 50 and PS/2 Model 60

These are desktop 80286 models (both use the 10 MHz version). They support the OS/2 Standard Edition, which is too slow to be practical. OS/2 Extended Edition will not run on these machines. Functions similar to Presentation Manager are provided by Windows/286, a Microsoft product being sold by IBM with its 286 systems. However, the 286 systems offer the RAM, disk storage, and video display capabilities of the 386 systems. The other models, the model 30 and the model 25, are not OS/2-compatible. They are designed for the educational and consumer markets and are not expected to play a role in MIS designs.

Fixed Disk Access Times

The following average access times are provided in the IBM publication entitled *IBM Personal Systems: Reference Guide* (June 1988):

Capacity (megabytes)	Size (inches)	Controller Type	Data Transfer Rate (megabits per second)	Average Access Time (microseconds)
20	3.5	ST-506	5	80
30	3.5	ST-506	5	39
44	5.25	ST-506	5	40
60	3.5	ESDI	10	27
70	5.25	ESDI	10	30
115	5.25	ESDI	10	28
120	3.5	ESDI	10	23
314	5.25	ESDI	10	23

Selection of an appropriate PS/2 system for I/O-intensive operations, such as maintenance of large databases and operation as a network file or database server, requires attention to the speed with which data can be delivered from the disk to the user. The speed with which the disk controller can transfer data is measured in millions of bits per second (Mbps) and the time required for the read/write heads to find a sector (on the average) is reported in microseconds (thousandths of a second). Both of these must be taken into consideration to compare the speed with which disk data can be accessed. A low access time and high data transfer rate are desirable.

IBM Operating System/2

Among the distinctive features of OS/2 are the following:

1. *Overcomes the 640-kilobyte memory limitation of the PC*
   The memory map of the new OS/2 operating system takes full advantage of the addressing capabilities of the 80286 CPU and provides access to the full linear address space of 16 megabytes.

2. *An operating system for the advanced 80286 chip*
   Unlike PC DOS, which is an operating system for the 8088 chip, the new OS/2 from IBM is written for the more advanced and faster 80286 chip and does not support the 8088. The 8088 goes back to the roots of the PC. Microcomputers are so much more powerful today that it was necessary to finally wean the personal computer line from this granddaddy of Intel's 16-bit CPUs.

3. *Multi-tasking*

For many "power users," this will be an especially useful feature. Multi-tasking allows the user to run several programs at the same time or to run the same program several times on different files. A popular use of multi-tasking is to keep the most frequently used programs running at all times and to simply switch among them as needed, thus saving considerable time that would otherwise be spent in exiting one program and executing another.

4. *SAA compatibility*

How important IBM's System Application Architecture (SAA) will be in the future of MIS is still an educated guess. The possibilities are exciting. Could it actually be that someday all of IBM's machines, from the PS/2 to the System/3x, from the AS/400 to the 4381 and the 3090, would all be logically the same machine? Imagining the resulting software portability, the connectivity, and the multi-machine distributed processing boggles the mind.

5. *Macintosh-like point-and-click usability*

Away with command lines and cryptic "A:>" prompts! Enter now the world of mouse-driven command systems with windows, pull-down menus, icons, and a graphical user interface that Macintosh users have known and loved since 1984 (while IBM PC users scoffed). IBM has done Apple one better by building an extensive context-sensitive help system right into the operating system à la AS/400.

6. *Standardized user interface*

Conventional-operating systems such as PC DOS offer standardized disk access methods; standardized device addressing and display methods; and an array of system calls for application programs to access system routines. However, they do nothing to standardize the user interface. So, each application programmer is free to design dialogs, commands, and keyboard functions. For example, in Lotus 1-2-3, the user depresses the ESCAPE key to abort a command node and uses the F1 key to ask for help screens, while in WordPerfect the abort command is F7 and the help command is F3. What's more, the help facility works very differently in the two environments. Each software program is unique and thus potentially confusing to users of other programs. Like Macintosh before it, OS/2 has finally remedied this situation by standardizing the user interface of IBM's personal computers. OS/2 uses the CUA (Common User Access) of SAA, so that not only are the user interface of

PS/2 programs likely to be similar, but this similarity should hold for all IBM machines that support the SAA architecture.

7. *Built-in database system*
Contained within the operating system is an implementation of IBM's relational database system, DB2 with the SQL (Structured Query Language) interactive query and report writing program. The data structure and command syntax are compatible with IBM's mainframe DB2 system. Although the importance of DB2 in the future of PS/2 is unknown at present, it certainly will play an important role, even if only as a data structure master plan for other database programs.

8. *Connectivity*
OS/2 supports a range of communication methods and emulation modes, including IBM's System 3270, async links, X.25 and SNA support, and IBM's local area networks. Terminal emulation includes IBM 3270, 3101, and 5250, and DEC's VT100.

9. *32-megabyte disk volumes*
The PC's 32-megabyte disk volume size limitation has, sadly, been retained. This means that large disk drives are divided into multiple volumes of 32 megabytes or less.

Apple Macintosh Computers

The ideal tool is invisible.   — Dr. Donald Norman, Chairman
Cognitive Sciences Department
University of California, San Diego

Prior to the Macintosh, the computer as a tool has been anything but invisible. Many human endeavors, including college courses in engineering or finance, become so bogged down by the need to learn specific computer procedure that the complexity of the procedure becomes confused with the task itself.

The Apple Macintosh broke significant new ground in the design of personal computers, bringing innovations that have altered the course of personal computing and the personal computer industry. Before the Macintosh, computers, even personal computers, were designed for technically sophisticated users. Less sophisticated users attended classes and read books or otherwise attempted to become computer-literate so that they too could participate. Apple designed the Macintosh to surmount this barrier and to "put computing power in the hands of everyone, not just the technologically oriented."

The computer industry overcame its initial skepticism about such radical ideas and has adopted many of them. Even IBM is using the mouse-driven graphical interface in its new CUA/SAA and OS/2 Presentation Manager systems. From the gathering momentum, it seems fairly certain that this interface is the way computers of the future will look and feel to most users.

From an MIS manager's standpoint, the user interface alleviates three important concerns with respect to end-user computing: training, support, and overall user satisfaction. Computers that virtually anyone can use require very little training and support, and the MIS manager feels little apprehension with respect to "proliferation" of personal computers if no large staff and overhead budget will be required to train and support the users to a very large extent. *User satisfaction* is becoming an increasingly important buzzword in MIS as more MIS managers realize that EIS, DSS, and other end-user intensive systems are utilized only to the extent that the users enjoy using them. It is difficult to win over users who have become intimidated by the need for more and more manuals and training. What's more, executives and managers frequently do not have the time to read through manuals or to participate in extensive training sessions.

The Macintosh Graphical User Interface

Instead of the abstract command line interpretation used by older systems, the Macintosh uses a system of metaphors that draws analogies between the computer's functions and those of familiar objects. The physical display screen is presented as a desktop containing a menu and several windows, objects, and tools. The tools differ in function and only one tool is active at a given time. The most common tool on the desktop is the arrowhead which, like other tools, is manipulated by moving and clicking the mouse. The objects can represent disk volumes, folders (subdirectories), files, application programs, and specific functions (such as the trash can). Windows are virtual screens that hold the display of data from any of these objects that has been "opened" by the mouse action. Many windows can be opened and left on the desktop. The user can use the mouse to alter the size and location of the windows, to rearrange the windows to form a convenient display, and to select which window will be the active one. Many actions can be taken simply by manipulating the objects. Other actions may require commands issued from a system of pull-down menus. The menu on top of the desktop is actually a list of menus grouped according to function. Thus, most functions of the computer are realized simply by manipulating objects in a graphical layout instead by typing commands.

An important property of the Macintosh that may not be immediately apparent is its consistency. The Macintosh looks the same and works the same, whether the user is in the operating system desktop or any one of thousands of application programs. To ensure this consistency, Apple has built a standardized user interface into the operating system instead of leaving to the whims of programmers the definition of command systems and screen designs. Application programs communicate with the user by making system calls (that is, by calling the system routines provided) that automatically perform the window, menu, and icon management according to a single consistent set of rules.

Motorola 68000 Series Microprocessors

While the IBM personal computers employ the iAPX 86 line of processors from Intel (8088, 8086, 80286, 80386), Apple's Macintosh line of computers uses the 68xxx series of processors from Motorola. These include the 68000, the 68020, and the 68030. The new Motorola 88000 series of chips has not yet been incorporated into a personal computer. The 8-MHz 68000 CPU is used in the Macintosh Plus and the Macintosh SE models. These chips have a 32-bit internal architecture, a 16-bit wide data path, and 24-bit addressing capabilities. The standard processor in the Macintosh II is the 16-MHz 68020. The more advanced 68020 and 68030 are full 32-bit chips and offer much faster processing speeds. They have a 32-bit data path and 32-bit addressing modes. The computing power these chips bring to the desktop exceeds that of the minicomputers produced only a few years ago. The Macintosh II also includes a 68881 floating point math co-processor.

Communications and Connectivity

The Macintosh was designed to be a networked computer. In addition to standard serial and parallel ports, the Macintosh contains an AppleTalk network connector and an SCSI (small computer systems interface) port as standard equipment. The Apple-Talk network, initially supplied to allow several Mac users to share a common laser printer, has matured into a very powerful and fast local area network with file servers (for example, AppleShare), print-queuing routines (Laserserve), and bridges and gateways to Ethernet and other large-scale networks (Fastpath). The SCSI connector brings out a data bus that has gained widespread industry support. It allows expansion by the addition of up to eight peripheral devices, including hard disks, tape drives, and CD/ROM drives, which can be attached to the SCSI port.

The Macintosh SE

The low-end Macintosh is the SE, which retains the size and look of the original Macintosh. The main system board, the video display, and the disk drives are integrated into one compact unit. The keyboard and mouse are separate components that need to be connected to the system unit prior to operation. A key feature of the Macintosh is the high-resolution graphics display of 512 x 342 pixels. The 9-inch (diagonal) monochrome display has been criticized by some industry observers, but it offers some very important advantages: it is light and compact, and for a given pixel resolution it provides a high pixel density in terms of dots per inch. Pictures, icons, and graphics on the Mac's screen owe their crisp appearance to the high pixel density. Standard mass storage on the SE consists of an 800-kilobyte 3½-inch removable media FDD and a 20-megabyte fixed disk. A 40-megabyte drive is optional. The SE comes with 1 megabyte of main memory (RAM) using 1-megabit chips. Although this memory is adequate for most applications, Apple's MultiFinder multi-tasker requires at least 2 megabytes. The memory can be expanded to 4 megabytes on the system board. An expansion slot is provided for later addition of more memory or other devices. The clock/calendar is battery-backed so that the date does not evaporate every time the computer is turned off. A four-voice sound generator uses an 8-bit D/A (digital/analog) converter and a 22-KHz sampling rate. A sound port is provided for external connection to an audio amplifier. A recent enhancement, the SE/30, uses the faster 68030 chip.

The Macintosh II

This full 32-bit machine comes with impressive credentials, including a 640 x 480 color display, the capability to perform very fast computations with its 68020 (or optional 68030) processor and 68881 floating point math processor, and six expansion slots on Apple's NuBus design. In addition to the standard Mac operating system, Apple also offers a version of UNIX with a Mac-like graphical user interface called A/UX. The main memory capacity is 1 megabyte (standard) to on-board expansion to 8 megabytes. Additional memory can be added by using expansion boards. The Mac II includes an 800-kilobyte 3½-inch FDD and a 40-megabyte hard disk unit. An 80-megabyte hard disk is optional. Much larger sizes of mass storage are available from third-party vendors. Mass storage volumes and system files are not limited to 32 megabytes, as in the PS/2.

Macintosh Software and Applications

Large-scale MIS settings generally utilize Macintosh computers to take advantage of their connectivity and graphics. Most Macintosh computers are networked using AppleTalk clusters that are connected via a main corporate backbone. Each Apple-Talk cluster is normally equipped with a laser printer. Desktop publishing is still a big reason to use Macintosh but other business applications are gaining in importance. Microsoft Excel, a spreadsheet-modelling program, with its superior graphics and Macintosh-like usability, is normally considered to be the premier spreadsheet program in the industry. Microsoft Word (word processing), Hypercard, Helix, and 4th Dimension (database), and PageMaker (desktop publishing) are some of the programs normally found in a Mac environment.

Univac 1100 Series Mainframes

In our case studies we found that both Bechtel and Tyson were Univac "houses"; that is, their main corporate MIS base was on large Univac mainframes. These machines, the Univac 1100/80 and its more recent cousin the Unisys 1100/90, are the products of the Unisys Corporation, formed in 1986 by the merger of Sperry Univac and Burroughs. Unlike companies such as DEC and Sun that created their own market, or firms such as CDC, Cray, and Tandem that address niche markets, or firms such as Amdahl that produce IBM-compatible mainframes, Unisys sought through this merger (and the "power of two") to challenge IBM toe-to-toe on its home turf — the mainframe MIS market.

These machines are not IBM-compatible and face a stiff uphill battle in terms of IBM's deeply entrenched and trusted MIS application software. Their operating systems, file systems, and database structures are different from IBM's and many MIS managers complain about being "boxed" into Unisys systems. But Unisys competes on price, offering mainframe packages comparable to IBM systems in performance and capacity at substantially lower cost. No MIS manager can afford not to investigate such offers.

Unisys offers an IMS-like hierarchical database environment called DMS. An interactive front-end to DMS called MAPPER allows users to interact with DMS using 4GL-type queries. Even end-users can be trained to use MAPPER. Normally, HDBMS is considered to be very user-hostile and not conducive to 4GL/ad hoc access.

In addition to their line of smart terminals, Unisys offers a PC-compatible microstation that can be used as a Unisys terminal with the addition of a special communication board. Like all mainframe manufacturers (IBM 3270, DEC VT100), Unisys ties its customers into their own terminals and terminal protocol. These terminals are of little use outside the Univac world, and other terminals can communicate in only limited ways with these computers.

The Unisys 1100/92 is equipped with dual CPUs each with a capacity of 7.5 MIPS. A normal configuration has 16 to 32 megabytes of main memory and about a dozen disk drives, each with a capacity of 600 megabytes.

5000 Series Minis (Departmental Computers)

These small UNIX-based minicomputers are designed to address the "departmental computer" market. A single installation can serve many MIS and workstation users and can communicate with the 1100 mainframes. In large installations, it is possible to use a hierarchical architecture, with a number of these minis being served by the mainframe. Although Bechtel does not use this architecture, Tyson does use the 5000 machines as remote servers and data collectors in their production units.

DEC VAX and MicroVAX

The VAX line of computers from Digital (DEC) has been extremely successful for many reasons, not the least of which is that they offer virtually trouble-free operation, high performance, and a completely compatible growth path from a super micro-type desktop machine (MicroVAX) to a full mainframe environment (VAX Clusters). This compatibility across machines and the extensive networking support of these machines have made them MIS workhorses in many medium-sized companies. A rich base of software for MIS applications has evolved to support the VAX installations.

The VAX 8800 Series

The VAX 8810, 8820, 8830, and 8840 computers are the most powerful computers made by DEC. The 8840 is about four times as fast as the 8810 but is similar in other respects, offering up to 512 megabytes of main memory, 20 gigabytes of disk storage, and 30 megabytes per second data transfer rate. These models are all based on the 8810 architecture but vary with respect to the number of parallel processors installed and therefore with respect to computing power in terms of MIPS capability. Any of these can be upgraded to the more powerful versions by field modifications, a feature that is important to MIS designers looking for easy upward migration paths. (See the Autodesk case on page 166.)

As do all VAX machines, the 8800 series uses the VMS operating system that supports both DECnet and Ethernet networking standards and the X-Window iconic user interface. Although the operating system is very flexible and popular with users, it suffers from the apparent disadvantage that it is a proprietary (vendor-specific) software package without industry-wide support. This contrasts with operating systems such as MS DOS and UNIX that don't tie users in with a specific hardware vendor and that generally offer a better selection of software that is less expensive.

The VAX 8978 Cluster

A unique feature of VAX machines is the Cluster configuration. In installations for which the capacity requirements exceed that of the 8800 series, DEC can configure a logical machine that consists of up to eight VAX 8700 computers to achieve computing power and storage capacity in excess of many large-scale mainframes. The VAX 8978 Cluster, for example, offers eight times the CPU performance of the 8700 with a memory capacity of 4 gigabytes. The clusters are cleverly engineered so that they appear to be a single machine to the programmer and applications user, who become aware only of the increased power and capacity without having to worry about how the machines communicate or where a given memory segment is physically located.

The MicroVAX 3600

On the other end of the spectrum of VAX machines is the MicroVAX line, DEC's entry-level, low-cost machines. They allow small organizations to adopt VAX systems at a budget price and may also act as small development stations for programmers who are writing applications for VAX/VMS. In large-scale MIS environments, MicroVAX computers are widely used for departmental computing. In VAX networks, the MicroVAX machines are appealing as peripheral servers and controllers.

Departmental computing is a buzzword that you will see more and more in the MIS literature. The concept can be viewed as part of the continuum that stretches from corporate mainframes on one end to personal computers on the other, with varying degrees of control. Just as individuals have direct control over their PCs, so departments can exert more control over the selection and application of the departmental computers than they possibly can with corporate mainframe behemoths. Yet the departments are able to avail themselves of the features of the large-scale computers such as sophisticated multi-user systems, databases, and MIS applications.

MicroVAX machines are also used as "branch office" computers in WAN-distributed (wide area network) MIS architecture. In a typical WAN system, the central mainframe maintains the primary corporate database but is connected via satellite (or other means) to branch office minis. These minis, in turn, support a network of PCs or terminals. Large banks and hotel and retail chains would use this sort of overall MIS structure.

A particularly important feature of the MicroVAX is that it is just as much a VMS machine as the 8800, since DEC maintains complete software compatibility across VAX models. Yet, MicroVAX machines are little more than glorified microcomputers, comparable in computing power and cost to the Sun-3, Macintosh II, and IBM PS/2-type machines. The 3600 model can be configured with 32 megabytes of memory and up to 560 megabytes of disk capacity. The computing power or overall CPU performance of the machine is slightly less than one-third that of the 8800 systems.

Thousands of VAX applications developed for the VMS operating system are available for the MicroVAX. These include CAD/CAM, MRP, database, order entry, inventory, project management, and accounting software packages.

It should be noted that the distinction between micro and mini in terms of computing power and storage capacity is becoming obscure and even academic. Ultimately, the real difference may lie in the applications and user interface that each machine targets; for example, micros as workstations and minis as number crunchers. John Jacobs, the late great computer specialist at Bechtel, once lamented that a microcomputer can be defined as "any computer that is sold at a low price with little documentation and no support." There may be not much distinction beyond that.

PC Workstations and Networks

Two very attractive features of VAX systems are (a) their high level of connectivity and extensive network support, and (b) DEC's aggressiveness and success in implementing personal computers (both IBM and Apple) as workstations on their network.

Like other vendors of mainframe equipment, DEC does have its own line of terminals, the VT100, VT220, and VT241. However, to the company's immense credit, instead of doing battle with the micros in the workstation arena, it became a vanguard in the quest for integrating micros and mainframes. Both IBM PCs and Apple Macintosh computers have been fully integrated as VAX workstations. This is very attractive to potential customers who wish to utilize their investment in PCs while following a migration path to mainframes. Additional details about this sort of micro-mini synergy are presented in "The VAX-MAC Connection" on page 236.

Sun Microsystems

Sun Microsystems of Mountain View, California, are makers of the very popular Sun-3 and Sun-4 "super micro" workstations. These systems are characterized by phenomenal raw computing power, superior graphics display, UNIX operating systems, and intrinsic and extensive network support. These "workstation" machines were originally conceived to meet the needs of design engineers who required fast floating point number crunching in conjunction with graphics display. The graphics display on workstations normally produces very crisp, (high-resolution) three-dimensional renderings for solids modeling. However, the speed and versatility of these machines have spread their application base to include desktop publishing, animation, CAD/-CAM, artificial intelligence, expert systems, graphical user interface, and even MIS (see the Autodesk case on page 166).

Graphics display needed for solids modeling requires many colors and shades of colors to be displayed. Normally, this means that an analog RGB display must be used. The voltage to the three guns (red, green, blue) can be varied over a range to control the color. Sun workstations use this sort of display to produce 256 colors on an image from a palette of a possible 16.7 million colors. The result is a stunning rendering of lifelike images in three dimensions.

The Sun-3/200 Workstation

This machine has a 19-inch color display with a resolution of 1600 x 1280 — 1600 dots across and 1280 dots down. Compared to the IBM Enhanced Graphics resolution of 480 by 320, one of the Sun-3 screens could display twelve of the IBM screens!

The main (CPU) processor for this unit is the MC68020 CPU chip made by Motorola, the same processor that powers the Apple Macintosh II computer. It is a true 32-bit CPU in that it has 32-bit registers and is able to transfer 32-bit chunks of data in and out of these registers at a time. The MC68020 also uses 32-bit main memory addressing, which gives it an immense sea of linear address space to work with. In the Sun-3 implementation, this processor runs at 25 MHz (very fast) and uses the MC68881 in tandem to help speed up engineering and math computations. (General-purpose CPUs are designed for integer arithmetic. Floating point calculations performed in software are slow and cumbersome.)

The Sun-3 is normally configured with 8 to 32 megabytes of main memory (RAM). Hard disk storage capacities vary from 280 megabytes to 3.6 gigabytes. Operating at 25MHz, the powerful MC68020 is able to crank out 4 million instructions per second (MIPS). As you can guess, this computing power is far in excess of "normal" microcomputers such as the IBM PC (it equals the computing power of more than 50 PCs, if they could work together). For these reason, machines such as the Sun-3, for which the overall design strategy is that of a micro but that packs extraordinary power, are called *supermicros*. The Sun-3 costs twice as much as a normally configured IBM PS/2 model 70.

Although the workstation concept is mainly for engineering and graphics applications, the high graphics resolution, combined with computing power and network compatibility, makes these machines suitable for certain MIS and DSS needs such as network servers, development systems, and utilization of the sophisticated graphics for building "natural" graphical and iconic user interfaces to DSS software. A particular application of CAD technology to MIS and DSS is the use of graphics to build iconic models of real-world situations that are automatically converted to mathematical models by the machine in real time.

In addition, the extensive software base of the UNIX operating system makes many database, accounting, order processing, MRP, and other software packages accessible to the MIS designer. In an MIS environment, the high graphics resolution of the machine can be exploited with the use of windows, or "virtual screens" to combine a number of different textual and graphics displays into one screen. This is particularly useful when the user is working on a number of different files at a time.

Sun-4/200 Workstation

The 4/200, the most powerful machine produced by Sun, uses a proprietary reduced instruction set computer (RISC) processor, the M886900, to crank out an incredible 10 MIPS. It can be configured with up to 128 megabytes of main memory and 3.6 gigabytes of disk storage. This power, although supplied by a 32-bit CPU, is comparable to that available with mainframe computers and large-scale mini-computers. The same graphics display and UNIX operating system available for the Sun-3 are also provided with the Sun-4. However, an aggravating problem for Sun users is that because the Sun-3 and Sun-4 use different CPUs, compiled (machine) code is not portable between the two machines. Source code must be transported and recompiled under a different compiler and linker. The Sun-4 costs about twice as much as the Sun-3.

When the computers were first invented and its inventors boasted that they could perform thousands of additions per minute, critics of the new contraptions asked why anyone would want to do that many additions in the first place. The same sort of logic would question the search for more and more computer power when the power we have now seems perfectly suitable for all the word processing and spreadsheet calculations we wish to do.

The fact is that heavy MIS users and computer professionals are demanding more and more power from desktop machines as their applications transgress the rarefied atmosphere of mainframe applications. Also, as new computer power is made available to programmers, wholly new paradigms of computer usage are defined. We conceive new uses for the computer, as well as new ways that computers and humans should relate. Every time this has happened (first word processing, then the spreadsheet, then the Macintosh iconic user interface, and desktop publishing), we have seen quantum leaps in individual and organizational productivity.

The RISC Processor

Sun's SPARC processors use the reduced instruction set architecture (RISC). The power and popularity of the RISC processor lies in its simplicity. The best way to understand the RISC concept is to put yourself in the position of the CPU designer. Since functions that are built in to the hardware of the chip are more efficient than those that are software-driven, you try, of course, to pack in as many hardwired functions as possible. But there is a trade-off. The more hardware functions you put in, the slower the chip becomes. Everything becomes slower, even the simplest ADD instructions. A designer needs to make a decision as to how much to pack into the CPU. As an analogy, consider the person who drives a motor home all year so when he goes on vacation he won't need to stay at motels.

One way to make this determination is to find out how much of this hardwired functionality is actually being used by software engineers. (How often do you go on vacation?) As it turns out, the vast majority of software uses only the simplest of CPU instructions such as fetch, store, add, and compare. (Once a year for a week.) Radical hardware designers therefore conceived of a CPU that provided only these essential (a reduced set) instructions, thereby achieving huge gains in processor speed. (Drive an economy car and stay at motels.) The operations that were sacrificed have to be done "in software" and thus take longer. However, these are so rare that overall there is a speed advantage. This rationale turned out to be a very good idea and is behind the speed and success of Sun's SPARC RISC processor.

Sun's Window and Mouse Interface

Sun offers a Window and Mouse interface for their UNIX systems that many believe is showing the way to UNIX systems of the future. The familiar "point and click" iconic interface, developed at Xerox's PARC think tank and popularized by the Macintosh, has proven to be the man/machine interface most usable by lay users and has been adopted by IBM in their new PS/2 with the OS/2 operating system. The Sun window and icon interface has been implemented across their Open System Network and allows for easy access of icons and files on other nodes in a way that makes the network transparent to the user. This interface is a very exciting development that is being closely watched by the industry.

Sun's Network Implementation

Sun computers, designed as "workstations," have been from their inception windows network resources. In this regard, Sun shares Apple Computer's view that "the network is the system" and everything else is either a workstation (human interface) or a device (resource interface).

Sun's Open System Network (OSN) is a network protocol designed to accommodate a variety of computers and network access hardware and software components. In addition, Sun's TOPS network and NEWS network window implementation have enhanced application of Sun computers in networks, both with other Sun machines and in a highly heterogeneous environment.

Application Software Available for Sun Computers

Along with most UNIX operating system software, specific implementations of the UNIFY and INGRES database management programs are available on the Sun machines. Also available are office automation software (this usually means word processing, calendar and appointment management, and electronic mail), and project management and project scheduling aids for PERT, GANTT, and CPM charts. More than 500 other applications are listed in a publication called *Catalyst,* available free from Sun.

In addition to the normal arsenal of compilers such as C, Pascal, FORTRAN, LISP, and FORTH third-party vendors also market CASE and AI software.

As one would expect for workstations, there is a good selection of graphics applications such as CAD, solids modeling, desktop publishing, animation, and windowing utilities.

Cognition, Heuristics, and Decision-Making Styles

The design and implementation of decision support systems must consider the user in a particular sort of way. For instance, if we are to design the best system to support the decision-making process, we must understand something about the manner in which the user, that is, the decision maker, makes decisions.

One useful way to categorize decision makers is to place them in the so-called preceptive/receptive space (see the figure on page 261). In terms of two-dimensional Cartesian space, the x-axis places decision makers with respect to his or her reliance on mathematics, data, and analysis on the extreme left side of the line, through a continuum of increasing reliance on intuition to total reliance on intuitive decision making on the extreme right side of the line. The y-axis similarly places decision makers in preceptive/receptive space with respect to their total reliance on details in the extreme bottom of the graph (receptive) to the ability to see the whole or the big picture and little reliance on details at the top of the graph (preceptive). (See McKenney, J.L., and Keen, P.G.W., "How Managers' Minds Work," *Harvard Business Review,* May-June, 1974.)

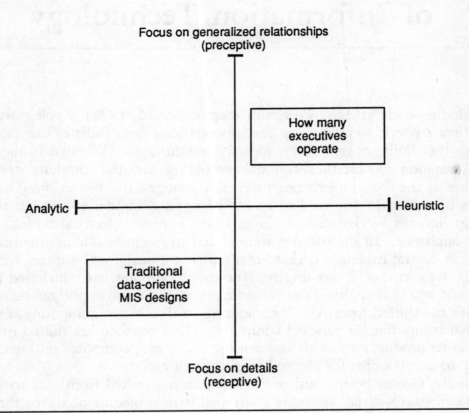

Preceptive-Receptive Space

Focus on generalized relationships
(preceptive)

Analytic ⊢————————————————⊣ Heuristic

How many
executives
operate

Traditional
data-oriented
MIS designs

Focus on details
(receptive)

Fault-Tolerant Computers

Tandem Computers of Sunnyvale, California, and Stratus Computer of Marlboro, Massachusetts, are two vendors in the niche market of fault-tolerant computers. These systems are built with mirror components in critical service such as CPU, main memory, and main DASD. When a service unit fails, the mirror unit automatically takes over and flags the operator. These systems are normally used in critical service such as OLTP, real-time critical processes, or monitoring of dangerous activities. Apple uses Tandems to run its flexible manufacturing lines.

The Changing Priorities
of Information Technology

In a wonderful article in *Apple Viewpoints* (September 26, 1988), Apple's Stuart Greene offers a poetic view of some fundamental long-term shifts in our priorities underneath the shuffle of new technological breakthroughs. Whereas in the past we sought automation and used institutional computing with the computer operator or programmer as the focus, microcomputers have changed this hierarchy. There are computers now that do not need to be locked up in computer rooms but that can be brought into the workplace and plugged into a regular electrical outlet just like any other appliance. In the past we were forced to organize our information systems around large central machines because that's what the mainframe makers wanted to sell us. Today's market is user-driven. The microcomputer has transferred power to the end user, who has replaced the programmer as the most important user. The architecture has shifted from central computing to distributed computing, from institutional computing to personal computing. Our purpose has shifted from automation to productivity. Our concern for conserving computer resources has given way to our concern for the end-user's overall experience.

Similarly, Greene points out, our orientation has shifted from data to information. MIS managers today are more concerned with providing access to the computing resources than with controlling access. And with our increased concern for the end user, the emphasis has shifted from computation to presentation. Whereas in the past the users submitted jobs to the machine, today users interact with the machines and have a session. The user interface engendered by micros for end users allows the user to select an action (menu driven) instead of specifying it (command driven). We have gone from following rules to using methods.

PART 5

Glossary

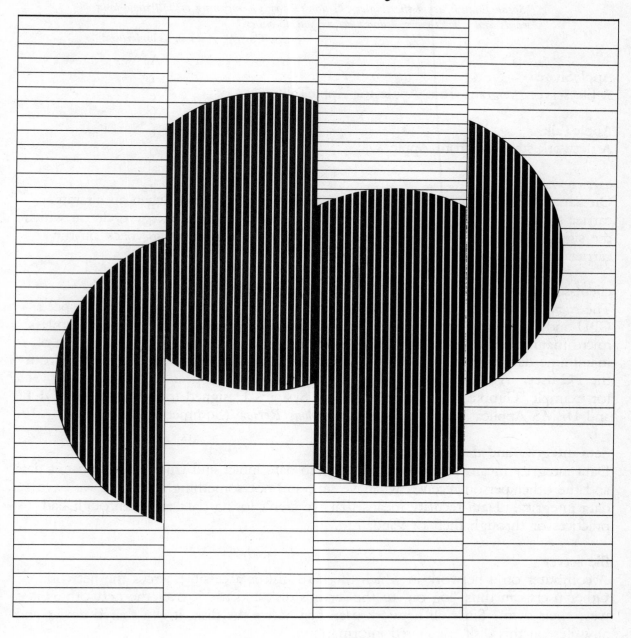

Buzzwords

"Speak English," said the Eaglet. "I don't know the meaning of half those long words and what's more, I don't believe you do either."
                                                              — Lewis Carroll, *Alice in Wonderland.*

AppleShare
A file server program from Apple for AppleTalk.

AppleTalk
A network standard from Apple.

carrier wave
On San Francisco Bay, that which causes your sailboat to rock when an aircraft carrier steams by. In signal transmission, the electromagnetic energy cycle on which the signals are placed. The signal can be thought of as riding piggyback on the carrier or as distortions in the carrier wave.

client-server systems
The *client* is a PC or PC user. The *server* is a mainframe or mini with high-speed CPU and large disk storage. This buzz-phrase refers to database design in seamless micro-mainframe networks in which the database is designed for PC-type access of mainframe data with application programs that hide the mainframe complexity from the PC user. A number of good articles on the subject appear in the literature. See, for example, Gimple, William, et al, "Unix Systems Designed for Client-Server OLTP and DBMS Applications," *Computer Technology Review* (Summer 1988).

data integrity and data security
Data integrity means that we expect to keep data intact and true. If we transmit data and the other person receives what we sent and not something else, then we have data integrity. Data security means that we aren't losing data either through bad practices or through theft or vandalism.

file server
A computer on a network in which the hard disk is accessible across the network. Other users can thus "log on" to the server's disk and use it over the network as if it were their own. Since all network users can access the disk, it is a shared device and any files on this disk are shared information.

hacker
A programmer who does not produce original code but who changes or "hacks" other people's code, usually with inferior results. The media like to use the term to describe network vandals.

host resident
Host resident software is on the mainframe rather than on the micro. The term is used in conjunction with micro-mainframe communications and refers to programs written on the mainframe to facilitate such a link.

icon
An on-screen pictorial representation of a familiar object to designate computer system components or functions. For example, the picture of the familiar trash can is used to represent file deletions.

microcode
A sequence of machine instructions that can be executed as single instruction. These are stored in a special segment of RAM that is not otherwise addressable.

noise
In network data communications, *noise* refers to random electrical activity on the line that is not the signal. When the signal strength is low or when the noise level is high, it is difficult to make out the incoming data, which may appear to be garbage.

object-oriented programming (OOP)
Conventional programming uses a procedural method; that is, the programmer codes up a sequence of procedures and expects that the computer will arrive at the desired objective when it follows the procedures. Each procedure performs a specific task and expects the data passed to it to conform to a syntax. As the program grows in complexity, the data passing from procedure to procedure become difficult to keep track of. The result? Long maintenance cycle times and difficulty in porting software to other hardware environments.

An alternative approach is object-oriented programming, one of the many clever innovations of Xerox PARC. Instead of defining the problem in terms of procedures, it is defined in terms of objects. Objects are categorized into *classes,* assigned a subset of data, and supplied with an internal set of procedures. The object is thus made *smart* in that it knows what to do with the data. The important difference is that when the objects call each other to perform tasks, no object knows or needs to know the other object's data. What is gained is simplicity of code in generating otherwise complex software systems. The Macintosh user interface (Finder) is written in this style of programming.

peer-to-peer network
A network of computers of similar size and power, unlike networks in which smaller "workstations" are used as access devices to larger "servers." A peer-to-peer network can be thought of as a network of servers with the capability for all machines to access data on any machine. The term, normally used in conjunction with mini and mainframe computers, is topical in distributed and departmental computing circles.

printer server
Like a file server, a printer server is a computer on a network that makes one or more printers attached to it available to all network users.

protocol
In data communications, a set of rules observed by sender and receiver designed to retain data integrity. For example, if I talk with you, it is understood that you will not talk while I am speaking, that I will be using vibrations of air to communicate sounds to your ear, that these sounds are to be interpreted as English words, that we both subscribe to the same dictionary, that certain pauses and intonations will delineate sentences, and that longer pauses and facial expressions and gestures will indicate that I have finished transmitting the message and that I am awaiting a reply. Verbal communication between us is possible only because both of us utilize a common set of rules of speech. The same is true of data communications between computers. The rules of communication are collectively referred to as protocol.

transactions per second
An index of activity in transaction processing systems. In large companies, this rate ranges from 5 to 50 transactions per second (tp/s). Vendors will usually quote a tp/s rating for systems specifically designed for transaction processing. The rate is especially critical in the design of OLTP systems.

wait states
The number of CPU clock cycles that must pass between memory access; needed when the processor is very fast and memory is slower.

Alphabet Soup

AFP
AppleTalk Filing Protocol
AFP supports the Mac's visual filing system and user interface over the AppleTalk network.

ANSI
American National Standards Institute
An organization that sets many MIS standards.

ASCII
American Standard Code for Information Interchange
A set of binary codes corresponding to letters of the English alphabet, Arabic numerals, and other symbols normally used in typed communication.

CICS
Customer Information Control System
A software platform for building transaction processing systems. The program is written by IBM and is standard on most MIS installations that use the IBM 3083 or 3090 mainframes.

CMS
Conversational Monitor System
Conversational terminal access system for IBM mainframes.

CSMA/CD
carrier sense multiple access with collision detection
A data communications protocol commonly used in local area networks that use the bus topology.

DASD
direct access storage device
Frequently seen in IBM product literature; always refers to a hard disk.

DB2
Database 2
A relational database management system from IBM for its mainframes with PC support.

DOD
Department of Defense
Responsible for developing COBOL, ADA, TCP/IP, and other gems.

DMS
Display Management System
A screen design utility available on IBM mainframes. Used to design input and output screens for interactive application programs.

DOS
disk operating system
Any disk operating system in the generic sense.

EBCDIC
Extended Binary-Coded Decimal Interchange Code
IBM's set of binary codes to represent numerals, letters of the alphabet, and other symbols.

FDD
floppy disk drive

GB
gigabytes
One gigabyte is 1024 megabytes, or approximately a billion characters.

IEEE
Institute of Electrical and Electronics Engineers
Responsible for many standards in computer and networking systems. In particular, the 802 committee has been active in establishing network standards.

IMS
Information Management System
The old standard IBM database for large-scale transaction processing. IMS uses a hierarchical data structure. To what extent IMS will be replaced by IBM's newer relational database products such as dBASE II and SQL is not clear. Many IMS systems run up to 50,000 workstations and process 1,000 database transactions per second. IBM is currently working on increasing the capacity to 150,000 users and 4,000 transactions per second.

ISO
International Standards Organization
The people who came up with the Open System Interconnect model of data communications.

MAPICS
Manufacturing and Production Information Control System
An IBM System/38 MIS software for the manufacturing industry. It includes programs for production control and costing, accounting, inventory management, sales analysis, order entry, and MRP.

MB
megabytes
One megabyte is equal to 1024 kilobytes, or about a million characters of text.

MUSIC
Multi-User System for Interactive Computing
Conversational terminal access system for IBM mainframes.

MVS
Multiple Virtual Storage
An IBM mainframe operating system used in 4381, 3083, and 3090 systems; designed for OLTP systems.

OLTP
online transaction processing
A TPS system in which all files are automatically updated each time a transaction is entered. The alternative is to accumulate transaction data and then update the files in a batch run.

OSI
open system interconnect
A model for defining network standards.

PARC
Palo Alto Research Center
The now legendary Prometheus of computer science, at Xerox in Palo Alto, where many of the new ideas in computing were born. The Macintosh user interface and object-oriented programming are derived from ideas germinated in this think tank. Ironically, Xerox itself has yet to reap a direct benefit from this work.

PC
personal computer
Not necessarily an IBM personal computer, although IBM has usurped the term. Throughout this text, PC is used to refer to any personal computer, including the IBM PC, IBM AT, IBM PS/2, and all Macintosh systems.

RACF

Resource Access Control Facility

An IBM program for the VM and MVS environments in 3090 and 3083 mainframes designed for security against unauthorized access to data system resources.

RISC

reduced instruction set computer

Computers designed with fewer instructions and faster operating capability.

SAA

Systems Application Architecture (IBM)

A framework for logical design of a computer system that presents a consistent view to programmers and end users and that supports a cross section of IBM systems, devices, and network protocols. An effort by Big Blue to integrate the worlds of OS/2, System/370, System/3, and AS/400.

SDF

Screen Definition Facility

A system utility accessed by application programs to control CRT displays.

SCSI

small computer systems interface

A host adapter and peripheral controller standard and bus that can be used to daisy chain up to eight disk or tape drives to one connector on the computer. A very inexpensive and efficient way of extending the expansion capacity of small computers. Apple Macintosh computers are equipped with an SCSI interface.

SDLC

systems development life cycle

In systems analysis, the stages in the incarnation of information systems from birth, through systems analysis, systems design, implementation, and maintenance to rebirth.

synchronous data link control

In data communications, a method of packaging data into frames. Used by many network protocols, including AppleTalk.

SNA

System Network Architecture

IBM's specifications for high-speed data communications between mainframes.

SQL/DS

Structured Query Language Data System

IBM's relational database management system with query and report writing facilities.

TCP/IP
transmission control protocol and internet protocol
A DOD specification for data communications that is very popular with Unix users and at most large universities.

TSO
Time Sharing Option
Conversational terminal access system for IBM mainframes.

VAX
Virtual Address Extended
A line of computers made by DEC.

VAX/VMS
VAX Virtual Memory System
The operating system of VAX computers and the networks in which they are assumed to reside.

VM
Virtual Memory
Operating system environment in IBM mainframes.

VS
Virtual Storage
IBM mainframe operating system for 4381, 3083, and 3090 systems. CMS (conversational monitor support) supports terminal users while CP (control program) allocates resources. Each user appears to have control of the computer.

VSAM
Virtual Storage Access Method
A file access method used in IBM mainframe operating systems.

VTAM
Virtual Telecommunications Access Method
Network operating system from IBM that takes care of resource allocation and user requests on IBM networks.

Trademarks

Software	Manufacturer
1-2-3	Lotus Development Corporation
3Com Network	3Com
A/UX	Apple Computer, Inc.
Adabas	Software AG
ADI (AutoCAD Device Interface)	Autodesk, Inc.
AFP	Apple Computer, Inc.
AlisaShare	Alisa
Apollo	Apollo
Apple II	Apple Computer, Inc.
AppleLink	Apple Computer, Inc.
AppleShare	Apple Computer, Inc.
AppleTalk for VMS	Alisa
AppleTalk	Apple Computer, Inc.
ARCNet	Datapoint
AS400	International Business Machines Corporation
ASK	ASK Software
AutoCAD	Autodesk, Inc.
AutoCAD/AEC	Autodesk, Inc.
AutoFlix	Autodesk, Inc.
Autograf4	MOMS Computing
AutoShade	Autodesk, Inc.
AutoSketch	Autodesk, Inc.
AutoSolid	Autodesk, Inc.
Brunig	Brunig
CADAM	International Business Machines Corporation
CICS	International Business Machines Corporation
CL/1	Network Innovations
Compumotor Plus	Compumotor-A Parker Hannifin Corporation
Computervision	Computervision
CPI	International Business Machines Corporation
CPS	International Business Machines Corporation
Cray XMP	Cray Research, Inc.
CUA	International Business Machines Corporation
DATA-3	Data 3 Systems
DB2	International Business Machines Corporation

dBASE II and dBASE III	Ashton-Tate
DECNet	Digital Equipment Corporation
DMS	Unisys
Double Helix	Odesta
DPS	Unisys
Ethernet	Xerox Corporation
FastPath	Kinetics
Federal Express	Federal Express
FoxBase	Fox and Geller
Generic CAD	Autodesk, Inc.
HFS (Hierarchical File System)	Apple Computer, Inc.
HP3000	Hewlett-Packard Company
HP9845	Hewlett-Packard Company
Hypercard	Apple Computer, Inc.
Hypermart USA	Wal-Mart Stores, Inc.
IBM 9370	International Business Machines Corporation
IBM 4381	International Business Machines Corporation
IBM 3090	International Business Machines Corporation
IMAP (Industry Marketing Assistance Program)	International Business Machines Corporation
Informix	Informix
Ingres	Ingres
Intergraph	Intergraph
LA (Lending Adviser)	Syntelligence
LaserWriter	Apple Computer, Inc.
Mac Workstation	Apple Computer, Inc.
Macintosh Plus	Apple Computer, Inc.
Macintosh IIx	Apple Computer, Inc.
Macintosh	Apple Computer, Inc.
Macintosh SE/30	Apple Computer, Inc.
Macintosh SE	Apple Computer, Inc.
Macintosh II	Apple Computer, Inc.
MAPICS	International Business Machines Corporation
MAPPER	Unisys
MFF (Math Function Facility)	International Business Machines Corporation
Microsoft Word	Microsoft Corporation
MicroVAX	Digital Equipment Corporation
Multimate	Multimate International
MVS and MVS/XA	International Business Machines Corporation
NEWS (Network Window System)	Sun Microsystems, Inc.
Nomad	D&B Computing Services
Oracle	Oracle
OS/2	International Business Machines Corporation
OSN (Open System Network)	Sun Microsystems, Inc.

PARC	Xerox Corporation
PC Support (AS400 software)	International Business Machines Corporation
PhoneNet	Farallon
PRISM	Apple Computer, Inc.
PS/2	International Business Machines Corporation
Query (System/38 program)	International Business Machines Corporation
R:Base 4000 and 5000	Microrim
Revelation	Cosmos
SAA	International Business Machines Corporation
Sam's Wholesale Club	Wal-Mart Stores, Inc.
SBT	SBT
SNA	International Business Machines Corporation
SPARC	Sun Microsystems, Inc.
SperryCalc	Unisys
SQL/DS	International Business Machines Corporation
SQL	International Business Machines Corporation
Sun/3, Sun/4	Sun Microsystems, Inc.
Supercalc 2	SORCIM Corporation
Syntel	Syntelligence
System/3	International Business Machines Corporation
System/36	International Business Machines Corporation
System/34	International Business Machines Corporation
System/38	International Business Machines Corporation
Team-Up	Unlimited Processing
Tee-Bird	Taylor-Dunn
TIP	Unisys
Token Ring Network	International Business Machines Corporation
TOPS	Sun Microsystems, Inc.
TopView	International Business Machines Corporation
UA (Underwriter Adviser)	Syntelligence
Unify	Relational
Univac 1100/xx	Unisys
Unix	AT&T Bell Laboratories
VAX/VMS	Digital Equipment Corporation
VAX	Digital Equipment Corporation
Versacad	Autodesk, Inc.
Visicalc	Personal Software, Inc., VisiCorp
VT100, VT220, VT241	Digital Equipment Corporation
Windows	Microsoft Corporation
X-Window	Digital Equipment Corporation
Xerox 1186	Xerox Corporation